The Development of Universities in Nigeria

The Development of Universities in Nigeria (DISCARDED)

Dedicated to Obiajulu and Ugochukwu
and
"A"

The Development of Universities in Nigeria

A study of the influence of political and other factors on
university development in Nigeria, 1868–1967

NDUKA OKAFOR, B.Sc.(Lond.), Ph.D.(Cantab.),
The University of Nigeria, Nsukka

Longman

LONGMAN GROUP LTD
London
*Associated companies, branches and representatives
throughout the world*

© Nduka Okafor 1971

First published 1971

ISBN 0 582 64060 1

Printed in Great Britain by
The Camelot Press Ltd., London and Southampton

Acknowledgements

The author and publishers are grateful to the following for permission to reproduce copyright material:

Ahmadu Bello University for the table 'Composition of Appointment Boards as established by the University of Ahmadu Bello Law, 1962', and 'Degree courses offered and Certificates and Diplomas awarded in Nigerian Universities as in 1965/66' from the *1964/65 Calendar* of the University; Cambridge University Press for extracts from *Awo* by Obafemi Awolowo; Author for extracts from *Renascent Africa* and *My Odyssey* by Dr. Nnamdi Azikiwe; the Clarendon Press for the table 'Universities in Europe at the end of the fifteenth century' from *The Universities of Europe in the Middle Ages* by Hastings Rashdall (ed. Powicke & Emden); the Daily Times of Nigeria Ltd. for an extract from an editorial on the Yaba Higher College, January 1934, and for an extract from an article on the Yaba Higher College, March 1934; The Federal Ministry of Education, Lagos, for extracts from *Investment in Education: Report of the Commission on Post-School Certificate and Higher Education in Nigeria*, Lagos, 1960; Harcourt Brace and World Inc. for the table 'Nigerian political organisations and parties, 1908/66' modified from R. L. Sklar in *Politics in Africa*, ed. Gwendoline Carter, New York, 1966; the National Universities Commission of Nigeria for the tables 'Nigerian College: Planned courses and enrolment, 1953' from *Proposals for the Future Financing of Nigerian College*, Lagos, 1953, 'Distribution of students among Faculties by 1967/68 and 'Proposal for contributions towards the . . . grants to the Universities 1963/68' from *Universities Development in Nigeria*, Lagos, 1963, 'Total Enrolment in Nigerian Universities 1964/5' 'Staff situation on 1st October, 1965', 'Student/Staff Ratio 1964/65', 'Geographical Distribution of students in Nigerian Universities by institution and sex 1964/65', all from *The Annual Review of Nigerian Universities 1964/65*; Oxford University Press for an extract from *Sierra Leone Inheritance*, by Christopher Fyfe; George Philip & Son Ltd. for extracts from *Ethiopia Unbound* by J. E. Casely Hayford; University of California Press for extracts from *Nigeria: Background to Nationalism* by James Coleman; Universities of Ibadan, Ife and Lagos for parts of the table 'Degree courses offered in Nigerian Universities as in 1965/66' from *1954/65 Calendars* of these Universities.

We have received no objection to our request to the Negro Printing

Office for our inclusion of an extract from Letters by E. W. Blyden, 1872 (the West African University), or from the Military Governor, Ibadan, for our inclusion of extracts from the Government White Paper on the Establishment of a University in Western Nigeria (Sessional Paper No. 12, 1960).

In view of the difficulties in Nigeria at the present time, we have been unable to obtain permission from the University of Nigeria for inclusions in the table 'Degree courses offered and Certificates and Diplomas awarded in Nigerian Universities as in 1965/66' from the *1964/65 Calendar* of the University. We have also been unable to obtain replies from the editors of the *Lagos Weekly Record,* the *Lagos Standard* and the *Daily Express* of Lagos in respect of our reproduction of extracts from an editorial on the importance of Manual Skills to the West African Negro (*Lagos Weekly Record,* 7th March 1896); correspondence between E. W. Blyden and Sir Gilbert Carter, 1896, and extracts from a letter from Governor Carter of the 20th May 1896 (*Lagos Standard*); extracts from an article on the V. A. Oyenuga Affair at the University of Ife (*Daily Express,* 25th November 1963).

Preface

The script of this book was ready early in 1967. The political crisis in Nigeria which started with the military *coup* of January 1966, however, greatly delayed its appearance. Even before war broke out in July 1967 between the Eastern Region of Nigeria, where I reside, and which had declared itself the Republic of Biafra* in May 1967, and the rest of the Nigerian Federation, communication had been difficult because of the crisis. With the war it became virtually impossible. Numerous letters written between the publishers and myself were lost in transit; for instance after a year, corrections to the proofs had not reached the publishers. These delays and the political changes that may follow the war may make certain parts of the book less topical than they might have been. These sections must be seen as a record of the state of universities at the time the book was written.

But only some of the faults of the book can be blamed on the crisis. I hope that, whatever shortcomings there may be, the reader will share some of the enjoyment I had in writing the book. Even more, I hope that the shortcomings will stimulate the writing of a more thorough and more professional work.

I should like to thank the following who read and criticised all or part of the script: Mr. Ralph Nwamefor, Dr. Peter Esedebe, Dr. Hollis Lynch, Professor J. F. Ade Ajayi, Mazi Ray Ofoegbu, Dr. Ikenna Nzimiro, Dr. F. Ogakwu and a host of others.

Professors Babs Fafunwa and Edward Blyden III allowed me to use their unpublished doctoral theses. Professor Edward Blyden III also allowed me use of his vast collection of books on or by his illustrious grandfather. I thank both of them as well as the Nsukka Philosophical Society, who discussed sections of the book at two of their meetings.

I would also like to thank Miss Mary Ike who typed most of the script, and the staff of the University Library at Nsukka. The Publishers deserve thanks for their co-operation in extremely difficult circumstances.

Finally, I would like to thank my wife, Chinyelu, for her encouragement.

N. O.

Obudike Villa
Nri, Awka Province
November 1968

* The Republic of Biafra was proclaimed extinct on 14 January, 1970, following the end of the war.

Contents

List of Tables

Figure

1   Universities:
Their Nature and Origins

It is difficult to define in detailed universal terms what constitutes a 'university'. This difficulty arises from the very diverse ecological and historical factors which have operated to shape universities and to decide where they may exist.[1] There are, however, a number of important characteristics by which a university may usually be distinguished from other institutions.

One essential feature of a university is the simultaneous presence of senior and junior scholars. Indeed a university has been described as 'a society of scholars, all of whom are learning, but the more senior scholars spend part of their time teaching the junior scholars, and they also increase their own knowledge by adding to the store of human knowledge. This they do by research.'[2]

Though varying from place to place, the name evokes in the modern mind the ideal of

> a place where those who hate ignorance may strive to know, where those who perceive truth may strive to make others see; where seekers and learners alike, banded together in the search for knowledge, will honour thought in all its finer ways, will welcome thinkers in distress or in exile, will uphold ever the dignity of thought and learning and will exact standards in these things.[3]

A university must seek to increase the bounds of knowledge through research; it must act as a repository of such knowledge and must also disseminate it.[4] It is essential to make this distinction and thus to contrast the university with institutions which possess some attributes of a university proper. For instance there is a gradual growth in some parts of the world of institutions devoted solely to the furtherance of knowledge. Although research of the highest kind may be carried out in these institutions and such knowledge disseminated, these institutions cannot be considered universities because 'junior' scholars are absent. Similarly some of the colleges devoted entirely to undergraduate teaching cannot be considered universities[5] if the teachers are not engaged in research.

This book is concerned with tracing the establishment of universities in Nigeria.

The origin of universities

Learning and scholarship are not new to the indigenes of West Africa.

Jenne, and Timbuctoo in what is now Mali, were renowned as centres of commerce and learning, having grown into cities by the twelfth century.[6] The name Sankore is connected with the scholarship of Timbuctoo. Sankore was attached to the mosque of the same name and was connected both by letter and by personal visits with centres of learning in Spain and North Africa, including Egypt. The subjects studied included law, literature, grammar and theology, rather than the natural sciences. Leo Africanus, the sixteenth-century traveller, records of Timbuctoo, 'Here are great stores of doctors, judges, priests and other learned men.'[7] There is extremely scanty information on the Sankore centre of learning in Timbuctoo. It has been referred to as 'the University of Sankore' where 'the more distinguished professors would seem to have had schools in which they gave courses of lectures, attended by students, who afterwards received diplomas from the hands of masters.'[8] Trimingham in his *History of Islam in West Africa* claims, however, that the 'University of Sankore' did not exist. According to him, Sankore was simply the quarter where the majority of the teaching clerics had their houses, though some taught in the mosque there.[9]

Whatever be the case, the university as we know it today in Nigeria and as we have defined it, has its ancestry not in West Africa, but in the Middle Ages in Europe.

The exact origins of universities are not known and probably never will be. It is believed, however, that they began with a great revival of learning in the twelfth century, partly through the scholars of Italy and Sicily, but chiefly through the Arab Scholars of Spain, who studied the works of Aristotle, Euclid, Ptolemy, the new arithmetic and those texts of the Roman law which had lain hidden through the Dark Ages.[10]

The two earliest universities were in Italy, Salerno in the south and Bologna in the north. Bologna was already highly reputed for medicine—the only subject it taught—by the middle of the eleventh century. Salerno developed shortly after Bologna and although it became better known from the early twelfth century for civil (Roman) Law it taught other subjects as well.[11] Before this, learning and scholarly work were carried out (at least in England) in three types of institutions: in monasteries, where scholarly commentary on the scriptures and other learned works was already being produced; in cathedral 'schools' which taught pupils of all ages over a wide field of studies, and finally in centres of learning built around individual teachers to whom students flocked.[12]

With the new knowledge, however, the old cathedral and monastery schools became inadequate. For instance, Paris, the third university, grew out of the Cathedral Schools of Notre Dame.

Europe's fourth university, Oxford, developed about 1167. It is generally believed today that it came into existence partly because King Henry II of England, as a result of a quarrel with Archbishop Thomas à Becket, forbade all English clergy from travelling to the continent of Europe and simultaneously ordered those already there to return.

The name 'university' originated from the Latin *universitas*, which applied to a corporation. It did not refer exclusively to institutions of learning and when it did was qualified. As Rashdall says:

> At the end of the twelfth and beginning of the thirteenth centuries, we find the word applied to corporations either of masters or of students; but it long continued to be applied to other corporations as well, particularly to the then newly formed guilds and to the municipalities of towns. . . . In the earliest period it is never used absolutely [when referring to scholastic guilds]. The phrase is always 'University of Scholars', 'University of Teachers', 'University of Masters and Scholars', 'University of Study' or the like.[13]

It is thus accidental that the term has become restricted to one kind of organisation.

The term which, however, denoted the physical institution, i.e. the schools or the town which held them, was *studium generale*; it described not the generality of subjects taught, but rather a place where students from all parts, and not a particular district, were received. Since students sometimes travelled from far-off districts or countries, they formed themselves into corporations of students, *universitas scholarium*, for mutual protection from exploitation by the local inhabitants. They employed their own teachers and formulated regulations which ensured that such teachers discharged their duties satisfactorily. And since teachers lived on their students' fees they had to abide by these regulations. At Bologna it was the students, who were often mature men, and lawyers in established practice who formed the corporation.

In contrast to Bologna, Paris developed as a corporation of teachers and was therefore a *universitas magistrorum*. Oxford and most present-day universities followed the Paris set-up. Organisations of the Bologna type were far less copied among modern universities except in a few instances, for example in Scotland.[14]

The *universitas magistrorum* required certain qualifications of the student for admission; these he obtained by examination. The student ultimately sought the licence to teach, *licentia docendi*, irrespective of what was to be his future career; logically, of course, the ability to teach a subject presupposed knowing that subject. To obtain the *licentia docendi* he had to become a Master of Arts, a process which demanded competence, ascertained by examinations, in the liberal arts.

The first three, the *Trivium*, were grammar, logic and rhetoric. The student usually began the *Trivium* at about fourteen at which time he had acquired a working knowledge of Latin, then the language of scholarship. The next stage was the *Quadrivium*, normally a four-year course consisting of arithmetic, geometry, music and astronomy. The successful candidates became Masters of Arts with the right to teach. The Doctorate was obtained by Masters of Arts, after further periods of study, lasting eight or more years, in canon (church) law, civil law, medicine or theology.[15]

The above is a most sketchy excursion into the European origins of universities. But although universities have a common origin they have today come to vary according to the histories of the countries harbouring them; even within the same country differences in many aspects may be found, as the briefest consultation of the *International Handbook of Universities* will demonstrate.

A particular university has not in fact remained the same from one age to another. In other words, although universities have a common European origin they have adapted themselves to new places and times. Not even where the founder laid down specific injunctions, as for instance at the founding of the University of Heidelberg in 1386, has the university retained its original character:

> [The University of Heidelberg]
> Shall be ruled, disposed and regulated according to the modes and matters accustomed to be observed in the University of Paris and that as a handmaid of Paris—a worthy one let us hope—it shall imitate the steps of Paris in every way possible so that there shall be four faculties.[16]

As Flexner puts it:

> Universities differ in different countries . . . as a matter of history, they have changed profoundly—and commonly in the direction of social evolution of which they are a part. The Paris of 1900 has little in common with the Paris of 1700; the Oxford of the twentieth century, externally so largely the same, is nevertheless a very different thing from the Oxford of the 18th century.[17]

What resemblance then does the modern university bear to its ancestor? It is not, as Haskins points out, in the dress and (certainly not in the Nigerian context) in the buildings. Rather it is in the institution that this ancestry may be most clearly discerned. One can do no better than to quote Haskins:

> First, the very name university, as an association of masters and scholars leading the common life of learning. . . . Next, the notion of a curriculum of study, definitely laid down as regard time and subjects, tested by an examination leading to a degree, as well as the degrees themselves. . . . Then the faculties, four or more, with their deans, and the higher officers such as chancellors and rectors . . . [and finally] the training of scholars and the maintenance of the tradition of learning and investigation.[18]

The Universities of Nigeria

There are today (February 1967) in Nigeria five universities, in order of age:

University of Ibadan (1948)
University of Nigeria, Nsukka (1960)
Ahmadu Bello University, Zaria (1962)

University of Ife (1962)
University of Lagos (1962)

Ibadan, the oldest of the five, was started in 1948, nearly nine centuries after the first universities developed in Europe. Yet it preserves the essential features of a university. For according to Sir Eric Ashby:

Over a stretch of six centuries, university organization has preserved a recognizable identity of pattern, through periods of high prestige and ascendancy and through periods of decadence and insignificance. It has preserved its identity not only in time but in space: the features which today distinguish it from other social institutions in Ghana, in Germany, and in Australia, are similar to those which distinguish it from other social institutions in the fourteenth century. This survival of identity is a sign that the university has adapted itself to successive cultural environments.[19]

What are the factors which, up to early 1966, have decided the character that the universities in Nigeria have assumed? What factors, social and historic, have influenced the nature and numbers of Nigerian universities? These and other questions are the concern of the succeeding chapters.

Notes

[1] See for instance A. KERR, *Universities of Europe*, Cambridge, 1962.

[2] BRUCE TRUSCOT, *First year at the University*, London, 1946, *passim*.

[3] From a speech by John Masefield at the installation of the Chancellor of the University of Sheffield, 25 June 1946, quoted by A. W. CHAPMAN, *The Story of a Modern University*, Oxford, 1955.

[4] Cf. ABRAHAM FLEXNER, *Universities: American, English, German*, Oxford, 1930, p. 7: 'The conservation of knowledge and ideas is and has always been recognized as the business of universities, sometimes, perhaps, as almost their only business.'

[5] H. C. JOHNSON, 'Are Our Universities Schools?', *Harvard Educational Review 35*, 1965, pp. 165–73.

[6] BASIL DAVIDSON, *Old Africa Rediscovered*, London, 1961, pp. 90–91.

[7] FLORA SHAW, *A Tropical Dependency*, London, 1906, p. 202–8.

[8] SHAW, *loc. cit.*

[9] J. SPENCER TRIMINGHAM, *A History of Islam in West Africa*, Oxford, 1962, p. 98n.

[10] H. C. HASKINS, *The Rise of the Universities*, Cornell, 1963, p. 4.

[11] H. C. DENT, *Universities in Transition*, London, 1961, p. 15.

[12] DENT, *ibid.*, pp. 19–20.

[13] H. RASHDALL (1895), *The Universities of Europe in the Middle Ages*, ed. F. M. POWICKE and A. B. EMDEN, Oxford, 1936, p. 5.

[14] KERR, *op. cit.*, p. 125.

[15] HASKINS, *op. cit.*, p. 4.

[16] E. F. HENDERSON, (1892) quoted from HASKINS, *op. cit.*, p. 20.

[17] ABRAHAM FLEXNER, *op. cit.*, pp. 4–5.

[18] HASKINS, *op. cit.*, pp. 21–25.

[19] SIR ERIC ASHBY, *Technology and the Academics*, London 1958, p. 3.

2 Contacts with Europe: Introduction of Western Education in Nigeria

Universities as we know them today developed in Europe. In order that the concept might be transported to Nigeria, contact was necessary at some point.

The earliest direct contacts between West Africa and Europe

Until the fifteenth century A.D. rapport between Europe and West Africa was indirect and operated through the transportation of West African goods, especially gold, through North Africa.[1]

Between 1434 and 1482, Europeans mainly from Portugal and Castile visited the whole of the West African coastline. The aims of the Portuguese exploration which took place under Henry the Navigator of Portugal, were numerous, according to the Prince's contemporary chronicler. First, there was the mere curiosity, scientific in inspiration, to discover what lay in the unknown areas; second, Henry wished to conduct trade with West Africa, while avoiding the Muslim middlemen of North Africa, with whom trade with the Orient had had to be conducted; third, he wanted to discover and create Christian allies with whom he could resist the onslaught of Islam, the adherents of which, for the greater part of two centuries since the eighth, had endeavoured to conquer and occupy the Iberian Peninsula.[2]

Religion (including the philanthropy it inspired) and trade appear, however, to have been the most impelling factors in the relationship between Europe and West Africa from the very beginnings of contact. Indeed these two appear to be the overriding reasons for relationships between Europe and West Africa for the three centuries following the first arrival of the Iberians in West Africa.

From their earliest period in the Gulf of Guinea, the Portuguese had regarded these coastal regions as promising areas for missionary work. They were attracted to the extensive Kingdom of Benin by the Binis' belief in a supreme God, which fact they thought would favourably dispose the Binis to the acceptance of Christianity. The reigning Oba of Benin showed a passing interest, but only to enable him to obtain arms, the delivery of which to 'infidels' had been forbidden by the Pope. Thus the early Benin Missions failed.[3]

In the succeeding century the Portuguese made greater progress in near-by Warri, where the Portuguese had been invited by the Itsekiri in order to enable them to gain independence from their overlord, the Oba of Benin. The exact date of the Portuguese mission is uncertain but appears to be between 1571 and 1574. Under Father Francisco, an Augustinian priest sent out from Sao Tomé by Bishop Gaspar Cao, a Christian settlement was founded in Warri. Father Francisco succeeded in baptising the Olu (King) of Warri's eldest son and heir, naming him Sebastian after the reigning King in Portugal. Soon after its founding the Warri mission ran into trouble because of shortage of funds and of the difficulty of finding priests able to stand mosquitoes and malaria.[4] A later Bishop of Sao Tomé therefore persuaded Sebastian, who had become King, to send his son, Domingos, to Portugal to study for the priesthood. Domingos studied at the Hieronymite College in Coimbra and later at an Augustinian and a Jesuit College, both in Lisbon. After eight years he returned home, having married a Portuguese noblewoman, and within a short time after succeeding his father, turned against the Portuguese.[5]

The Warri, like the Benin mission, was short-lived. But we see an early, probably the earliest, example of the pursuit of higher education in Europe by a Nigerian. When, towards the end of the fifteenth century, European contacts were being established with Nigeria, Europe was already well-studded with universities and had (or had had) a total of about sixty (Table 1). Domingos therefore had the opportunity of living and studying for some time in a continent already used to universities. These institutions were not demanded, however, by a West African until about four centuries later.

Table 1

Universities in Europe at the end of the fifteenth century

Italy	20
France	18
England	2
Scotland	3
Spain and Portugal	3
Germany, Bohemia and the low countries	16
Other countries	6

Source: H. RASHDALL, *Universities of the Middle Ages of Europe*, Oxford, Vol. I, p. xxiv.

If religion was important in determining the pattern of contact between West Africa and Europe, an even more important factor was trade. Indeed as Professor Kenneth Dike says, 'The history of modern West Africa is largely the history of five centuries of trade with European nations; commerce was the fundamental relationship that bound Europe to Africa.'[6] In the very early stages of this trade, the presence of gold along the West Coast encouraged the Portuguese to establish trade posts and contacts there. But it was in the Gold Coast (Ghana) that the quantities of the metal produced were largest and most regular. Naturally it was there they first built their forts. As A. W. Lawrence points out in his *Trade Castles and Forts of West Africa*, European strongholds had existed in other lands, as in Moslem lands during and after the Crusades, and trade flourished under their protection; but none had been built solely with commercial intent.[7]

The earliest of these forts, the Elmina—the 'mine' of gold—was built on the Gold Coast in 1482, before Columbus had sailed to America or Vasco da Gama to the Indian Ocean. Eventually eight European countries or their national chartered companies kept forts at one time or another in West Africa. For instance, in 1618 the British founded Fort James on the Gambia River, while the Dutch increased their trading settlements and actually occupied Elmina.[8]

The importance of these forts is twofold. First, they provided a strong foothold from which the Europeans not only prosecuted trade but eventually colonised and dominated the hinterland. Progressive pacification of the hinterland gradually rendered the forts superfluous; one European government after another took over responsibility for administering them, leaving the companies to pursue strictly commercial matters.[9]

Second, it was in some of the forts that the earliest schools in West Africa were founded and thus a formalised contact with western ideas first established. These early schools were destined to provide the foundation of forces which were eventually to overthrow foreign domination, and also to demand and initiate universities in West Africa. The earliest of these 'Castle Schools' were started in what is now Ghana in the Elmina (1644), Christiansbourg (1722), and in Cape Coast castles by the Dutch, Danes and Portuguese respectively. The schools at Elmina and Christiansbourg were built for mulatto children and the instruction was usually given by chaplains and meant for the inmates of the castles, although the children of an Ashanti chief were admitted at one time to the Elmina school.

The Cape Coast School was the first real mission school. Its founder was the Rev. Thomas Thompson, educated at Cambridge University in England, and sent out by the Society for the Propagation of the Gospel. He stayed only four months, due to ill-health, but succeeded in sending three Gold Coast children to England. The only survivor of the three, Philip Quque, was ordained and on his return, managed the Castle School for mulatto and African children.[10]

The Castle Schools, however, stand apart from the general development of education in West Africa; being sporadic they did not provide the

permanent foundations of West African education.[11] They, however, produced a tradition of Western education in the Gold Coast, and it is perhaps
not surprising that that country was the first of the former British West
African colonies to gain independence. Until the Gold Coast became
independent in 1957, the British West African countries shared many
aspects of their existence in common and thereby the other territories,
including Nigeria, enjoyed some of the consequences of the Gold Coast's
longer association with Western education. British West African education, however, spread from Sierra Leone *via* returned slaves and their
descendants.

England and the slave trade in West Africa: the founding of Sierra Leone

The Portuguese, as the first arrivals in West Africa, had a great initial
advantage over all the other nations of Europe and were determined to
maintain the monopoly conferred on them by the Papal Bull (the Pope's
authority). This sway was not seriously challenged until the sixteenth
century; the Protestant countries of northern Europe who had no allegiance
to the Pope could not be held back indefinitely. Of these the Dutch and
English were the earliest newcomers.[12] The first English voyage to West
Africa was in 1553 under Thomas Wyndham and although he died before
it was over, the voyage was a commercial success. The hope of further
profits stimulated another voyage under John Lock in 1554. It was another
thirty years before an Englishman made two voyages there in 1588 and
1590, returning at the end of the second with pepper, elephant tusks and
palm-oil. Trade in slaves did not start until 1562, when John Hawkins made
the first of his three voyages. Prior to this time the Portuguese had had the
monopoly of trade in this human commodity.[13]

Thus by the seventeenth century the centre of political gravity had
shifted from southern Europe to the north-west—to England, Holland and
France. Possessions of Portugal, which once claimed the whole of the West
African Coast, were now restricted, as they virtually are today, to Angola
and Mozambique.

The expansion of Europe to America had introduced a new factor in
West Africa. The new plantations in the Americas, but especially in the
West Indies, could not adequately be manned by the indigenes of those
lands. Slaves from Africa were therefore transported to them. In this way
a trade was begun in the sixteenth century which reached its climax in the
eighteenth.[14] There is no doubt at all about the odiousness of this trade,
which has been described (before the advent of Hitler) as 'the greatest
crime in history.'[15] The problems created thereby are still being settled
today in the United States and in other parts of the world. Nevertheless,

throughout the book it will be seen that the slave trade provided the means which were to lead directly or indirectly to the political independence of Nigeria and of the other former British West African countries; and to the demand for, and the eventual establishment of, universities in the country.

There were many Africans in England in the eighteenth century, mostly imported for domestic work straight from the West African Coast or reimported across the Atlantic. Lord Masefield's judgement in 1771, that whatever their status these Africans were free, created a social problem as many Negroes became homeless and destitute, having been released by their former masters. Their numbers were swelled by ex-service men from the American Revolutionary War who had escaped from slavery. The British Government was persuaded to accept responsibility for them and to give them free passages to Sierra Leone, where it was proposed that they found the Province of Freedom, a free, self-governing African community. The moving spirit behind the proposal was an opponent of the slave trade, Granville Sharp. The proposal to found the Province of Freedom failed for a number of reasons, including heavy rains and a high death-rate among the settlers (411 had sailed from Plymouth), and the hostility of the original inhabitants. Sharp, who had put much of his own resources into the venture, could not afford to refound the Province, and neither was the British Government willing. A trading company, The Sierra Leone Company, was therefore incorporated in London in 1791 to take charge of it.[16] The *Report*[17] of the Court of Directors shows abundantly that the Company had not only commercial but also philanthropic motives. It notes that 'Schools for reading, writing and accounts, will be set up by the Company, who will be ready to receive and instruct the children of such natives as shall be willing to put them in their care.'[18] A school was probably started soon after the arrival of the Company's ship *Lapwing* in January 1791, for by early 1793 the Company was already employing European school-masters.[19]

The Sierra Leone Company's schools were always closely associated with religious teaching. Chaplains had been sent out regularly from London.[20] In the early history of Sierra Leone, various bodies, including Methodists and Baptists, tried to found societies, but with little success. The point of interest for this book dates from 1795, when the London Missionary Society was started. In 1799 this Society changed its name to the Church Missionary Society to Africa and the East (later in 1813, to the Church Missionary Society). It is to be noted in passing that these were troubled periods for England, as the Napoleonic war was raging. A parallel to this occurred about a century and half later, when in 1943, in the midst of World War II, Britain appointed the two commissions which led to the founding of Ibadan and Legon Universities in West Africa. It is probably good psychology to divert attention from a national emergency as is shown by the fact that 'many successful efforts for the promotion of human happiness have been made amidst the clouds and tempests of national calamity'.[21] In 1804, the C.M.S. opened a mission in Sierra Leone and started schools. Three years later slavery was abolished and declared illegal for British subjects. After a series of misfortunes the Sierra Leone Company was finally taken over in 1808 by the British Government which immediately provided assistance for the mission schools.

The C.M.S. was finding difficulties in recruiting Europeans for its work in Sierra Leone and therefore built a Christian Institution in 1815 where recaptive children could be trained in useful trades or in farming, and the better ones as pastors and teachers. It closed in 1826. It was revived in 1827 and transferred to Fourah Bay, east of Freetown. This Institution was to play an important part in the development of education in Nigeria, including higher education. Not only was it the predecessor of Fourah Bay College, West Africa's first university, but the Institution itself was the training ground for many of Nigeria's early Anglican missionaries and teachers. This digression on Sierra Leone is essential here, for this country (especially its Creoles) played a great part in transmitting contact with Europeans to Nigeria and other British West African countries.[22] Indeed it is seen that even by the 1860's

> Creoles of Sierra Leone occupy lucrative subordinate positions of trust in both military and civil service of Government in four colonies and settlements of the Coast—viz. Sierra Leone, the Gambia, the Gold Coast and Lagos . . . Besides this they are to be found in every part of the Coast . . . in the capacity of merchants, traders, and clerks—in the French colony of Senegal; on the rivers Gambia, Cassamanza, Nunez, Pongas, Shebro, and Gallinas; in the Liberian Republic; on the Gold Coast; in the Kingdom of Dahomey; in Lagos and Abeokuta; in the Niger; at Bonny; Old and New Calabar, the Cameroons, Fernando Po, the Gaboons, and the Islands of St. Helens and Ascension. . . .[23]

Dr. James Africanus Beale Horton, a Creole who wrote the above passage in 1868, was himself working in the Gold Coast (Ghana) as a military surgeon at the time.

Nigeria's educational debt to Sierra Leone is reinforced by the fact that the inspiration for the earliest missionary education came from the latter. Again the actualisation was preceded by trade. Some of the enterprising liberated Africans found that Sierra Leone provided only limited opportunities for them. In 1839 three of them bought a ship renamed the *Wilberforce* and sailed to Badagry in what is now Western Nigeria. The majority of the recaptives in Sierra Leone were Yorubas captured after the Owu War of 1821. In Sierra Leone, they were known as the 'Aku' after their manner of greeting. Some of them had petitioned the Governor and received his permission for a colony to be started in Badagry.[24] That was the beginning of a minor exodus, during which, according to a contemporary report:

> Many Akoos have lately returned to their country, in vessels freighted by themselves, having obtained from Government passports obtained to that effect. I understand they

landed at Badagry. Many of these individuals were zealous followers of Christianity, and will doubtless carry with them the doctrines and rules of civilised life. May civilization and religion mark their footsteps![25]

Whether 'civilisation' marked their footsteps is outside the present discussion, but religion certainly did. Among the first liberated emigrants to Badagry was James Fergusson. He it was who wrote requesting the Western Missionary Society in London to send a missionary. In 1842 the energetic and tactful Rev. Thomas Freeman, a Wesleyan missionary, (the first Wesleyan General Superintendent at Cape Coast), was sent to investigate. That year he visited Abeokuta as well as other parts of Yorubaland. By 1845 the C.M.S. had established a boarding school at Badagry, which combined literary with some vocational training, Within five years, in 1850, the introduction of education and a more lasting contact with Europe were well-begun: the C.M.S. and Wesleyans had opened centres in various parts of Yorubaland, the Scottish Mission had been started in Calabar, and Onitsha was already being set up as a centre by the Niger.[26]

'The Bible and the Plough'

Although the slave trade was abolished in 1807 in England, it was some time before it was completely stopped. National steps towards the abolition of slavery were accompanied by the search for new markets for Britain's growing industries. Trade had been conducted through African businessmen at the Coast, but following the contributions of such explorers as Mungo Park and particularly the Lander brothers,[27] a desire to trade directly with the interior opened up great possibilities. No sooner had the Lander brothers returned than an enterprising Liverpool merchant, Macgregor Laird, sent out two ships with commercial goods. The enterprise failed owing to heavy death tolls resulting from malaria.[28]

The humanitarians[29] also came to realise that stopping the slave trade was not enough; it had to be attacked at its very beginnings. This attitude was put in book form in T. F. Buxton's *The African Slave Trade and its Remedy* (London, 1840). He argued that the efforts of Britain to stop the slave trade through diplomacy in Europe and the naval patrols of the Atlantic had not done much to reduce the number of slaves removed from Africa. His theory was that Christianity and trade, working *pari passu*, would destroy the slave trade and 'civilise' African thinking, thus making legitimate trade more profitable than the slave trade. The task was to be carried out by Africans themselves, who because of their adaptation to the climate were to be trained as teachers and technical and agricultural agents, in industrial schools operated by the missions. Buxton's plan was popularly christened 'The Bible and the Plough'.[30] Buxton urged the British government to undertake pioneer journeys into the interior through the newly discovered waterways in order to sign treaties with chiefs and to show what possibilities there were for trade. Africans from Sierra Leone and the Americas should be used as agents, who, protected by Britain, guided by the missionaries, and working with capital from European merchants, would start little settlements from which this new light was to be shed.[31] The result of this was the government-backed 'civilising' mission of 1841.[32] Again many on the expedition died, but treaties were signed with the rulers of Aboh and Igalla, and a short-lived model farm set up at Lokoja.[33] Although the mission failed, it had some far-reaching effects in other directions. First, the government, formerly averse to being involved in West African politics, now began to encourage the signing of slave trade treaties to strengthen the hands of its naval officers by obtaining for them the support of favourably-disposed rulers in the African mainland.[34] This was to lead eventually to the acquisition of ports such as Lagos in 1861. Second, wide publicity given to the mission in Sierra Leone led to the return of many liberated Africans and to the extension of missionary activity in the country[35] as a major source of Western christian contact with the interior. Indeed the failure of the mission meant that the initiative in the application of Buxton's ideas passed to the missions themselves. Missionary enterprise was advanced on three fronts: the Church of Scotland Mission at Calabar, the C.M.S. in the Niger Delta and up Niger, and the Methodists, the C.M.S. and the Baptists moving into Yorubaland. Freed slaves played prominent parts throughout.[36]

Notes

[1] Ivor Wilks writes:

Although the production of gold in Europe, notably in Hungary, rose in the fourteenth century, consumption rose still more rapidly—principally due to the minting of new gold coinages, and to the loss of the metal through the overland trade with the East. European gold merchants looked to Africa for increased supplies, and their demands were felt first at the North African ports, and later, via the trans-Saharan routes, in the gold entrepôts of the Western Soudan.

'A medieval trade-route from the Niger to the Gulf of Guinea', *Journal of African History*, 3, 1962, p. 337.

[2] G. DE AZURA, *Chronica de Guine*, quoted in C. P. GROVES, *The Planting of Christianity in Africa*, London, 1946; I, pp. 118–19.

Azura's full name was Gomes Eanes De Zurara. A.F.C.RYDER (*Journal of African History* 3, 1962, p. 505) writes in his review of Professor Leon Bourdon's translation of *Chronique de Guinée*:

Zurara took no part in the Portuguese expeditions to Guinea, but he was a contemporary of the events he relates, and he witnessed from a privileged position the impact of this new geographical dimension upon the life and feelings of his fellow countrymen. He frequented the Court of the Infante Dom Henrique [Henry the Navigator]; he talked to the leaders of expeditions; even more important, as official chronicler of the Kingdom from 1450 and as custodian of the royal archives in the Torro do Tombo from 1454, he had access to a wide variety of documents.

[3] A.F.C.RYDER, 'Missionary activity in the Kingdom of Warri to the early nineteenth century', *Journal of the Historical Society of Nigeria*, 2, 1960, pp. 1–2.

[4] RYDER, *ibid.* p. 3.

[5] *Ibid.*, pp. 4–7.

[6] K. O. DIKE, *Trade and Politics in the Niger Delta 1830–1885*, Oxford, 1959, p. 1. Also J. D. FAGE, *An Introduction to the History of West Africa*, Cambridge, 1962, pp. 39–56.

Compare also A.F.C.RYDER's statement in 'An early Portuguese trading voyage to the Forcados River' in *The Journal of the Historical Society of Nigeria*, 1, p. 294:

> Certainly they [the Portuguese] knew of the existence [of the Forcados River] earlier than 1485, for in December of that year Joãs II of Portugal issued a privilege to the first settlers embarking for Sao Thomé which permitted them to trade the produce of that island . . .

[7] A. W. LAWRENCE, *Trade Castles and Forts of West Africa*, London, 1963, p. 25; also IVOR WILKS, *op. cit.*, pp. 337–41.

[8] For an account of the factors which led to the decline of Portuguese power in West Africa and their subsequent attempt to re-open trade, see A.F.C.RYDER, 'The establishment of Portuguese factories on the Costa da Mina to the mid-nineteenth century', *Journal of the Historical Society of Nigeria*, 1, pp. 157–81. During this period the Portuguese actually *imported* gold to West Africa!

[9] I. L. EVANS, *The British in Tropical Africa*, Cambridge, 1929, p. 12.

[10] G. G. WISE, *A History of Education in British West Africa*, London, 1956, pp. 1–4.

[11] *Ibid.*, p. 13.

[12] A. N. COOK, *British Enterprise in Nigeria*, London, 1964, pp. 18–20; also EVANS, *op. cit.*, pp. 10–13.

[13] COOK, *op. cit.*, pp. 21–23.

[14] EVANS, *op. cit.*, pp. 13–15.

[15] R. COUPLAND, *The British Anti-Slavery Movement*, London, 1933; quoted by DIKE, *op. cit.*, p. 3.

[16] For a detailed account of the events leading to the landing of the first settlers on 14 May 1787, and the formation of the Sierra Leone Company, see CHRISTOPHER FYFE, *A History of Sierra Leone*, Oxford, 1962. pp. 13–30.

[17] Held in London, on Wednesday, 19th October, 1791; quoted in CHRISTOPHER FYFE, *Sierra Leone Inheritance*, Oxford, 1964, pp. 116–18.

[18] FYFE, *Sierra Leone Inheritance*, p. 117.

[19] FYFE, *History of Sierra Leone*, p. 69.

[20] C. P. GROVES, *The Planting of Christianity in Africa*, Vol. I, p. 204.

[21] *Ibid.*, p. 200.

[22] K. A. B. JONES-QUARTEY, The Debt of Sierra Leone to the Gold Coast, *Sierra Leone Studies*, New Series, 10, 1958.

[23] J. A. B. HORTON, *West African Peoples*, London, 1868, pp. 61–62.

[24] FYFE, *Sierra Leone Inheritance*, pp. 147–50.

[25] CLARK, *Sierra Leone*, London, 1843, p. 40; quoted in FYFE, *Sierra Leone Inheritance* p. 150.

[26] WISE, *op. cit.*, pp. 10–11; FYFE, *History of Sierra Leone*, p. 227.

[27] The nineteenth century witnessed a series of British expeditions to gain knowledge of the interior of the country and to pave the way for the influx of traders and missionaries. The first of these was undertaken by Major Houghton in 1791 under the auspices of the Royal Geographical Society. He died a few years after setting out. More successful was Mungo Park's 1795 expedition during which he reached the Niger. He died in 1804 during his second expedition. Other expeditions include those by Major Peddie and

Captain Turkey (1816), Major Denham and Captain Clapperton (1821), visiting various parts of Northern Nigeria. The Lander brothers, Richard and John, reached the mouth of the Niger in 1830.

COOK, *op. cit.*, pp. 24–38; EVANS, *op. cit.*, Ch. 11 *passim;* MICHAEL CROWDER, *The Story of Nigeria*, London, 1962 pp. 118–23.

²⁸ CROWDER, *op cit.*, pp. 123–4.

²⁹ *Ibid.*, p. 118.

³⁰ J. B. WEBSTER, 'The Bible and the Plough', *Journal of the Historical Society of Nigeria*, 2, 1960, p. 418.

³¹ J. F. ADE AJAYI: *Christian Missions in Nigeria, 1841–1891*, London, 1965, pp. 10–12.

³² C. C. IFEMESIA, 'The "Civilising" Mission of 1841', *Journal of the Historical Society of Nigeria*, 2, 1962.

³³ AJAYI, *op. cit.*, p. 12.

³⁴ *Ibid.*

³⁵ *Ibid.*

³⁶ CROWDER, *op. cit.*, pp. 126–9.

3   Nationalism and the Demand for Universities in Nigeria

In 1914 the Northern and Southern Nigeria Protectorates were joined with the Colony of Lagos, but not without some resistance from the Nigerians. Indeed long after this union the government still had to subdue dissenting states in various parts of the country. Some of these occurrences were the Egba Uprising (or the 'Adubi War') of 1918, the Arochuku Riots of 1925 and the Aba Riots of 1929.[1]

But opposition to foreign influence can be traced much further back than 1914. Foreign (in this case, European) influence can take, and has, taken other forms besides the political; resistance to it has therefore occurred at the various points of contact with the foreign powers. This opposition to outside influence may be termed nationalism and it must be emphasised in passing that nationalism and nationalist movements as here defined may or may not be contemporaneous with political movements aimed at liberation from foreign political domination. This broad definition is not universally accepted. Some have used nationalism in the restricted sense of a protest against foreign domination aimed specifically at securing political autonomy. Dr. James Coleman, for instance, gives the following as the distinguishing features of nationalism in the Nigerian context:

a) the explicit goal of Nigerian self-government
b) the concept of Nigerian unity
c) the predominance of a westernised élite in leadership groups
d) the development of permanent political associations to pursue nationalist objectives
e) the predominance of modern political values and ideals.[2]

This view, however, is restricted, and does not take account of earlier manifestations, although Coleman himself agrees that 'all these [earlier] forms of resistance and assertion might legitimately come under the rubric of "nationalism",' and 'are not without relevance for an understanding of later developments.'[3] This restricted concept of nationalism has recently been criticised by Ayandele: 'Evidence shows that there was a forceful awakening in Nigeria before 1914: that it was constructive, purposeful, inspiring and fruitful and that it prepared the ground for the better-known post-World War 1 nationalism...'[4] It seems appropriate for the purposes of this discussion then to regard nationalism in the broader sense, relating to 'any organisation or group that explicitly asserts the rights, claims, and aspirations of a given African society (from the level of the language-group to that of "Pan Africa") in opposition to European authority, whatever its institutional form and objectives'. [5] It is also important to note at this point that the term nationalism may also encompass 'the organised movement of a people, irrespective of whether or not they comprise a truly *national group*, towards self-government or independence'. [6] Indeed nationalism in the African context stemmed from the African's desire to demonstrate that his individuality is so different from the Euoropean's that he is ready to claim not only freedom from European control, but also to adopt only those European institutions which may suit his own peculiar circumstances. [7]

Nationalism and the demand for universities

Nationalism thus appeared in diverse forms. The demand for universities by West African nationalists could not arise until these nationalists themselves had come into contact with, and understood the power of the university—the peak of the educational pyramid. As mentioned earlier the devastating slave trade also brought Africa into faster and more intimate contact with western Europe than would otherwise have been possible. Slaves or their descendants were the pioneers of Christianity and western education in Sierra Leone and thence through all English-speaking West Africa. They were also pioneers of nationalism in British West Africa. As Shepperson aptly put it:

> The first British Empire owed much to the triangular trade between Africa, the West Indies and North Africa. The last British Empire [the Commonwealth?] has not been uninfluenced by another triangular trade, a trade not of pocatille, slaves and molasses but a commerce of ideas and politics between the descendants of slaves in the West Indies and North America and their ancestral continent. [8]

Four West African nationalists stand out clearly from among their companions for their part in the demand for universities in West Africa: Horton, Blyden, Hayford and Azikiwe. They had different reasons for their actions; each was influenced by his general background, profession, and the constitutional stage at which the various British West African countries had arrived at the time.

HORTON
The earliest initiative of which there is any record was that of James Africanus Beale Horton. He was born in 1835, the son of an Ibo recaptive carpenter, in Gloucester, Sierra Leone. In the 1850s the (British) War Office was alarmed at the expense of maintaining the medical corps on the West African coast. Although a double staff was provided to give the employees regular home leave, mortality was still high. It was then decided that young Africans should be trained as doctors and given commissions. The C.M.S.

was asked to help and it chose three youths who were already at the Fourah Bay Institution: James Horton, William Davies and Samuel Campbell, who were sent to England. Campbell died soon afterwards, but Horton and Davies went on, and took their medical qualifications. Both obtained the M.R.C.S., London, in 1858; a year later, Horton took the M.D. of Edinburgh and Davies that of St. Andrews. Also in 1859, they entered the army and were posted to the Gold Coast with the rank of Staff-Assistant Surgeon.[9] The two contrasted vigorously in character: Davies was mild and soft-voiced, whereas Horton was forceful and outspoken.[10] Horton was a many-sided man. Not only did he publish many books and pamphlets,[11] medical and non-medical, but he was also interested in political[12] and financial matters. For instance, after his retirement in 1880, he founded in 1882 the Commercial Bank of West Africa (the first indigenous bank) with headquarters in Freetown. He had planned branches in other parts of West Africa, but unfortunately he died in 1883, a year after its opening, and the bank was closed.[13]

Horton's nationalism found expression in his *West African Countries and Peoples, British and Native, with the Requirements necessary for the establishment of that Self-Government recommended by the Committee of the House of Commons, 1865 and Vindication of the African Race*, which was published in 1868. The book may be divided into three parts. The first dealt with a description of the topography and the peoples. The second was a refutation of the currently held view of the African's innate inferiority. The third part was concerned with proposals for the self-government of West Africa, especially Sierra Leone. The framework for Horton's demands reflects the political situation in British West Africa at the time. There were in the early 1860s four British colonies: Gambia, Sierra Leone, Gold Coast and the 'Settlement' of Lagos. At this time the British government had apparently still not made up its mind whether to keep colonies in West Africa.

In 1865 a Select Committee of the British House of Commons was appointed to study whether or not the four West African colonies should be retained. Following the *Report* of the Committee, the House of Commons resolved that it was not possible for the British government to withdraw wholly or immediately from any settlements or engagements on the West African Coast. But at the same time it stated that:

> all further assumption of territory or assumption of Government, or new treaties, offering any protection to native tribes would be inexpedient; and that the object of our policy should be to encourage in the natives the exercise of those qualities which may render it possible more and more to transfer to them the administration of all the Governments, with a view to our ultimate withdrawal from all, except, probably Sierra Leone.

However, there was the loophole:

> that this policy of non-extension admits of no exception, as regards new settlements,

but cannot amount to an absolute prohibition of measures which in peculiar cases, may be necessary for the more efficient and economical administration of the settlements we already possess.[14]

The background to the setting up of the Committee and its subsequent function explains to a large extent Horton's motives for writing *West African Countries*. Early in 1864 it was suddenly realised by the British public that heavy losses of life and money were being experienced in the Ashanti War which the Governor of the Gold Coast had been fighting for some months. There was, however, both inside and outside Parliament a division of opinion. Some felt that the colonies were useless, neither suppressing the slave trade nor encouraging legitimate trade and therefore should be abandoned. Others felt that the colonies should be kept. Some of those who wanted the colonies abandoned accused the mission-educated colonials of being 'notorious rogues' and 'dishonest trouble-makers'.[15] The Chairman and most members of the 1865 Select Committee were members of this group. It was not surprising therefore that all but one of the Committee 'tended in their questions to show prejudice against West Africa, and particularly Sierra Leone.'[16]

Shortly before the Committee was appointed, prejudice had been mounting in England against the West African Settlements and most especially Sierra Leone. This was due mainly to superficial travel books written by Englishmen who had visited the Coast, the contents of which were swallowed unquestioningly by the British public.[17] These writers described West Africans (especially those in Sierra Leone) as lazy, and as haters of Europeans.[18] Missionaries were attacked for being harmful and useless and for having led educated Africans to think themselves equal to Europeans. Instead Muslims were looked up to for the civilisation of Africa.[19] Indeed it was prophesied by Winwood Reade and others that the African race must eventually die out by natural selection and young ladies 'will read with tears *The Last of the Negroes*'.[20]

At about this time also the Anthropological Society of London was founded (1863) with Richard Burton as Vice-President and Reade, a member. The Society was founded to examine objectively the racial characteristics of mankind. In practice, however, it devoted its attention to proving the superiority of the European over the non-European, using superficial medical evidence.[21] In short this was a time when the idea of the racial inferiority of the Negro was being much discussed. Hence Dr. Horton's sub-title of *Vindication of the Negro Race*, under which, in a very pertinent passage, he defended the race thus:

> But the Creoles of Sierra Leone have been stigmatised as the most impertinent rogues in all the coast, even by men who know nothing of them. They will not wait for the truth, the whole truth and nothing but the truth. . . . There is undoubtedly among the low, reckless class, a certain amount of roguery, such as is found among a parallel portion of the population of the world; but the stigma is here applied to the whole

population. . . . But we find nevertheless that these Creoles of Sierra Leone occupy lucrative subordinate positions of trust in both the military and civil service of the Government in the four colonies and settlements of the coast. . . . If they were not an industrious, exploring race, determined to advance their position in life by speculation and other legitimate means, would they not have confined themselves within the limits of the Peninsula of Sierra Leone; and do not the exertions above alluded to, point to a similar trait in the character of Englishmen, who are to be found in every part of the known world where money is to be made?[22]

Being a medical man he was also able to refute in the language of science the alleged anatomical similarity of the Negro with the ape:

But it is in the development of the most important organ of the body—the brain and its investing parieties—that much stress has been laid to prove the simian or ape-like character of the negro race. . . . Among the negro race, at least among the thousands that have come under my notice, the posterior sutures first close, then the frontal and coronal, and the contrary has never been observed by me in ever a single instance, not even among negro idiots; and yet M. Gratiolet and Carl Vogt, without an opportunity of investigating the subject to any extent, have unhesitatingly propagated the most absurd and erroneous doctrine—that the closing of the sutures of the negro follows the simious or animal arrangement, differing from that already given as the governing condition in man.[23]

He then went on to quote scientific works which proved his opponents wrong.

'On every occasion,' lamented Horton, 'modern anthropologists delight to descant on the inferiority of the negro race as regards their intellectual and moral improvement . . . In Dr. Hunt's brochure *On the Negroes' Place in Nature* [for instance] he endeavoured to prove that the Negro, being in his opinion intellectually inferior to the European or white race, should occupy a servile position in nature.[24] But, argued Horton, these detractors of the Negro race withheld the fact that Negroes had been exposed to what Horton called 'influences not calculated to develop either the moral, or the intellectual faculties but on the contrary to destroy them'. It was not Negroes alone who under pernicious influences become altered, 'but animals and Europeans also. M. Dupins has conclusively proved this in his report on the effect of long captivity and severe treatment on European Christians among the Arabs. They lost their reason and feelings; their spirits broke and their faculties sank in an undescribable stupor; and when subject to a succession of hardships, they lost all their spirit of exertion and hope, became indifferent, abject, servile and brutish.'[25]

If bondage and a depraved life had such damnifying influence on the moral and intellectual condition of man in general, how could men be elevated while the (climatic and geographic) burdens which oppressed them were so great? How could they be expected to discover anything like even a 'virtuous emulation' while precluded by their circumstances of slavery? Indeed, Horton wondered, could any other people have endured the privations or the sufferings to which Negroes had been subjected without being even more degraded?[26]

In such terms Dr. Horton defended the Negro race. It must be mentioned that the West Africans had their supporters amongst Englishmen, notable among them Lord Alfred Churchill and his African Aid Society.[27]

Resolution 3 of the 1865 Committee had indicated that natives would be encouraged to engage in those activities which would eventually make them fit for self-government. Horton jumped at the opportunity and included in his book the following *Requirements necessary for establishing that self-government recommended by the Committee of the House of Commons, 1865*:

> But as it is proposed to teach the people self-government, to the ultimate withdrawal of British influence or power, and to leave natives to govern themselves, there must be chosen either a monarchical or a republican form of government. As in the Gambia a republic is unsuited to the taste of the people, so it is at Sierra Leone. It will never survive among the native inhabitants, who have always looked up to their King, to the same influence and effect. A national government, then, will be the only form, and the King should be elected by universal suffrage, supported for some time by the British Government; he should for a short period be initiated into the art of governing, by serving the subordinate position of a governor over the Colony and its Dependencies, whilst the English Governor should act as Governor-General of all the Coast.
>
> His first policy would be to show himself to be on the popular side identifying himself with the growth of the peoples' liberties, by which means he will secure an under-basis of popular affection, which will be an important anxillary in his infant Kingdom, where, at the commencement, conflicting views and opinions are possible. He should make merit the great high road to public trusts, honours, and rewards, thus proving to everyone that measures the intellectual worth and dignity of man, not by the truths which he possesses, or fancies he possesses, but by the sincere and honest pains which he takes to discover them. He should be a native-born Sierra Leonist or a citizen by constitutional adoption. . . . A constitutional form of government must form the basis of his administration, consisting of a House of Assembly which should be composed of men elected by the people, as it will be difficult for his Government to stand without confidence. . . . Besides the House of Assembly there should be the Senate, consisting of men above the age of 35 years and having extensive means, and who may be recognized by all as possessing good practical common sense. . . . Gold and silver should be made the legal tender for the payment of debts; English money be recognized for a period as the state coin, until such time as the country will be able to establish a mint. . . .[28]

Horton believed that Sierra Leone had already many of the necessities for independent existence:

> On accession he [the King] will find that his treasury is not impoverished, that his people are intelligent, industrious and willing to give him every assistance in establishing and completing the national edifice. He will have a population comparatively well advanced and progressing in civilization, who by the zealous effort of the missionary societies, have nearly one-fifth of the whole inhabitants at school, which is an unusually large proportion in any country. By the census of 1860 the 'percentage of the population under education was 22, whereas the percentage in Prussia was 16 and in England 13'; and the effect is manifested in the intellectual, moral and religious improvements visible in the country.[29]

The setting out of the above served the dual purpose of recording the presence of institutions and conditions favourable to self-government and of defending the Sierra Leonian against attacks prevalent at this time.

He recognised, however, that certain institutions needed some, if only slight, modifications to fit them for the needs of the new Sierra Leone:

> The schools [which] are supported in some measure by fees and endowments obtained by the exertions of the people . . . are good and useful establishments but are open to great improvements. In Sierra Leone there is a good self-supporting grammar school where Latin, Greek, Mathematics and other branches of English education are taught by a native Clergyman, which bears most profitable fruit and is fully self-supporting. Besides this there is a large theological college, where the higher branches of learning are taught under the C.M.S. and which the King can do no better than to convert to a university. . . .[30]

Horton's more positive demands for a university were embodied in the section dealing with 'General Improvement in the Educational and Ecclesiastical Department of the Colony':

> We want a University for Western Africa, and the Church Missionary Society has long ago taken the initiative and built an expensive college, which should now be made the focus of learning for all West Africa. . . . Fourah Bay College should henceforth be made the University of Western Africa, and endowed by the Local Government.[31]

He then made suggestions on the curricula and method of study in the proposed university:

> A systematic course of instruction should be given to the students, and regius professors appointed; for it is high time to abolish that system of Lancastrian school-boy teaching, and a professor should be appointed to one or two subjects, and should give lectures on the result of extensive reading and research. The subjects will be better mastered by the teachers themselves, and the students would reap largely the benefit. Lectures should be given in the theory and practice of education, classics, mathematics, natural philosophy, mensuration and book-keeping, English language and literature, French, German, Hebrew, history in general, mineralogy, physiology, civil and commercial law, drawing and music; besides the various subjects which might be included under the term of theology.
>
> But the study of the physical sciences which are closely connected with our daily wants and conveniencies, should form an essential part of the curriculum. . . . Algebra, arithmetic differential calculus, trigonometry, and geometry [should be included].[32]

Horton's demand for a university was thus prompted by the expectation that British withdrawal and concommitant self-government were imminent. It has been suggested, however, by Professor Dike and others that Horton 'took the recommendations [of the 1865 Committee] literally and agitated for their implementation'; that 'In its origin the Select Committee was called forth largely by considerations of economy and not solely by the desire to abandon West Africa or her trade.'[33] There are other views on the matter, and indeed there are good grounds for believing as Professor J. F. Ade Ajayi points out, that the Committee took seriously their recommendation that the Africans be trained for self-government as an alternative to intermittent British political intervention. Professor Ajayi continues:

The implication was that in the colonies Britain wished to retain, Africans, who cost less to maintain than Europeans, should be taught the European art of government. Owing to the difficulty of wars about which Britain could do nothing constructive, and to problems of economy and climate, self-government was being urged as a positive thing good in itself, good for the interests both of Britain and of the local communities.[34]

The real intentions of the British government or the subsequent expansion of trade despite the Resolutions of the 1865 Committee may be seen retrospectively to have been outside Horton's knowledge at the time he wrote his book. It is rather more useful at this point to look at the background of the writer. This may be summarised by saying that Horton was a typical product of the 'Bible and Plough' policy[35] (see Ch. 2).

The chief implementer of this policy was Henry Venn, the Secretary of the C.M.S. from 1841 to 1872. Venn's desire was to encourage the growth of an African middle class. It was not enough that trade with Europe should increase; it was necessary that trade should also lead to social change and the development of a middle class. This was the only sure way to eradicate slavery permanently in Africa.[36] The Church must move with the times and keep pace with the social change; the Church must be self-supporting, self-governing, self-propagating, employing African personnel, stressing the vernacular and incorporating African ceremonies and rites. Indeed, the wind of change in secular affairs must also affect the Church. Although enunciated for the C.M.S., the change inevitably reached other denominations, pressed as they were by their African membership.[37]

How did the missionaries bring about the new social order, this building-up of a middle class? First, they introduced western education, training local people and creating a local body of educated people. Second, they sought to introduce to their wards ideas of nation-building which were current in Europe at that time. The ideals of European nationhood presented to them had three characteristics: the Europeans were Christian, they had an advanced technology consequent on the Industrial Revolution, and finally, small states had given way to larger units.[38] Education and nation-building may be seen as direct consequences of the 'Bible and Plough' policy. They were in practical terms a result of high mortality rates amongst Europeans and determined to considerable extent the whole future of Afro-European relations.[39] There is no doubt that this development influenced the general attitude of the 1865 Committee.

The first generation of this educated middle class were slaves or their descendants and were at first mainly trained in Sierra Leone. In passing from slavery to freedom, many of them had had the opportunity of seeing other (especially European) lands and had become conscious of the technological and other gaps separating them as a people from others.[40] At this time it was common, as has been shown, for the alleged racial inferiority of the Negro to be thrown in their faces in the writings of Europeans. It was therefore natural that they should develop a form of nationalism.

C

This nationalism of the 'Bible and Plough' middle class had two distinct features. First, it was not specifically national in the territorial sense, as present-day states like Sierra Leone and Nigeria were either non-existent or else had not expanded to their present form; rather, racial consciousness gave rise to this nationalism. Their loyalty was therefore to the 'African Race', and since most of them knew only a part of Africa, they usually had their home area in mind. The dispersal of their descendants in different parts of West Africa gave reality to West Africa as a basis for their nationalism.[41] An added factor was the unifying influence of missionary activity and British colonial policy which often tended to treat the embryo British West Africa as one unit.

A second feature of this nationalism was that it desired some association with Britain. This is easy to understand as most of these educated elements or their forbears had been liberated only through the kindly intervention of the British.[42]

Dr. James Horton was the archetype of this mid-nineteenth century educated West African. He had already been trained by the C.M.S. in their Fourah Bay Institution before being sent to England to study medicine. His *West African Countries* is the very picture of Professor Ajayi's description. The book was not only intended to vindicate, in Horton's terms, the African race from the racially inferior position to which it was generally relegated by Europeans. It was also concerned with suggestions for establishing self-government, but these were virtually concerned with Sierra Leone alone. For instance, although his university was proposed for all Western Africa, the lower rungs of the educational ladder from which the university was to be fed were designed only for Sierra Leone:

> The whole Colony [of Sierra Leone] should be divided into educational districts. In each there should be a free grammar-school, where scholars should be prepared either for a foundation school, to be established in the city, or for the University. . . .
> The Government should also establish a preparatory school at Freetown for the express purpose of training up teachers, or forming a corps of well-trained teachers, who should give instruction both in theory and in the practical application of the Sciences; if very proficient in these studies some might be transferred to the University.

Other areas of West Africa[43] came in for only brief consideration:

> It will not be out of place if a minister or officer of public instruction be created, with suitable councils, to regulate and improve the educational branch, not only of the Colony of Sierra Leone, but also of the other Colonies in West Africa.[44]

Horton's self-governing 'West Africa' was not to become so without British supervision. Although the King of 'West Africa' was to be elected by universal suffrage he was to be supervised for some time, and initiated into the art of governing by the British government.[45]

Horton's university was thus to serve the needs of the new 'West African' nation. He had, however, prior to the publication of *West African Countries*, advocated in 1861 the creation of a small training school in Freetown where prospective medical students could be introduced into their studies before proceeding to England to qualify. In a letter to the War Office on the matter, on 13 July 1861, he praised the British government for the scheme whereby young Africans were sent to England to study medicine, and under which he himself and Davies had qualified. The scheme was important because Africans survived the West African climate better than Europeans. In consequence Europeans stayed for only short periods and so could not acquire sufficiently long experience to make them competent in treating peculiarly West African diseases. The African properly trained in medicine acquired this experience and stayed longer on the job in West Africa.

Furthermore 'The immortal Sir Fowell Buxton [of the "Bible and Plough" fame] has truly affirmed that if Africa is to be civilised and evangelized it must be by her progeny.' It would therefore be of very great importance to the country and to the people that the government continue to provide the Coast of Africa with well-educated natives, to serve there as scientific and professional personnel.

Finally, argued Horton, the scientific resources of Western Africa were 'entirely in embryo' and ignorance about them was prevalent. There were vast treasures in the bowels of this extensive continent, potent medicines in its picturesque fields, and objects of great importance to naturalists, as yet unknown to the scientific world. The short stay of the European would not permit him to study them adequately, but the African could. Horton suggested that for the training of doctors a small Government Medical Establishment be put at Sierra Leone, where youths with qualifications in Latin, Greek and mathematics, from the four colonies and settlements—Gambia, Sierra Leone, Lagos and Cape Coast—could be given preliminary courses in Anatomy, Physiology, Chemistry, Botany ('of Africa'), Natural History, Hospital Practice and Pharmacy, while at the same time continuing with their classical studies. The Master of the Establishment should be African.[46] In this way Horton hoped the African student would, once in England, catch up more easily with his English counterparts.[47]

According to Horton, a favourable reply was received from the War Office, but when European Army Officers on the Coast were consulted, 'the subject received a combined and warm opposition, which nipped it in the bud.'[48]

But Horton had another reason for suggesting the founding of the small Medical Establishment, one which it would have been imprudent to state in his letter to the War Office, but which he mentions in his *West African Peoples*. The proposed establishment was only apparently a beginning. His real desire was to open something which would ultimately attain the status of a medical school. In this way he hoped that African scientists would themselves be able to prove to the scientific world the falsity of the assertions being made about the Negroes' anatomy, et cetera.[49]

We must depend upon the direct investigations and experiments among natives of Africa, who have mastered their subjects in European Universities to make these experiments in Africa upon dead and living subjects. This can only be achieved by a Medical School being established in Africa, and facilities offered for obtaining subjects for dissection and experiments. The Author, feeling certain of the immense advantages which Africa would derive from so important an establishment, . . . proposed the Scheme to the Home Government for a Medical School in Sierra Leone.

When this failed he provided in his will for the establishment of 'Horton's Collegiate High School', primarily to teach science. This he hoped would develop into a university. Once again his plans fell through: his will was disputed, the shares in which he had invested his money depreciated and when his assets were finally wound up little was left for the endowment.[50]

BLYDEN

At the time of Horton's death in 1883 a contemporary of his, Edward Wilmot Blyden, had already made his mark on West African affairs. Blyden was born in St. Thomas, in the then Danish West Indies, in August 1832, three years before Horton. At the age of twelve he was apprenticed to a tailor, working in the afternoon after attending school in the morning. His interest in English composition caught the attention of the Rev. Knox who was in charge of the Dutch Reformed Church, and in 1850, when the gentleman was about to return to the United States, Mrs. Knox encouraged the young Blyden to come with them in the hope that he might gain admission to an American college and eventually enter the ministry. Blyden found, however, a

deep-seated prejudice against my race, exercising so controlling an influence in the institutions of learning, that admission to them was almost impossible. Discouraged by difficulties in my path, I proposed to return to St. Thomas and abandon the hope of an education. . . .[51]

Fortunately for West Africa, Blyden did not abandon hope, for encouraged by Mrs. Knox, he decided to accept the offer of the New York Colonisation Society of a passage to Monrovia, arriving there on 26 January 1851. He was admitted into the Alexander High School, where he learnt Latin, Greek, Geography, and Mathematics. Hebrew was not taught in the school and he mastered the subject in his leisure, 'being anxious to read the entire Scriptures in the original languages, especially those passages of the Old Testament which have reference to the African race.'

Three years after Blyden's admission, the Rev. Wilson, who was Principal of the school, left for the United States on account of ill-health, and young Blyden, having performed very well, was put in charge. While thus engaged, he also undertook public service, when he accepted an invitation to be the assistant editor of the *Liberia Herald*. When the Rev. Wilson retired in 1858, Blyden was put completely in charge of the school and in the same year he was ordained in the Presbytery of West Africa.

In 1861, while still teaching in the school, he was appointed Professor of Latin and Greek at the newly-established Liberia College. His age was twenty-nine.[52] Blyden was hopeful of the success of the new College and rightly saw the justification of its establishment to serve the young Liberian state:

> To say, as has been too often said by persons abroad and persons here, that the establishment of a college in Liberia at present is premature, is to set aside the experience of other countries . . . showing the indispensableness of institutions of a higher order, to send down, through all the ramifications of society, the streams of wholesome and elevating influence. . . . It cannot be denied, that the studies which shall be pursued in this Institution are of great utility to the country just now.[53]

This institution of higher learning was to serve the mundane needs of the Liberia to which he had migrated some ten years earlier. At the same time it was to provide an 'elevating influence' on the populace. This influence was not spelt out in full, but his subsequent writings develop it. Probably at this stage the teaching he was to propagate throughout his long life was already forming. His idea, as seen from his writings, was that the African had an identity different from that of any and every other race. In particular he considered that the European missionaries who had introduced Christianity had arrogated to themselves the form Christianity was to take in Africa. Like Horton his ideas sprang partly from the contemporary denunciation of the African race as inferior. The forms which their nationalism was to take were naturally dictated by their backgrounds. Horton was a medical man and his refutation of the nineteenth century attacks on the Africans was based mainly on scientific evidence. Blyden, on the other hand, was liberally educated as well as being an ordained minister of the American Presbyterian Mission. For instance, in 'Noah's Offering', one of his earliest published speeches, he said:

> Various theories have been stated as furnishing satisfactory explanation of curses upon this unfortunate [African] race. Of these none has been more strenuously urged by the opposers of the race than that which refers its condition to a malediction recorded in Genesis 9; 25, 26, 27. They who support this theory take the ground that the curse was denounced against Ham, the progenitor of the African race, [and] all his posterity. . . .
> Now it seems to us that the most natural inference which a candid reader would make from this passage is that the curse denounced Ham in that branch of his posterity which descended from Canaan. To establish the hypothesis that the curse included all the posterity of Ham, it appears to us necessary that one of three things be proved to have been the fact. First, it must be proved that the curse was upon Ham himself; second, that it was pronounced upon each of his sons individually; or third, if pronounced upon Canaan, that he was the only offspring of Ham. But we know that no one of these was the fact: whence the inference is obvious.[54]

With devastating scholarship he attacked these 'opposers of the race', as he called them, in the language he and they understood.

The *Liberia Herald* founded by Russworm, a Negro who had emigrated to Liberia from New England, had from its beginning in the 1830s initiated what may be described as the first stirring of West African nationalism. Liberia provided the Negro ex-slave with an atmosphere of development, free from the white man's presence. The tone of the *Herald* was strongly evangelical until 1855, when Blyden was invited to be its assistant editor.[55]

In that year Blyden published in the *Herald* the first of a steady stream of literary works, embodying the true origin of West Africa's latterday nationalist thought. These writings, which continued from 1855 to his death in 1912, contained what Blyden's grandson, Professor E. W. Blyden III, has called 'The Blyden Thesis' and has summarised thus:

> [It was] that the black man had a unique contribution to make to universal history and world civilization as had other peoples and races of the world; that such contribution could only be made by Africans and not by Europeans who tried to interpret the African's culture; that while literacy in English and education patterned after the systems of Europe and the West are recognized as *sine qua non* for progress and survival in the modern world, such exotic systems of thought and social behaviour were of small effect in bringing out the very best in the African or his society, if imposed upon, rather than adapted to, the indigeneous institutions and traditional forms of . . . cultural activity long established by the African himself within his own society; that the process of adaptation to and modification of European ideas and beliefs, if merely imposed upon African society, would fail to serve the needs of the one, and would destroy the life and fire of the other; that, in the final analysis, the reproduction of the European and western way of life in the African tribal society would fail to survive the test of the true criterion of 'civilization' if the 'trammels' and not the 'essential creeds' of that culture were given the greater emphasis.[56]

He repeatedly stressed that the African should not ape Europeans, but should seek to develop along lines best suited to his environment, the missionaries being continuously blamed for the African's miseducation. He contrasted these Africans to those in the hinterland, away from the Coast, who were Muslims. His book, *Christianity, Islam and the Negro Race*, dealt with this topic and aroused great interest in West Africa among his friends and followers. Naturally this gave rise to speculation among his opponents that he was becoming a Muslim, which he refuted.

> The rumours of my having embraced Mohammedanism are based chiefly upon my book, and my travels and labours among that people have been over and over again contradicted in English and American newspapers.
> I believe Christianity to be the ultimate and final religion of humanity. Indeed I believe that it has always been and always will be the system which raises mankind to the highest level. 'Before Abraham was, I am,' said Christ; and my labours and efforts among Mohammedans are to assist them to understand Him whom the Koran describes as the 'Spirit of God'.[57]

Blyden then states why he saw so much in Islam: it had done for the vast tribes of Africa what Christianity in the hands of Europeans had not yet done:

> It [Islam] has cast out demons of fetishism, general ignorance of God, drunkenness, [and] gambling, and has introduced customs which subserve for the people the highest purposes of growth and preservation. I do not think that a system which has done such things can be outside of God's beneficent plans for the evolution of humanity.[58]

Horton had concerned himself very much with political matters. He was a civil servant and indeed had once held the post of Civil Administrator in the Gold Coast. He therefore saw the improvement of colonial West Africa in terms of politics and administration. Blyden, however, was a cleric, and his interest was naturally concerned with religious and cultural matters. To him politics were secondary; cultural improvement of the race was supreme.

> We are rising to a loftier, purer and clearer atmosphere, and arriving at the conviction that the political and commercial aggrandizement of this country is of less importance than the improvement and integrity of the people. [59]

One sure means of rising to this 'purer, loftier, clearer atmosphere' was, in Blyden's view, the establishment of a university in West Africa.

On 22 May 1872, the editor of *The Negro* wrote to the Honourable William Grant, Member of the Legislative Council of Sierra Leone on 'the establishment in this colony of a good educational Institution to be conducted by trained and experienced Negroes [and] of importance, vital importance—not only to the people of this colony, but of the whole West Coast of Africa.'[60]

Sierra Leone had the most promising position in the world for the erection of an education system adapted to the Negroes' peculiar needs. Everywhere else (especially in the United States of America) influences that tended to confuse the instincts of the race were paramount. But in Sierra Leone the Negro would be surrounded by people in whom it was possible to produce a 'race sentiment'. No factitious restraints growing out of the predominating presence of a foreign race could limit the expression, the investigation or the experimentation of the Sierra Leone Negroes who were just as much at home there as they might be in their original homes on the banks of the Niger or in the Yoruba plains.

It seemed therefore to the editor of *The Negro* that a common duty devolved upon the influential natives of Sierra Leone to endeavour to secure for the indigenous youth the means of proper training at home. Such an institution would generate 'a general diffusion of that higher intelligence which originates public measures, which stimulates the people, moderates their impulses, sustains and gives weight to noble enterprises, creates and expounds a healthy public sentiment, and accelerates the normal and spiritual progress of the race'.[61]

In reply, Grant suggested that the Editor should publish the letter in *The Negro* in order that the subject should be thoroughly ventilated and discussed, 'trusting that such discussion may lead to the adoption of such measures as will promote the educational interests of our people'.[62] Subsequently therefore the letter was published in a supplement to *The Negro* for 5 June 1872.

To put the significance of this event in its proper perspective, it is important to point out that the editor of *The Negro* was Blyden himself and, that William Grant, a self-made, rich and influential businessman, was one of five Sierra Leone leaders who had helped Blyden found *The Negro*. Grant had been appointed to the Sierra Leone Legislative Council in 1869.[63] This clever tactic of remaining in anonymity behind a public figure at the beginning of a project appears to have been one of which Blyden was very fond (see also Ch. 4).

Six months after the appearance of Blyden's letter in *The Negro* supplement, Blyden opened a correspondence with the Governor of Sierra Leone, J. Pope Hennessy, on the establishment of a West African University.

In his first letter, dated 6 December 1872, Blyden stressed the importance of a liberal education to the youth of the country:

> If in the Governments of these settlements, native agency is to be welcomed and encouraged and not despised and excluded; if the people are ever to become fit to be entrusted with the functions of self-government; if they are ever to become ripe for free and progressive institutions, it must be by a system of education adopted to the exigencies of the country and race; such a system as shall prepare the intelligent youth for the responsibilities which must devolve upon them; and, without interfering with their native instincts, and throwing them altogether out of harmony and sympathy with their own countrymen, shall qualify them to be the efficient guides and counsellors and rulers of the people.[64]

Blyden argued that to give the people the opportunity of a free and healthy development which would civilise and sharpen the character and originality of the individual, a university was necessary.

> The presence of such an Institution with able African teachers brought, if necessary, from different parts of the world—even a Negro Arabic Professor from Egypt, Timbuctoo or Futah—would have great influence in exposing and correcting the fallacies upon which our foreign teachers have proceeded in their misapprehension, and perhaps contempt, of African character.

Blyden implored the Governor to obtain the co-operation of the government in England[65] to found an educational institution 'to give shelter and nutriment to these struggling views, so as to make them a property of the masses; and by gradually developing and extending them, make them a permanent element of moral and even religious power on the whole coast'.[66]

The university Blyden had in view, as he noted in his second letter, would assist in the creation and building up of an indigenous literature.

Blyden could not persuade Governor Hennessy to promise government support for the university, which, according to the Governor, must be the work of the Africans themselves'.[67] Blyden politely asserted that

> Europeans owe us a great debt, not only for the unrequited physical labours we have performed in all parts of the world, but for the unnumbered miseries and untold demoralization they have brought upon Africa by the prosecution . . . of the horrible traffic to promote their own selfish ends; and we do not simply ask it as a favour but claim it as a right when we entreat their aid as civilized and Christian Governments in the work of unfettering and enlightening the Negro mind.[68]

All he received, however, was the Governor's agreement to transmit the letter to the Home Office and also his permission to publish the correspondence.[69]

This limited success, if success it can be called at all, did not, however, stop Blyden from exclaiming optimistically:

> Pegasus will now be unbound. The tropical African blood that beats passionately in the heart of every Negro will manifest itself in a new social force, in new institutions and a new literature. The present straight-jacket of unmodified European training holds back the hand of many a master. We are racked and torn on the bed of Procrustes. The idea that he must always conform in his views to the canons of European taste produces upon the mind of the cultivated Negro a practical paralysis, preventing it from acting naturally or freely. The intelligent few who ought to guide their people are thus hampered and rendered inefficient by the very conditions of their existence. The masses not being able to avail themselves of the intelligence, wisdom and ability of the few, except through the channel of European thoughts and prejudices, and the few being therefore cut off from the strength, support and reverence of the masses, are deprived of all incentive to independent exertion and self-reliance; while the masses are altogether estranged from habits of self-respect. It is this that gives to all Negro communities . . . that deep tinge of servility and that spirit of self-conscious inferiority which are really more degrading and emasculating than the alleged intellectual sterility.[70]

The Colonial Office was not, however, agreeable to Blyden's demand to establish a university.

Both Horton and Blyden were influenced by the House of Commons' 1865 resolutions, which had promised self-government to West Africa, and by a desire to vindicate the African race. But Blyden's influence was far more widespread in West Africa than Horton's, which was restricted mainly to the Gold Coast and Sierra Leone.[71] One reason for this was probably Blyden's longer life. Horton lived for forty-eight years (1835–1883) whereas Blyden, who was born three years before Horton, died in 1912, having lived eighty years. Moreover, Blyden occupied public offices through which he inevitably became well-known in West Africa.[72] In addition, his immense intellectual energy resulted in regular production of writings and speeches. But undoubtedly Blyden's greatest asset in the West African context was the theme of his mission. He was highly critical of the attitude of European missionary activity in West Africa and urged missionaries to adapt their teaching to the African environment.[73] This period, the mid-nineteenth century, was the period during which Venn was implementing his policy of encouraging missionaries to train Africans to replace them. The self-government for which Horton's *West African Countries* was to prepare was political. Blyden's self-government was cultural and religious.[74] He looked forward to an independent African Church much in the same way as Venn did. Indeed, in 1891 he was to urge the setting-up of an independent African Church with Bishop Crowther as head.[75] The political event was secondary.

The reason the educated class in West Africa was easily won over by Blyden was that at this time the Church itself was the scene of a 'struggle for power' between the white missionaries and the African clergy. This African nationalism, as expressed within the Church, is generally described as 'Ethiopianism',[76] which derives from the Bible (Ps. 68:31): 'Ethiopia shall stretch forth her hand to God.'

Ethiopianism in West Africa was different, however, from that prevalent in South and Central Africa, where it was racial and arose from the colour-bar policy of the white settlers. Whereas in those areas Ethiopianism involved secession from the Church, and anti-government and subterranean movements, in West Africa these elements were absent or reduced in intensity. Unlike South and Central Africa, West Africa had an African middle class within the Missions; the African therefore could express himself and did not need, as it were, to go underground.[77] Indeed 'the Christian church was almost the only public institution in which the educated African could give free and unfettered expression to his own personality.'[78] Ethiopianism whipped up Negro racialism and become a beacon of hope which educated Africans believed would be fulfilled in the future.[79] This hope was directed first towards administrative independence or self-government in the Church and consequent elevation of Africans to higher posts, and second, towards adaptation of Christian teachings to the African environment. These were at the very core of Blyden's writings.

It was not therefore surprising that he had such a following in West Africa, to the extent that his writings became treasured possessions among educated Africans.[80] One of his many friends and followers was Bishop James Johnson, a nationalist in his own right.

James Johnson was born in Freetown in 1838, at about the same time as Blyden, a son of recaptive Nigerian parents: his father was an Ijesha and his mother an Ijebu (both clans of the Yoruba tribe).[81] He received his secondary education at the C.M.S. Grammar School, Freetown and entered Fourah Bay, from which he graduated in 1857. For the next six years he was first a Catechist and later taught in his old school.[82] During the period from 1863 to 1874 he was a priest in Pademba and he played an important role in the demand for a University of West Africa.

The native pastors and educated natives of Sierra Leone in the last three or four decades of the nineteenth century had been encouraged to hope, like their counterparts on the West African Coast, that independence, secular and religious, was at hand. This hope was raised by the Resolutions of the 1865 Committee and Henry Venn's enlightened policy of the 'Bible and Plough'. It soon became clear, however, that European missionaries had little confidence in their African counterparts. The head of the C.M.S. missionaries at this time, Bishop Henry Cheetham, rated the ability of Africans *vis-à-vis* that of an Englishman as '100 to 3'.[83] This led to an agitation within the rank and file of the pastors, and the subsequent demand for the control of education and the Church, the two most potent sources of Western contact.[84]

The publication of the letter addressed to Grant in *The Negro* on the need for a university, and the subsequent publication of the Blyden-Hennessy correspondence on the matter in booklet form, *The West African University*, fostered a great deal of discussion among the educated classes in Sierra Leone at this time. Prominent among these classes were the native pastors, for whom the creation of a university along the lines advocated by Blyden would have provided a means of controlling education and hence achieving one of their aims. For example, Johnson wrote:

> It has been forgotten that European ideas, tastes, languages, and social habits, like those of other nations, have been influenced . . . by geographical position and climatic peculiarities; that what is esteemed by one country polite, may be justly esteemed by another rude and barbarous; and that God does not intend to have the race confounded, but that the Negro or African should be raised upon his idiosyncrasies.[85]

Blyden, the initiator of the agitation, was roundly condemned by the Bishop as 'the great source of evil' who 'has so dwelt upon this race feeling that a most strong and virulent anti-white feeling has arisen'.[86] Blyden, having founded *The Negro* in 1871, after his initial appointment as linguist at Fourah Bay had been turned down,[87] continued from the pages of this newspaper his campaign on behalf of a West African university and the race generally. During his absence in the interior, Johnson became editor of *The Negro*, and together they advocated a university which would lead to the 'formation of a national intellect from which respect for the race has not been eliminated'.[88]

The feelings generated by the discussion of Blyden's ideas prompted the parent committee of the C.M.S. to invite Johnson, who was described by Cheetham as the champion of the native pastors, to London in 1873.[89] Both laymen and pastors were initially optimistic that this invitation would lead to a granting of their demands, but both groups were soon to lose interest in their demand for the university of Blyden's dreams. The pastors asked as an alternative that Fourah Bay College, the C.M.S. institution, be converted to a centre of higher learning in West Africa.[90] Much as Grant was stirred by Blyden's ideas, he and his other lay colleagues were not able to provide the funds for the university. Influential in Church and state affairs, Grant therefore asked for the development of Fourah Bay into a centre of higher studies open to all.[91] Above all Bishop Cheetham was afraid that his arch-enemy, Blyden, might succeed in founding a 'godless' university, and therefore suggested in 1874 that the C.M.S. extend the scope of Fourah Bay.[92]

In 1875 the parent committee of the C.M.S. agreed to open the College to any student of good behaviour, no matter what his religious affiliation, provided he passed the matriculation examination. On 1 February 1876 it opened in its new form and like Codrington College, Barbados, was

affiliated to Durham University. Students took examinations set in
Durham, the papers being sent by post to Fourah Bay.[93]

Thus a compromise was reached; Fourah Bay, though not a university,
was affiliated to one. The arrangement no doubt satisfied the laymen and
pastors who had demanded or agreed to the new form. It is clear from
this that the pastors were never quite as convinced as Johnson and Blyden
of the dangers of European education. The pastors had even asked Johnson
to 'suggest the education in England by the government of a few selected
youths in various branches'[94] Blyden's object in joining the C.M.S. in 1871
had been to reform missionary activities, of which he was so critical, from
within. He hoped he might thereby persuade that Society to appreciate
better the African way of life. To achieve this objective he was to teach
Arabic, the language of learning, to a few students in the West African
interior, while he himself was to study and reduce to writing certain West
African languages which were necessary for missionary work away from
the Coast. In fact, he was dismissed even before he took up the job, because
of an allegation that he had committed adultery. Despite proof to the
contrary he was not reinstated: the missionaries led by Cheetham had
succeeded in beating off a threat to their ideas.[95] After his failure to persuade the government to start a university, and to obtain a teaching post at
Fourah Bay, Blyden returned to Liberia; his friend Johnson, who did not
succeed in winning ecclesiastical independence from London for the pastors,
was transferred to Breadfruit Church in January 1874.[96] Their departure
brought to an end the first phase of nationalist demand for a university,
both in Sierra Leone and in West Africa.

But neither Blyden nor Johnson had been daunted. After his return to
Liberia, Blyden held a number of posts and in 1881 was appointed President
of Liberia College. As if to remind the missionaries that the fight was not
over, he said on assumption of office:

> A college in West Africa, for the education of African youth by African instructors,
> under a Christian government conducted by Negroes, is something so unique in the
> history of Christian civilization, that wherever in the civilized world the existence of
> such an institution is heard of there will be curiosity as to its character, its work, and
> its prospects. . . . Every thinking man will [however] allow that *all we have been doing*
> *in this country so far, whether in church, in state or in school, is only temporary and*
> *transitional.*[97]

But even a college such as the one he was to head was not necessarily the
best for the natives in the interior, since 'the civilisation of that vast population untouched by foreign influence, not yet affected by European habits,
is yet to organise itself according to the nature of the people and the
country'.[98] A quarter of a century later, Blyden and Johnson were again to
spearhead the demand for another educational institution in another West
African territory. This was the Training College and Industrial Institute in
Lagos—an embryo university that never was.[99]

CASELY HAYFORD

The torch of nationalism lit by the descendants of slaves removed from parts of West Africa was soon to be handed to the other West Africans; so also was the demand for the creation of a university. The first prominent figure in this latter group was James Ephraim Casely Hayford, who was born on 3 September 1866 in Cape Coast, the son of the Rev. J. de Graft Hayford, 'cleric, intellectual and patriot'. He received his primary education in Cape Coast and his secondary in Freetown, Sierra Leone, before proceeding to study law in England.[100]

Hayford, along with John M. Sarbah, was later to play a leading role in nationalist activities in the Gold Coast in the late nineteenth and early twentieth centuries. Hayford, partly because he lived longer, continued the Blyden tradition, transmitting this to later men like Azikiwe. Hayford was able to institutionalise his nationalistic ideas in the National Congress of West Africa which he founded in 1920. He has aptly been described as probably representing 'the epitome of that breed of African intellectual nationalist leaders of whom . . . [it might be said] the college rooms and halls of British academic institutions provided inspirations for anti-imperalist sentiment.[101]

Perhaps nowhere in Hayford's works is this inspiration better depicted than in *Ethiopia Unbound*.[102] Sub-titled 'A study in Race Emancipation', *Ethiopia Unbound* was an allegory with its initial setting in London. The two principal characters were law students. The real purpose emerges almost at the end of the book, when Hayford gave consideration to what he called 'African nationality':

> In the name of African nationality the thinker would, through the medium of *Ethiopia Unbound*, greet members of the race everywhere throughout the world. Whether in the east, south, or west of the African continent, or yet among the teeming millions of Ethiopia's sons in America, the cry of the African, in its last analysis, is for scope and freedom in the struggle for existence, and it would seem as if the care of the leaders of the race has been to discover those avenues of right and natural endeavour which would in the end ensure for the race due recognition of its individuality.[103]

Hayford's nationalistic sentiment burst and flowed in the pages of *Ethiopia Unbound*. One reads the book with the impression that Hayford's feelings, pent up for so long, had gradually swollen like a river which a dam can hold back no longer, and which, breaking through, sweeps all over the neighbouring land. For as Hayford writes in the first chapter of his allegory,

> At the dawn of the twentieth century, men of light and learning both in Europe and in America, had not yet made up their minds as to what place to assign to the spiritual aspirations of the blackman; . . . the Nations were casting about for an answer to the wail which went up from the heart of the oppressed for opportunity. And yet it was at best but an impotent cry. For there has never lived a people worth writing about who have not shaped . . . a destiny for themselves, or carved out their own opportunity.

Before this time, however, it had been discovered that the black man was not necessarily the missing link between man and ape. It had even been granted that in intellectual endowments he had nothing to be ashamed of in an open competition with the
Aryan or any other type. He was anatomically perfect, adaptive and adaptable to any
and every sphere of the struggle for life. Sociologically he had succeeded in recording
upon contemporary history a conception of family life unknown to western ideas. . . .
    And there were sons of God among them, men whom the Gods visited as of yore;
for . . . three continents were ringing with the names of men like Du Bois, Booker T.
Washington, Blyden, Dunbar, Coleridge Taylor and others—men who had distinguished themselves in the fields of activity and intellectuality—and it was by no
means an uncommon thing to meet in the universities of Europe and America the
sons of Ethiopia in the quest of the golden tree of knowledge.[104]

Like Horton and Blyden before him, Hayford had set for himself the
task of placing his fellow Negroes at par with the Europeans in the thinking
of the western world. He wished to point out to the world that 'Africa has
nothing to be ashamed of in its place among the nations of the earth,'[105]
nothing to be ashamed of in her religion or her marriage custom:

With respect to marriage a great blunder has been committed by the meddlesome
missionaries. . . . There is a vulgar way of approaching the question of polygamy; there
is a scientific way; and lastly there is the spiritual way. It may appear strange that the
average man that there is a spiritual side to polygamy.[106]

With feelings such as he had, he was naturally impatient with the more
docile of the American Negroes:

To be born an African in America . . . is to be entangled in conditions which give no
room for the assertion of the highest manhood. African manhood demands that the
Ethiopian should not seek his opportunity or ask for elbow room from the white
man, but that he should create the one or the other for himself.[107]

The central figure of the book, Kwamankrah, voiced Hayford's dreams
and deeds. This mythical character was a man of remarkable intelligence
who, after receiving the best available education of his day, so impressed
the community that at the age of nineteen he was entrusted with the editor-
ship of a national newspaper (echoes of Blyden!).[108]

Hayford was a great friend and admirer of Blyden. So close were they
that Hayford was to have been the elder man's biographer,[109] and one of
the main chapters of *Ethiopia Unbound* is in fact devoted to a consideration
of Blyden's role in race emancipation. In the Introduction to Blyden's
West Africa Before Europe, published in 1905, Hayford summarised in
glowing terms the place of Blyden in the 'emancipation' of the Negro race.
Six years later Kwamankrah repeats this *verbatim* in *Ethiopia Unbound*:

The claim of Edward Wilmot Blyden to the esteem and regard of all thinking Africans
rests not so much upon the special work he has done for any particular people of the
African race, as upon the general work he has done for the race as a whole. The work
of men like Booker T. Washington and W. E. Burghart Du Bois is exclusive and
provincial in a sense. The work of Edward Wilmot Blyden is universal, covering the
entire race and the entire race problem. . . . While Booker T. Washington seeks to
promote the material advancement of the black man in the United States, and W. E.
Burghart Du Bois his social enfranchisement, amid surroundings and in an atmosphere

uncongenial to racial development, Blyden has sought for more than a quarter of a century to reveal everywhere the African unto himself; to fix his attention upon original ideas and conceptions as to his place in the economy of the world; to point out his work as a race among races of men; [and] lastly and most importantly to lead him back to self-respect. . . . He is the greatest living exponent of the true spirit of African nationality and manhood. In the Afro-American school of thought the black man is seeking intellectually and materially to show himself a man, along the lines of progress of the white man. In the African school of thought represented by Dr. Blyden the black man is engaged upon a sublimer task, namely, the discovery of his true place in creation upon natural and rational lines. . . . The great influence of Dr. Blyden over the rising thinking youth of the race, lies in the fact that he has revealed in his writings and utterances the true motive power which shall carry the race from victory to victory.[110]

Hayford, like Blyden, believed that the crux of the education question was that western methods 'denationalised' the African, who subsequently became a slave to foreign ways of life and thought. The 'question of questions' was how the West African could be so trained that he preserved his 'national identity and race instinct.'[111] Hayford himself supplied the answer. First, Hayford would found a national university, for the simple reason that a people cannot be educated unless there is a suitable local training ground.[112]

Second, he would ensure, 'as a precautionary measure,' that the 'educational seminary' (i.e. the university) was placed in a region far beyond the reach of the influence of the Coast.[113]

Third, he would found Chairs of History and of African Languages. The history to be taught would be 'universal history with particular reference to the part Ethiopia (i.e. the Negro Race) has played in the affairs of the world, laying stress on the 'fact that Africa was the cradle of the world systems and philosophies and the nursing mother of its religions.'

Language professorships would be established in Fanti, Hausa and Yoruba. Should the idea appear odd and unusual, Hayford declared, 'I can only point to the examples of Ireland and Denmark, who have found the vehicle of national language much the safest and most natural way of natural conservancy and evolution.'[114]

The whole idea of the founding of the proposed university was to create a means of 'revising erroneous current ideas regarding the African; of raising him in self-respect; and of making him an efficient co-worker in the up-lifting of man to nobler effort'.[115]

Hayford's seat of learning would be so renowned and attractive that students from the United States, the West Indies, Sierra Leone, Liberia, Lagos and Gambia would flock to it:

And they come to this Mecca not in top hat and broad cloth, but in the sober garb in which the Romans conquered the material world, and in which we may conquer the spiritual world.[116]

Even before he described the above characteristics of his African

National University, Hayford had in the first chapter of his book discussed the 'good work' already being done in Fanti-land by a mythical Mfantsipim National University. According to Hayford,

> it had its origin in the national movement which swept over the country in the stormy days of 1897, when the people as if moved by a sudden impulse, rallied round the Aborigines Society and successfully established the principle of land tenure under which the country had since thriven.[117]

The people themselves subscribed enthusiastically to the National Educational Fund, during a vigorous campaign to solve the education question. Kwamankrah played an important part in the whole venture:

> Upon the opening of the National University, Kwamankrah gave up newspaper work and joined the University staff. He was foremost in bringing forward schemes to prevent the work of the University becoming a mere foreign imitation. He kept constantly before the Committee . . . the fact that no people could despise its own language, customs, and institutions and hope to avoid national death. . . . It was recognized that the best part of the teaching must be done in the people's own language and soon several textbooks of known authority had, with the kind permission of the authors and publishers, been translated into Fanti. . . . The scheme . . . involved the turning out of efficient teachers, and, as the University was affiliated to that of London and in working correspondence with some of the best institutions in Japan, England, Germany, and America, the work done was thorough.[118]

Some of Hayford's writing in this allegory has historical foundation. For example, an Aborigines Rights Protection Society was actually formed in 1897. According to Kimble, it was the first organised protest on anything approaching a national scale, although it was centred mainly in Cape Coast and the Western Province.[119] An Mfantsi National Education Fund, sponsored by the educated leaders of Cape Coast with the support of a few chiefs, is also an historical fact. The plan did not, however, include a university, but was limited to proposals to found primary and secondary schools for liberal and professional studies (cf. the literary and industrial sections of the Lagos Training College) and to encourage local literature. Little came of it, however.[120]

The Mfantsipim National University and the African National University must therefore be seen as aspirations for the proposed university—a university thoroughly conscious of, and adapted to, its environment but simultaneously maintaining an international standard.

In 1920, nine years after the publication of the book, the National Congress of British West Africa again returned to the education question and the creation of a university. In March of that year representatives from Nigeria, Sierra Leone, and the Gambia, with their Gold Coast counterparts, assembled in Accra for the first National Congress of British West Africa. The session lasted for over two weeks and eleven major subjects covering a wide range were discussed, each introduced by a different speaker, as follows:

FROM THE GOLD COAST

J. E. Casely Hayford	Legislative (including municipal) reforms and granting of franchise
W. E. G. Sekyi	Education, with particular reference to a West African University
A. Sawyer	Judicial reforms
Dr. F. V. Nanka-Bruce	West African Press Union
H. Van Hien	The inauguration of the Congress of Africans of British West Africa. Representation of West African views

SIERRA LEONE

F. V. Dove	Alien problems
L. E. V. M'Carthy	Commercial enterprise
Dr. H. C. Bankole-Bright	Sanitary and medical problems

NIGERIA

Patriarch J. G. Campbell	The policy of the government in relation to the land question

GAMBIA

E. F. Small	The right of the people to self-determination

Resolutions were made at the end of the conference on each of the above topics.[121] Only those on legislative reforms and the university are relevant here. On the first topic the Conference resolved *inter alia*:[122]

> That in the opinion of this Conference the time has arrived for a change in the Constitutions of the several British West African Colonies, so as to give the people an effective voice in their affairs, both in the Legislative and Municipal Governments. . . .
> That this Conference recommends a Constitution on the following lines:
> 1. An Executive Council as at present composed.
> 2. A Legislative Council composed of representatives of whom one-half shall be nominated by the Crown and the other half elected by the people, to deal with Legislation generally.
> 3. A House of Assembly, composed of members of the Legislative Council together with six financial members elected by the people.

On 'Education with particular reference to a West African University', seven resolutions were passed. These deserve quoting in full as they summarise the points made earlier by the West Africans, Horton and Blyden, and reflect some of those in Hayford's *Ethiopia Unbound*:

> 1. That this Conference is of the opinion that the system of Education best suited to the needs and conditions of the various British West African peoples under British influence is one which whilst enabling students to attain the highest proficiency in the many departments of learning, will least interfere with the development by the student of a proper spirit of reverence for indigenous institutions and modes of life not opposed to equity and good conscience.

D

2. That in the opinion of this Conference the time has come to found a British West African University on such lines as would preserve in the students a sense of African Nationality, and therefore recommends that all existing Secondary Schools throughout West Africa, or those about to be formed, should promote a course of training that shall best attain the end in view.
3. That with this object in view it recommends that the different Boards of Education of each Colony should admit . . . African Educationalists capable of contributing practical suggestions, and that in the submission of such suggestions they be guided by the experience of such communities as Japan which have encountered similar problems to those of West African communities.
4. That besides existing Secondary Schools the Conference recommends each section of it to promote a scheme in each Colony whereby sound Secondary Education on national lines supported by the people may be promoted, and which shall form a further nucleus for the formation of the proposed British West African University.
5. That compulsory Education throughout the British West African Colonies be introduced by law, and that the standard of both the Primary and the Secondary Schools be uniformly raised to meet the standard of the University.
6. That the Education Schemes of the Governments of the several British West African Dependencies be considered and incorporated in the scheme and given as far as practicable a more national tone by co-operation between the Educationists controlling the working of the scheme and such experienced educated Africans capable of suggesting lines of African National evolution.
7. That each British West African Colony promotes a National Educational Fund so as to ensure the development of a national Education Scheme, which Fund, when the Scheme is in operation, may be supplemented by Government subsidies.[123]

A delegation of the Congress went to London later in 1920 to present their petition to King George V, and met Professor Gilbert Murray, President of the League of Nations Union. The petition was a condensed form of the Memorandum; No. 25 therein asked for the establishment of a university.[124]

The Congress met with disappointment in London, as the Secretary of State would not see the delegation. There were a number of reasons for this. Some of the Chiefs of the Gold Coast, led by Nana Ofori Atta, were peeved because the intelligentsia, which the Congress was claiming to represent, was not comprised of all the people. Moreover, the Governors of West Africa were offended because they were not informed of the Congress's intention to meet the Secretary of State directly until too late; the Governors, in particular Sir Hugh Clifford of Nigeria, did not believe in the eventual possibility of the creation of a Nigerian, let alone a West African nation. The combined hostility of the Governors and Chiefs thus ensured the downfall of the Congress.[125]

Quite apart from general hostility to the Congress, the attitude of the British government, to which the demand was directed, was summed up by Lord Lugard, who in his *Dual Mandate* (1922) attacked

The African progressives, who lightly say[ing] that 'the time has come to found a West African university on lines of African nationality,' do not indicate a single donation from the wealthy members of their community towards its realization.[126]

In other words the British government asked the West Africans to foot the bill themselves. As will be seen later, the Colonial Office believed the West African to be unwilling to subscribe towards public appeals. (The Gold Coast however, was to pay for her own university college in 1948.)

Nevertheless, in 1923, Achimota College was founded and from the start it was to serve as the nucleus of a university. Hayford claimed during the Presidential address to the 4th Congress in Lagos in 1929, not without some truth, that the creation of Achimota was due partly to the demands of the West African Congress.[127]

Earlier demands for the development of universities in British West Africa had been made by non-Nigerians. It is important to note that loyalty prior to the 1920s was to 'West Africa', 'Africa' or the 'Negro Race'. These demands were for a university for, or in, West Africa. It is doubtful if the financial or the potential student population of any one Colony alone could have supported a university. There was some sound reason therefore for wanting a university for all four Colonies. But the more important reason was that until the thirties loyalty was to West Africa as a whole rather than to the individual Colonies.

AZIKIWE

The first Nigerian to call for university establishment was Benjamin Nnamdi Azikiwe.[128] Born in 1904 in Zungeru, Northern Nigeria, of Ibo parentage, he received his secondary education in the Hope Wadell Institute, Calabar, and the Methodist High School, Lagos. After a brief period as a clerk in the Treasury office in Lagos he sailed for the United States in 1925.

In 1934 he returned to West Africa and for three years worked in Accra, where he edited the *Morning Post*. In 1937 he went back to Nigeria and immediately entered the rough and tumble of politics, becoming in 1961 the first Nigerian Governor-General of an independent Nigeria. From 1963 until the army take over on 16 January 1966 he was the President of the Federal Republic of Nigeria. The above is sketchy but it speaks much for the place of this man in the history of Nigeria that even in his lifetime at least three respectable biographies[129] of him have appeared, not to mention articles and pamphlets about him or his activities. There are few aspects of life in Nigeria to which Dr. Azikiwe has not made some contribution; Nigerian politics, journalism, banking, sports, and education all bear the mark of his personality. But concern here centres on the interaction between his nationalism and the course of university development in Nigeria.

As has been shown, the three earlier demands for universities were made by nationalists and intellectuals. With perhaps the exception of Hayford, they were not men of action, their nationalistic activities being removed from the field of practical politics. Dr. Azikiwe was also an intellectual nationalist, but brought with him into West African politics a militancy and a dynamism hitherto absent.[130]

While Dr. Horton was concerned with proving the non-inferiority of the Negro *vis-à-vis* Europeans, Dr. Azikiwe seems to have assumed that they were in fact equal. If they were equal then no nation had a right to assert itself over another. Azikiwe's contribution to nationalist activity seems to have centred around a determination to overthrow what he would call 'imperialism'. Indeed as far back as 1931, when he was only twenty-seven, and the year in which he graduated as B.A. from Lincoln he was already discussing, in an article entitled *Ethics of Colonial Imperialism*,[131] the social, political, and economic origins of imperialism, no doubt as a preparation for his work in West Africa in the succeeding three decades. The same year he was also already defending Liberia against Euro-American writers who 'have delighted themselves in seeing chaos, disorder, hopeless anarchy and failure of the Liberian "experiment" whenever her case is before the bar of international opinion . . . but I submit . . . that eighty-four years of *de jure* existence are inadequate to pronounce definitely the success or failure of any political venture'.[132]

Dr. Azikiwe's writings and speeches on educational matters are numerous.[133] His earliest writings were directed toward the 'New' or 'Renascent' African. In his book *Renascent Africa*[134] he described the new African species as one which 'exists in a transitional stage between the old and the New Africans. This African refuses to view his future passively. He is articulate. He is destined to usher forth the New Africa.' The philosophy of the New African had five bases: (*a*) spiritual balance, (*b*) social regeneration, (*c*) economic determination, (*d*) mental emancipation and (*e*) national resurgence. Education was specially discussed under the two latter headings.

Mental emancipation was again an essential part of the New African's educational philosophy in much the same way as for Blyden and Hayford:

> This [mental emancipation] includes education of the sort which should teach African youth to have faith in his ability; to believe that he is the equal of the people of other races of mankind, mentally and physically; to look at no man as his superior simply because that man comes from the Antarctic or Arctic regions. It means that the Renascent African must be rid of the inferiority complex and all the trappings of hat-in-the-hand Uncle Tomism.
>
> Educate the Renascent African to be a man. Tell him that he has made definite contributions to history . . . that while Oxford and Cambridge were in their inchoate stages, the University of Sankore in Timbuctoo welcomed 'scholars and learned men from all over the Moslem world. . . .'[135]

Elaborating the emancipation theme further, Dr. Azikiwe claimed that the education of the African up to his (Azikiwe's) time was anachronistic, had prepared Africans for life in a stagnant and unprogressive social order, and had encouraged Africans to cultivate false values. It lacked 'moral stability,' emasculated Africans and was utterly useless as a preparation for leadership. With more than an overtone of Blyden he concluded: 'All that I have said can be summed up in these words: *Africans have been mis-educated. They need mental emancipation so as to be re-educated to the real needs of Renascent Africa.*'[136]

African philosophy, Dr. Azikiwe continued, had placed great emphasis on material things and had neglected the spiritual. But the greatness of an individual, as also with a nation, did not always lie in material possessions. Indeed 'things material cannot do without things intellectual or spiritual'. In other words spiritual and intellectual attributes were just as important, if not more so, as material ones in determining greatness.[137]

This argument seems to have been long held by Dr. Azikiwe, for in a speech delivered in 1934 at one of his old schools, the Methodist Boys' High School, Lagos, soon after his return from the United States, he said:

> I postulated at the outset that scholarship is coterminous with social progress. It is the scholar who makes or unmakes society. He may not be appreciated by his generation or even by generations after him. But time offers rewards to scholars who lay the foundations for the society of tomorrow, by immortalizing them in human history . . . Africans need to be scholars. We need to be creative. We must emulate, not imitate.[138]

The scholarship and intellectualism which Dr. Azikiwe was advocating are two pursuits more easily undertaken in a university than elsewhere. Dr. Azikiwe knew this. But there were no indigenous African universities at the time he wrote. Dr. Azikiwe lamented this fact thus:

> When I consider the fact that throughout the continent of Africa there is not an indigenous university sustained through African initiative, I am in a position to realize how most of the problems of Africa today are due to the intellectual poverty of Africans.
>
> Had African Universities been maintained at their expense, they could have had their curricula filled with important divisions of knowledge which could have hastened their intellectual emancipation.[139]

Azikiwe's African university was not only to emancipate the mind of the Renascent African, it was also to uplift him and help him shape the New Africa.

> Universities have been responsible for shaping the destinies of races, nations, and individuals. They are centres where things material are made to be subservient to things intellectual in all shapes and forms. No matter in what field of learning, at the university there is an aristocracy of mind over matter . . . The universities of Europe and America have been responsible for the great movements in the national history of these continents.
>
> [But] Black Africa has no university. Black Africa has no intellectual centre where the raw materials of African humanity may be reshaped into leaders in all fields of human endeavour. . . .
>
> With a taxation of one shilling *per capita* throughout British West Africa, an endowment fund of more than twelve million pounds can be raised. This is capable of supporting three or four first-class universities.
>
> Why should African youth depend upon Oxford, Cambridge, Harvard, Yale, the Sorbonne, Berlin, Heidelberg, for intellectual growth. These universities are mirrors which reflect their particular societal idiosyncrasies . . .

Give the Renascent African a University . . . and this continent can become over-
night, 'A Continent of Light'.[140]

As for curricula, Dr. Azikiwe was vague, and he seemed very much concerned that emphasis should not be laid on classics and philosophy—'The
Modern Greats' and 'The Bunkums' as, according to him, they were known
at Oxford and in the United States respectively—to the exclusion of science
('The Real Stuff' in the States). His ideal university was one in which the
curriculum was balanced and whose graduates 'know a little of the classics,
the humanities, and the sciences. This is the criterion of the efficacy of
university education, in any part of the world.'[141] Dr. Azikiwe got something near his ideal university in the University of Nigeria.

TO SUMMARISE

1. It is clear from the foregoing that the primary aim of the early nationalists in demanding a university was to help emancipate the Negro race.
2. The call was always for *a* University of Western Africa. The location of
the university depended on the domicile of the writer: Horton and Blyden
wanted their West African Universities located in Sierra Leone, Hayford
wanted his in Fanti-land, the Gold Coast. Azikiwe wanted his in Nigeria
(but see Ch. 8). It is interesting that the Minority Report of the Commission on Higher Education for West Africa, nearly a century after
Horton, recommended also *one* university for British Western Africa—but
for different reasons. The nationalists wanted one university because of
loyalty to the race, and the Commission, for reasons of economy and a
paucity of students.

How much success did their demands bring? Horton had asked that
Fourah Bay be made a university. Instead a compromise was reached.
Fourah Bay was not made a full-fledged university, although it granted
Durham degrees as from 1876. Blyden had asked for a university *de novo*
untied to the apron-strings of missionaries. He did not get one. Neither did
he succeed when he persuaded a group of Lagos citizens to plan 'The Lagos
Training College and Industrial Institute' in 1896 (see next chapter). All
Hayford achieved was Achimota, which in 1931 took the London Univer-
sity External B.Sc. in Engineering. Legon was not to be founded until 1948.

Only Dr. Azikiwe saw the foundation of his university, and was its
Chancellor for the first five years of its existence.

Notes

[1] J. S. COLEMAN, *Nigeria: Background to Nationalism*, California, 1958, pp. 172–5; see
also V. C. ONWUTEAKA, 'The Aba Riot of 1929 and its relation to the system of Indirect Rule' in *Nig. J. Econ. Soc.*, 7, 3, 1965 pp. 273–82.
[2] COLEMAN, *op. cit.*, pp. 169–70.
[3] *Ibid.*

[4] E. A. AYANDELE, 'An assessment of James Johnson and his place in Nigerian History', *Journal of the Historical Society of Nigeria*, **2**, 1963, p. 489; see also THOMAS HODGKIN, *Nationalism in Colonial Africa*, London, 1956, pp. 24–25.

[5] HODGKIN, *op. cit.*, p. 23.

[6] M. L. KILSON, 'The rise of Nationalist organizations and Parties in British West Africa', in *Africa as seen by American Negroes*, Paris, 1958, p. 37n.

[7] LORD HAILEY, 'Spotlight on Africa', in *Africa in the Modern World*, ed. by C. W. Stillman, Chicago, 1959, p. 9; see also J. F. ADE AJAYI's review of Coleman's *Nigeria* in *Ibadan*, **10**, 1960, pp. 16–18.

[8] GEORGE SHEPPERSON, 'Notes on Negro American influences on the emergence of African nationalism', *Journal of African History*, **1**, 1960, p. 299; see also ABIOSEH NICOL, 'West Indians in West Africa', *Sierra Leone Studies*, New Series, **4**, pp. 14–23.

[9] C. FYFE, *A History of Sierra Leone*, 1962, pp. 294–5; DAVID KIMBLE, *Political History of Ghana*, Oxford, 1963, p. 67.

[10] FYFE, *op. cit.*

[11] His publications included: *The Medical Topography of the West of Africa*, London, 1859; *The Physical and Medical Climate and Meteorology of the West Coast of Africa*, Edinburgh, 1867; *The Guinea worm or Dracunculus*, London, 1868; *West African Countries and Peoples . . .*, London, 1868; *The Diseases of Tropical Climates and their Treatment*, London, 1874 (2nd edn. 1879). These publications which drew from 'his own and other doctors's experience, were intended to advise the laymen coming to the Coast as well as inform the profession', FYFE, *op. cit.*, p. 295.

[12] Horton's political ideas were embodied in his *West African Peoples*. In 1870 he published in book form correspondence between himself and the Administrator in *Letters on the Political conditions of the Gold Coast*, London, 1865. His contribution has been appraised by KIMBLE, *op. cit.*, *passim*, but especially pp. 230–33 and pp. 243–6.

[13] FYFE, *op. cit.*, p. 437; KIMBLE, *op. cit.*, p. 38.

[14] *Parliamentary Papers 1865*, Vol. 5, p. 2, 'Report of the Select Committee on the State of British Settlements in West Africa', quoted in FYFE, *Sierra Leone Inheritance*, Oxford, 1964, pp. 190–1.

[15] FYFE, *History of Sierra Leone*, p. 337.

[16] *Ibid.*

[17] These included J. F. NAPIER's 'Garrulous, superficial' *European Settlements on the West Coast of Africa*, London, 1862; BURTON's 'gossiping' *Wanderings in West Africa and Abeokuta*, London, 1863, and WINWOOD READE's, *Savage Africa*, London, 1864.

[18] See FYFE, *History of Sierra Leone*, *passim* but especially pp. 292–3.

[19] *Ibid.*, pp. 333–4.

[20] *Ibid.*, p. 335.

[21] *Ibid.*

[22] HORTON, *West African Countries*, London, 1868, pp. 61–62.

[23] *Ibid.*, p. 44.

[24] *Ibid.*, p. 51; p. 45.

[25] *Ibid.*, p. 25.

[26] *Ibid.*, p. 51.

[27] J. F. ADE AJAYI, *Christian Missions in Nigeria, 1841–1891*, p. 168.

[28] HORTON, *West African Countries*, pp. 61–62.

[29] *Ibid.*

[30] *Ibid.*

[31] *Ibid.*, p. 201–2.

[32] *Ibid.*, p. 202.

[33] K. O. DIKE, *Trade and Politics in the Niger Delta, 1830–1885*, Oxford, 1959, pp. 166–7.

[34] AJAYI, *op. cit.*, p. 173.

[35] J. B. WEBSTER, 'The Bible and the Plough', *Journal of the Historical Society of Nigeria*, **2**, 1960, p. 418.

[36] J. F. ADE AJAYI, 'Henry Venn and the Policy of Development', *Journal of the Historical Society of Nigeria*, **1**, 1959, p. 335.

[37] WEBSTER, *op. cit.*

[38] J. F. ADE AYAYI, 'Nineteenth Century Origins of Nigerian Nationalism', *Journal of the Historical Society of Nigeria*, **2**, 1960.

[39] *Ibid.*, p. 199.

[40] *Ibid.*, p. 200.

[41] *Ibid.*

[42] HORTON, *West African Countries*, p. 203.

[43] Horton had worked in the Gold Coast and did make reference occasionally to that Colony.

[44] HORTON, *West African Countries*, p. 204.

[45] *Ibid.*, see fn. 24.

[46] *Ibid.*, pp. 46–50.

[47] *Ibid.*, p. 50.

[48] *Ibid.*; also FYFE, *History of Sierra Leone*, p. 342.

[49] HORTON, *West African Countries*, p. 46.

[50] FYFE, *History of Sierra Leone*, p. 472.

[51] E. W. BLYDEN, *Liberia's Offering*, London, 1862, author's 'Biographical Sketch', pp. i–iii.

[52] *Ibid.*

[53] BLYDEN, Inaugural address at Liberia College, *op. cit.*, p. 96.

[54] *Ibid.*, 'Noah's Malediction', pp. 31, 33–36; see also 'The Negro in ancient history' in *The people of Africa*, New York, 1871, pp. 1–34.

[55] E. W. BLYDEN, III, *Sierra Leone: The Pattern of Constitutional Development, 1924–1951*, unpublished Ph.D. thesis, Harvard, p. 63.

[56] *Ibid.*, p. 66.

[57] Letter in the Appendix from Dr. Blyden to Dr. Wilkinson acknowledging the dedication of Dr. Wilkinson's Book *The African and Christian Religion*, James Speirs, London, 1892, to the former, p. 243.

[58] *Ibid.*, p. 244.

[59] *The West African University:* Correspondence between Blyden and Hennessy, *The Negro* Printing Office, Freetown, 1872, p. 10.

[60] *Ibid.*, p. 1.

[61] *Ibid.*, pp. 1–4.

[62] *Ibid.*, p. 4.

[63] FYFE, *op. cit.*, *passim.*

[64] *The West African University*, *op. cit.*, pp. 6–7.

[65] *Ibid.*, pp. 7–8.

[66] *Ibid.*, p. 11.

[67] *Ibid.*, p. 12.

[68] *Ibid.*, pl 14.

[69] *Ibid.*, pp. 11–12.

[70] *Ibid.*, p. 16.

[71] See COLEMAN, *Nigeria*, p. 183–4; KIMBLE, *Ghana*, p. 538.

[72] He acted in various public offices. See Hollis R. Lynch, 'Edward Blyden: Pioneer African Nationalist, *Journal of African History*, 6, 1965.

[73] *Ibid.*, p. 383.

[74] See however LYNCH, *op. cit.*

[75] LYNCH, *op. cit.*

[76] AYANDELE, *op. cit.*, p. 489.

[77] *Ibid.*
[78] *Ibid.*, p. 495.
[79] *Ibid.*, p. 490.
[80] For example in Ghana; see KIMBLE, *Ghana*, p. 538; also AJAYI, *Christian Missions*, *passim*. James Johnson was also interested in educational affairs; as Ayandele wrote: 'James Johnson was unyielding in demanding a system of education suitable to Nigerian environment, [and] advocated in 1909, gratuitous education for clever Nigerians'. See ref. 71, above.
[81] AYANDELE, *op. cit.*, p. 490.
[82] *Ibid.*
[83] HOLLIS R. LYNCH, 'The native pastorate controversy and cultural ethnocentrism in Sierra Leone, 1781–1874', *Journal of African History*, 3, 1964, p. 398.
[84] *Ibid.*, p. 413.
[85] *Ibid.*, p. 405.
[86] *Ibid.*, p. 406.
[87] See PAUL HAIR, 'E. W. Blyden and the C.M.S., Freetown, 1871–1877', *Sierra Leone Bulletin of Religion*, 4, 1962, p. 22.
[88] AYANDELE, *op. cit.*, p. 498; quoted in the *The Negro*, 16 April 1873.
[89] LYNCH, *op. cit.*, p. 406.
[90] *Ibid.*, p. 409.
[91] FYFE, *op. cit.*, p. 505.
[92] *Ibid.*
[93] The first graduation three years later was described in *West African Reporter* of 23 April 1879 thus:

> On Wednesday the 16th instant there was an interesting gathering at Fourah Bay to witness the conferring by his Lord the Bishop of the Diocese [Bishop Cheetham] of degrees on some of the students of the college who had passed their final examinations in their connexion with Durham University. The circumstance was the first of its kind in the history of Sierra Leone as well as of Western Africa. . . . [The Principal said in a speech that] it gave him satisfaction to think that the ministry of the church in Western Africa will hereafter be filled by intelligent and qualified or properly educated men. The chief strength of those he was going to present lay in theology; in course of time he hoped he may be able to present one student in mathematics; but until the schools on the West Coast can show qualified scholars who have been properly trained to write verse and prose compositions in the classics, he had few hopes of doing anything in that branch.
>
> Five students were then presented as having obtained their Licentiates in Theology. These were S. Hughes, N. H. Boston, D. Brown, W. C. Morgan; the three others, namely N. Davis, O. Johnson, and Issac Olutvole, who had earned their degrees as Bachelor of Arts, were then presented.
>
> Quoted in FYFE, *Sierra Leone Inheritance*, pp. 211–13.

[94] LYNCH, *op. cit.*
[95] *Ibid.*, pp. 398–400.
[96] AYANDELE, *op. cit.*, p. 409.
[97] E. W. BLYDEN, *Christianity, Islam and the Negro Race*, London, Wittingham, 1887, p. 82. Italics in the quotation are mine.
[98] *Ibid.*
[99] AYANDELE, 'The relations between the Church Missionary Society and the Royal Niger Company, 1886–1900', *Journal of the Historical Society of Nigeria*, 1968, p. 90.
[100] K. A. B. JONES–QUARTEY: 'A note on J. M. Sarbah and J. E. Casely Hayford: Ghanaian Leaders, Politicians and Journalists, 1864–1930', *Sierra Leone Studies*, New Series 14, 1960, p. 75; see also Note 2.
[101] EDWARD BLYDEN III, *Sierra Leone, op. cit.*, p. 87.

[102] These included; *Gold Coast Native Institutions* (1903); *Ethiopia Unbound (1911);* *The Truth about the West African Land Question* (1913); *United West Africa* (1920).

[103] J. E. CASELY HAYFORD, *Ethiopia Unbound*, London, 1911, p. 167.

[104] *Ibid.*, pp. 1–3.

[105] *Ibid.*, pp. 194–5.

[106] *Ibid.*, p. 192.

[107] *Ibid.*, p. 182.

[108] *Ibid.*, p. 16.

[109] Edward Blyden III—personal communication.

[110] E. W. BLYDEN, *West Africa Before Europe*, London, 1905, pp. i–iii; HAYFORD, *Ethiopia Unbound*, pp. 163–5.

[111] HAYFORD, *ibid.*, pp. 192–4.

[112] *Ibid.*

[113] *Ibid.* Elsewhere Hayford says: 'Ashanti is my type, for the reason that Ashanti is yet "unspoilt" by the bad methods of the missionary', *Ethiopia Unbound*, p. 186. In this Hayford echoes Blyden's dislike of the coastal natives, who had adopted European ways, in contrast to those in the interior, who had not.

[114] *Ibid.*, p. 194.

[115] *Ibid.*, p. 195.

[116] *Ibid.*, p. 196.

[117] *Ibid.*, p. 15.

[118] *Ibid.*, p. 17.

[119] KIMBLE, *Ghana*, p. 330.

[120] *Ibid.*, p. 85.

[121] *Ibid.*, pp. 381–3; other Nigerian delegates included Dr. Akinwande Savage, 'Professor' Deniga, Prince Bassey Duke, Mr. Essien Offiong, Mr. Phillip Coker, Prince J. B. Lesi; PATRIARCH J. G. CAMPBELL, *Our West African Governors, The Congress Movement and Herbert Macaulay*, Lagos, 1921.

[122] *National Congress of West Africa, Accra, 11–29 March 1920: Resolutions*, London, 1920, p. 1.

[123] *Ibid.*, p. 3.

[124] *National Congress of British West Africa: Petition to King George V*, 19 October 1920 Petition No. 25. 'That your Petitioners desire the establishment of a British West African University, and are prepared to promote the necessary funds for its establishment, supported by Government subsidies.'

[125] PATRIARCH J. G. CAMPBELL states that the arguments adduced against the Congress were:

1. That the Congress was not representative of the chiefs and people.
2. That some amongst the important educated people of West African were absent.
3. That the West African Governors were not taken into confidence.
4. That the European elements were ignored.
5. That the Congress asked for Dominion self-government.

On Accusation No. 1, Campbell asks 'who invited the British Government to West Africa, was it the Chiefs?' On Accusation No. 2, Campbell accuses those who detract the Congress on that account as disgruntled people who wished that they rather than Hayford and others had gone to London.

CAMPBELL, *op. cit., passim;* see also KIMBLE, *Ghana*, pp. 389–92; COLEMAN, *Nigeria*, pp. 191–5.

[126] FREDERIC LUGARD, *The Dual Mandate in Tropical Africa*, Oxford, 1929, p. 456 fn.

[127] M. J. SAMPSON, *West African Leadership*, London, 1949, p. 86.

[128] In July 1934 he dropped the name Benjamin as a protest against discrimination at the British Empire Games, London. See his *Respect for Human Dignity*, Inaugural Address as Governor-General, Lagos 1960; also *My Odyssey*; autobiographical sketches, pub-

lished in *West African Pilot* 1938–39 and preserved in mimeographed form at University of Nigeria Library.

129 V. C. IKETUONYE, *Zik of New Africa*, London, 1961. K. A. B. JONES–QUARTEY, *A Life of Azikiwe*, London, 1965. F. C. OGBALU, *Dr. Zik of Africa*, African Literature Bureau, 1955.

130 See COLEMAN: *Nigeria*: 'During the fifteen-year period 1934–1949, Nnamdi Azikiwe was undoubtedly the most important and celebrated nationalist leader on the West Coast of Africa, if not in all tropical Africa.' p. 220.

131 NNAMDI AZIKIWE, 'Ethics of Colonialism', *Journal of Negro History*, 16, 1931, pp. 287–308.

132 AZIKIWE, 'In Defence of Liberia', *Journal of Negro History*, 17, 1932, pp. 46–47.

133 See AZIKIWE, *Zik: (Colected speeches)*, Cambridge, 1961, especially Chapter 2.

134 AZIKIWE, *Renascent Africa*, Lagos, 1937, pp. 7–8.

135 *Ibid.*, pp. 9–19.

136 *Ibid.*, pp. 134–5 (italics in the original).

137 *Ibid.*, p. 138.

138 AZIKIWE, *Zik*, pp. 23–24.

139 AZIKIWE, *Renascent Africa*, pp. 144–5.

140 *Ibid.*

141 *Ibid.*, p. 144.

4 The Proposed Lagos Training College and Industrial Institute, 1896

It is not generally known that an attempt was made by Nigerians resident in Lagos to found something in the nature of a vocational university as far back as the late nineteenth century. This chapter discusses that attempt and the type of institution visualised, and offers some explanation as to why it never materialised. Indeed this proposal was not limited in content to Lagos but was discussed all through the British West African colonies including the Gold Coast and Sierra Leone. *The Sierra Leone Weekly News* devoted successive columns of its pages to this question, and *The Lagos Weekly Record* and *The Lagos Standard* addressed themselves to the same problem.[1] A number of somewhat interrelated ideas appear to have stimulated interest in the question.

The first was the 'spirit of race' or the 'principle of race' which was described as 'the desideratum of the hour'.[2] This, like most of the factors which gave rise to the education controversy, was influenced by ideas of Negroes in America. The spirit or principle of race had as its central point that 'civilisation has its units of value of different orders, of which race is one that demands consideration in all successful efforts to improve the condition of our fellow men.'[3] According to this principle, the conception of race did not conflict with the broader idea of the common brotherhood of man; it demanded only a recognition of race differences. In other words what was good education for one race was not necessarily so for another. The Negro, therefore, demanded a different education from other races for his place in the order of things.

What sort of place, according to the race principle, did he deserve to occupy? It appears that the West African Negro by and large accepted the one into which he was put by white Europeans and Americans. And the education needed for this place, according to the then current view, was undoubtedly the industrial type, regarded as being essential to his development. This was enunciated very clearly in an editorial in *The Lagos Weekly Record*:

> The question as to whether mental education or manual skill should take precedence in the training of the African is a point around which a good deal of interest centres and upon which opinion widely differs. In an abstract sense, and by the natural order of things, the head is undoubtedly the guide of the hand; this natural and legitimate rule is [however] modified in a large degree by the influence of the environment and racial idiosyncrasies. A child who is surrounded by a healthy environment of industrial

activity as in Europe and America, needs the highest mental training to qualify him as a capable factor in the acutely keen competition of industrial activity in which he will have to contend.[4]

On the other hand, the surroundings of the African were just the reverse; in the African's case, 'indolence is imputed as a pronounced defect of his race, and his environment is in unmistakable agreement with the imputation'.

It was evident, the editorial continued, that with such surroundings, the first care in the training of the African should be to counteract as much as possible the untoward influence of the environment and to make up for the inherent disposition to indolence. According to this editorial:

This can only be accomplished by an early and continuous course of discipline in manual labour, thereby instilling the habits of regularity, industry and thrift. . . . We do not mean to imply that book knowledge should be ignored altogether, but we maintain that under the peculiar conditions of his surroundings, the African, in order to be properly developed, requires first and foremost to be subjected to a course of industrial discipline sufficient to overcome his innate indolent propensities and to instill into him the habits of regularity, diligence, and push.

In line with what must appear today to be extremely strange reasoning, 'the almost phenomenal mental progress' of the American Negro was attributable to two factors in his history: first, his subjection to industrial discipline as a slave, and second, the 'healthy environment of industrial activity' around him.

The editorial then went on to interpret the assertion published in a London weekly to the effect that the Negro had 'brain force' but not 'brain power'. This, the editorial continued, meant that while the Negro possessed mental capacity he lacked the power or energy to develop it. The chief object of the Negro's education should be to make up for this defect. *The Record* concluded:

And we apprehend that due and proper consideration must lead to the conviction that as regards the Negro in Africa, industrial discipline or training as initiatory steps is indispensable to his successful development.

That industrial education was generally highly regarded becomes evident from even a cursory perusal of educational materials published at this time. Leading citizens eagerly associated themselves with schemes for industrial education. When the Rev. Dr. Mojala Agbebi,[5] well known both in Lagos and in certain Negro circles in the United States, convened a meeting on 18 February 1895 in Lagos in connection with founding a Colwyn Bay (Industrial) Institute, those in attendance included such prominent figures as the Rev. W. B. Euba, Principal, Boys' High School; the Hon. and Rev. James Johnson, M.A. (formerly of Freetown); Mr. J. A. Otumba Payne, F.R.G.S., merchant and civil servant; C. A. Sapara Williams, B.L., leading lawyer; Dr. J. Randle, M.B., later of the Peoples Union; and G. A. Williams, Editor of *The Lagos Standard*.[6] The Congo Training

Institute situated in Colwyn Bay, North Wales, was, according to Agbebi, instituted in the interest of Africa. The principal feature of the school was the training in England of the most promising African youths in both industrial and literary pursuits for future usefulness to the country. By 1895 the Congo Institute had already opened the 'Alfred Jones' Institute at New Calabar under the principalship of the Rev. Dr. Scholes.[7] On 1 February 1896 another Colwyn Bay industrial mission was founded by the Rev. John E. Ricketts at Agboa in Ijebu Remo.[8] In a letter addressed to Lagos citizens he claimed that the children of the land 'will be able to receive an elementary education and at the same time be trained to become better farmers, carpenters, and in other useful arts'.[9]

Dr. Agbebi appears to have been a forceful advocate of this type of education. 'Industrial Education,' he told a group of Swedenborgians—a Christian sect founded by the Swede, Swedenborg—'is the watch-word of the hour [and] the present need of the great problem of African christianization is industrial evangelization . . . self-supporting, self-dependent churches.'[10] In a speech at Colwyn Bay itself he criticised the form of Christianity introduced by the Church of England, the Wesleyans, the Baptists and the Presybterians, for not establishing industrial schools.[11]

Another factor which lead to a discussion of the education question and moves for the establishment of the Lagos Training College was the growing dissatisfaction of the community with local youth trained in foreign institutions. Such youth were said to have copied the vices and not the virtues of the Europeans with whom they associated, and consequently became 'the laughing stock of foreigners and the ridicule of their . . . brethren'. They were said to be vandalistic, ostentatious, and their conduct presumptous.[12] One outspoken foreigner whose position and long contact with Africa entitled him to a hearing was the Governor of Lagos, Sir Gilbert Carter. From all accounts Carter was sympathetic to the local educational aspirations, including strenuous efforts to raise the standard of the primary schools in Lagos.[13] In an interview with *The African Review*, summarised approvingly by *The Lagos Standard*, Governor Carter attacked the *foreign-educated* Negro: he was a failure both as regards himself and his relationship to his people; he was filled with grotesque ideas; he spurned and looked down upon his former friends and acquaintances; he aped the shadow whilst he eschewed the substance.[14]

The foreign-educated youth was disapproved of not only in Lagos but also in Sierra Leone[15] and Liberia. Thus in a Report submitted to the Board of Trustees of Liberia College in 1881, Dr. Blyden wrote;

> The Negro [student] in exile labours under these three disadvantages: he is mis-
> understood by his enemies, which is a great misfortune; he is misunderstood by his
> friends, who think they understand him, which is a greater misfortune; and he is
> misunderstood by himself, which is the greatest misfortune. To correct these evils, a
> residence in the land of his fathers, and a liberal means of protracted culture therein

are indispensable. Hence the need of Liberia College and similar institutions. For the great work to be done in this vast country we must have men trained amid the scenes of their future labours—men who can enter at once into their work to do what is to be done; who need neither mental nor physical emancipation. [We need men] who know the specific methods in this country for performing industrial, commercial, educational and religious work; who will know how to live in the country and in the towns . . . who as missionaries can work from village to village, proclaiming the Gospel of Christ to the natives in a language they can understand, and [can] sit down on mats and skins in native huts . . . and then at meal-time can enjoy with their hosts palm-oil and rice, *palaver* sauce and *dumbouy*; who will not long and pine for bacon and greens, peaches and pears, broadcloth coats and beaver hats.[16]

In short, there was a demand for youth to be trained on the spot, owing to an 'apprehension of the ill-consequences of the effort to make Anglo-Saxons of Africans', which condition 'tended to extinction and death'.[17] What was *not* called education was, it was argued, more valuable than what *was* so called. 'This want of harmony of educational methods with the aim and tendency of nature has produced the unpleasant results which everybody is now beginning to deplore.'[18]

It was in the heat of the discussion of the education question that the appointment of the veteran Dr. Blyden, already well known all over West Africa as 'political officer for Yorubaland,' was announced towards the end of 1895. On 1 March 1896 Dr. Blyden sailed from England for Lagos in the *Bathurst*.[19] This was the second time Dr. Blyden had been appointed to a post of this nature. In 1871 he had been named the 'Agent for the Interior' in Sierra Leone by Sir Arthur Kennedy.[20] Blyden's reputation even in official circles was high; he had turned down the Lagos job in 1890 during his first visit to Lagos. This time the Governor was reported to have said that Dr. Blyden accepted the job on his own terms. He had visited the colony in 1894 when he was said to have taken great interest in the expensive new mosque.[21] Blyden was enthusiastically welcomed in Lagos and Sir Gilbert Carter was praised for his 'great foresight and deep interest in the aboriginal affairs of the Colony' and for 'a stroke of administrative wisdom and political sagacity unparalleled in the history of the Colony' in obtaining 'for Yorubaland an acquisition whose value is inestimable and whose suitability is indisputable'. Dr. Blyden's appointment met 'with general satisfaction' and would be 'of great use and much benefit to the colonial government, his country and his race'. Especially it was hoped that with the presence of so 'distinguished a thinker as the Hon. Dr. E. W. Blyden in the Colony we presume the question of education will not fail for want of a sponsor'.[22]

The expectations of the educated Lagos Africans were not disappointed, for no sooner had Dr. Blyden settled down than he set afoot plans for a Lagos Training College and Industrial Institute. Blyden first discussed the matter with the Governor and later corresponded with him, giving fuller details. The correspondence was discussed at a meeting of prominent

gentlemen in the town, after which a prospectus was issued. The Blyden–
Carter correspondence was later published,[23] appropriately prefaced by a
letter sent in 1872 from the Rev. James Johnson to the Governor of Sierra
Leone, Pope Hennessy, and by an extract from the preface by Sierra
Leone's Sir Samuel Lewis to Blyden's *Christianity, Islam and the Negro
Race*. Both these documents summarised the theme of the correspondence,
which was in general that the Negro should not necessarily be educated
along the well-worn European lines, but in ways appropriate to himself.

In his first letter, dated 14 May 1896,[24] Blyden stated that although
African youth had been going to England for about a century, nothing but
disappointment had resulted in almost every case. Of the first dozen or so
boys sent only one returned, the rest succumbing to the rigours of the
English climate.

Blyden reminded Governor Carter that in 1872 he, with other Africans
in Sierra Leone, had addressed a letter to the Governor of that territory on
the question of higher education in West Africa. But although the Governor had been sympathetic to the Sierra Leonians' cause he would not
commit the government to inaugurating a university because the Africans
were themselves not prepared to bear the initial contributions. Time, the
course of events and additional unpleasant developments, however, had
changed things: the leading natives of Lagos were willing to help the
government bear the initial financial burden, provided the matter was put
before them in a 'practical form' and 'with a probability of its being
sanctioned by the Secretary of State and becoming a part of government
policy'. The leading natives were anxious to have the means for the
thorough training of their youth at home, as it was an obvious peril for
young men in the most critical years of their lives to be away from their own
country. Parents were beginning to see the absurdity of this practice, but
they could do nothing about it since nothing suitable existed locally. A
similar situation in India had been rectified sixty years earlier when a
college had been founded by a wealthy native of that country. Blyden
suggested that the Botanic Station at Ebute Metta would be a splendid
site for carrying out the 'industrial' aspects of the scheme and hoped the
plan would be put into effect by the end of that century.

Replying, the Governor agreed that the practice of sending youth
abroad was a mistaken one. He himself had incurred the displeasure of
both Africans and English philanthropists 'whose knowledge of the African
is usually theoretical rather than practical'[25] for publicly saying so. He had
thought for a long time that a thoroughly good training institution for
Africans in Africa was the great educational need of the race. There was no
question that in general the young African educated in Europe imbibed
ideas which made him dissatisfied with the native environment and unfit
to live in it. He quoted as an example the practice of marrying English
women, which he said was encouraged by the publication of an unnamed

and pernicious book[26] by an intelligent and capable African. This book had encouraged the marrying of European women by African men in order to improve the features of the African race. 'Such an argument coming from an African,' continued the Governor, 'only tends to show the mind can become warped by being trained in an unsuitable atmosphere.' Although a capable man, the author had failed to see the implication of his arguments, which was the total extermination of his own country-women.

He then discussed the importance of the industrial aspects of the scheme. Although praising the contribution of missionaries to education, he criticised them on two grounds: first, for laying too much emphasis on religious training, the main efforts of which were directed to training recruits for missionary work, 'not the most urgent need of the African'. Second, the missionaries introduced dogmatic Christianity as expounded by the many Christian sects—a not 'unmixed blessing' which tended to confuse the simple African mind.

The young African did not come off lightly himself. Although skilled labour was in great demand in West Africa, manual labour was not popular with the young African who 'wants to be a Minister, a Lawyer, or a Doctor, and failing these occupations, he condescends to be a clerk'.

It was not until he came to the question of financial assistance that Sir Gilbert hesitated: 'You will of course understand that any possible assistance which might be expected from the Government in support of such a scheme must be dependent upon the assured successful establishment of an institution such as you have in mind.' The government already contributed a liberal yearly sum in aid of education conducted by the missionary societies.

Blyden hoped the Institution would attract Negro youth not only in the West Coast but also from across the Atlantic.[27] Before going into the details of the scheme, Blyden took time to discuss his favourite theme: the inadequacy of missionary education. With an impressive broad-mindedness he praised the missionaries' philanthropic and persistent efforts, through which public attention in Europe was fixed upon the African continent, and for diffusing information favourable to the Negro, in a way government officers ['birds of passage'] could not. 'But,' he argued,

> there has been marked advancement in all departments of life since they [the missionaries] performed those great and necessary labours, and Africans, for the work they now [must] do, need a different—a wider and deeper—training, industrially and intellectually, than the limits of the spheres and resources of the missionaries allow them to give. With gratitude for the past therefore, we are trying to take courage to face and deal with the unknown, and what appears to us pregnant, future.[28]

Blyden then gave in the rest of this, and most of the next, letter what was the blueprint of the College.

E

THE SITE
The site of the College should be at Ebute Metta[29] away from the town of Lagos and should be ample for industrial training and for 'practical illustrations of scientific teaching'.

THE CURRICULUM
There would be two Departments, the Literary and the Industrial.

1. *The Industrial Department* would include the 'usual mechanical trades', and scientific and practical agriculture. Every student would devote a certain number of hours in each week to 'such industrial work, either mechanical or agricultural, as his taste may select and as will give the necessary physical training and mental dexterity'.

2. *The Literary Department* would include 'such studies as would lead to the acquisition of good intellectual habits and exercise'. From his many years' experience as a teacher, Blyden felt what was learnt did not matter, once the student was grounded in reading and writing, as long as he acquired the 'habits of spontaneous and continued attention, self-control, and reflection'. These habits were *sine qua non* for African youth if they were to become capable and useful members of society.

From Blyden's experience the most effective of disciplinary studies were the ancient languages[30] and mathematics. The proper study of Greek and Latin was not limited to mere acquaintance with words in a foreign language but necessarily involved a good deal of history and geography, religion, and models of logic and oratory unparalleled in European [*sic*] literature. In addition, although the subjects might be difficult, they inculcated into the student the habits of memory, observation, abstraction, taste, judgement, and originality—indispensable qualities, irrespective of the student's final occupation.

As for mathematics, higher mathematics as such should be excluded, but enough should be taught the student to form the basis for understanding such other applied subjects as surveying, engineering, and cartography.

The African did not need to learn such subjects as astronomy—these were the prerogative of another race. The African ought to concentrate on branches of science useful to him—botany, mineralogy, geology—and literature.

Christianity should be taught but should be undenominational and based on love of God and man.

GOVERNMENT OF THE COLLEGE[31]
1. The government of the College would be invested in a Board of Trustees with the Governor as President *ex-officio*.

2. There would be fifteen members on the Board, six of whom were to be appointed by the Governor, and nine to be elected by the contributors to the scheme. Three of the members would be Europeans and twelve

natives, none of the latter of whom should have contributed less than £5.
3.   The Executive Government of the College would consist of five members, of whom one would be European.
4.   The financial aspects of the College were to be supervised by the local Bank of British West Africa.

THE FACULTY
1.   The Faculty, which would consist of the professors or teachers from the two departments, would elect one of their own number to be Principal. The Principal would be an *ex-officio* member of the Board of Trustees.
2.   The Governor as *ex-officio* President of the Institute might appoint any member of the Board of Trustees to preside in case of his inability to attend meetings.

In conclusion, Blyden hoped that the Governor would see his way

to recommend to the Secretary of State the grant to the Institute of such an annual sum as shall suffice for the payment of teachers and for the establishment of half a dozen or more scholarships to be bestowed upon indigenous and promising youths (a scholarship being £15 a year). . . . From the establishment of such an Institute in our own country under our own eyes, we look forward to the following economic or material results, viz.

1.   saving of the money of our youth
2.   saving of the time of our youth
3.   saving of the health and life of our youth.
From there must follow important moral consequences:
1.   saving the intellect of our youth
2.   saving of the character of our youth
3.   saving of the racial integrity and instincts of our youth.

Governor Carter's reply was again sympathetic. He would 'much like to see the idea zealously taken up and carried out by the more wealthy natives' and promised his support. But again the Governor would not be won over to give or recommend financial aid. It is clear that, even granting him sincerity in his utterances regarding the establishment of the proposed College, he was quite unwilling to commit the British government to give any financial help. He 'suggested' that the College be a 'National West African' one, as he did not think that Lagos alone, even with Government support, could run such an institution. Before any buildings were put up, an approximate calculation of fees should not be less than £30 *per annum* if the school were to be self-supporting. An endowment large enough for minimum staff of four should be available from the start.

However, in order to obtain government assistance it would be necessary to show strong reasons 'for the suggested departure from the present system of education'. The Governor then stated that the government already spent over £2,000 *per annum* on education in the Colony. Recently it had voted £1,500 for buildings at the Hussey Charity Institute[32] and had voted a £500 *per annum* grant to that institution for industrial education.

As for the land at Ebute Metta, he could promise nothing, as the Botanic Garden impinged on land in which the railway was being constructed.

Blyden could only reply that the Hussey Charity did work of a nature inferior to that of the proposed Institute. This indeed was true. For of the twenty boys in the Hussey Charity Institute in 1898, eleven were receiving primary instruction only and the remaining nine, together with twenty-four extra-mural students, were also taught mensuration, geometrical drawing, carpentry and smithery. Agriculture was not part of the curriculum, although a small vegetable garden was present on the school ground.

As the matter stood then, the ball was clearly in the court of the Lagos gentlemen. Blyden had convened a meeting of these men[33] on 27 May 1896, and from their number they had elected a Committee which then proceeded to draft a prospectus.[34] The prospectus summarised the points about the Institute as described in the Blyden–Carter Correspondence:

> There will be two departments, the Literary and the Industrial. The branches to be taught in the literary department will include Ancient and Modern Languages, Mathematics, History, Mental and Moral Philosophy and Natural Science.[35]

But it also included other features, such as fixing a date line for the contributions.

> If the sum of £1,000 be not secured before the end of the year, that is before 31 December 1896, and if there appear to be no reasonable prospect of raising the said amount so as to allow a beginning to be made on the buildings in the early part of 1897, with an assurance of completion, the monies contributed will be returned to the contributors—not one penny of which will be used for any preliminary expenses.[36]

Founders would be considered to be those who contributed £5 or more before the erection of buildings; they would also qualify to vote at meetings and might be elected to the Board of Trustees.[37]

The proposal of the Training College was hailed enthusiastically in the newspapers. Editorials in *The Standard* asserted that 'the youths of the country ought to sing and the maidens dance for joy, that for the first time in its history and that of West Africa an enterprise of such magnitude was set afoot as in a fair way of accomplishment'. The names of wealthy natives associated with it, Messrs R. B. Blaize, J. W. Cole, J. S. Leigh and J. Otumba Payne, 'were guarantees of success'.

When completed the College would serve as a training ground for the future self-government of the Colony and its Protectorate.[38] It was the answer to the 'education of the people', around which cluster all 'the ills that our political, religious and domestic life is heir to'.[39]

The more racially-conscious *Record* said:

> The proposed Institution will aim at intellectual excellence . . . but the question which is still asked is can they [the Africans] produce any effect upon the thought of the World? . . . To enable at least certain of the race to answer these questions satisfactorily is the object of the Lagos Training College. . . . We are sure that the proposed scheme of education is the greatest need of the race.[40] [Through the proposed Institute]

we shall be brought back to ourselves and be taught our true place in the economy of humanity—that we are not to be the tools or apes of others, but the producers of property both material and intellectual for the healthy exchange between nations which must be carried out if they are to respect each other.[41]

Indeed, feelings expressed at the time give the impression that the Lagos Training College was like a raft thrown to help a drowning man just when he had lost all hope of survival.

On paper the College was ready; the money, however, was still to come, and when the prospectus was published there were about six more months to reach the dateline. Every method of public persuasion appeared to have been used; the very setting of a dateline itself was calculated to give the scheme a practical form and to ensure that according to Blyden's hope it would be ready by the end of the century. The vanity of the educated gentlemen was appealed to—with a minimum contribution of only £5, one was entitled to be called a Founder and to be elected a Trustee. *The Standard* even appealed to religious rivalry:

We notice that the different denominations are represented in the Appeal issued, the people conspicuous by their absence being the Mohammedan population and our pagan majority. But we know from the characteristics already displayed by the Moslems [a reference to their expensive mosque] that they will muster forth in their native strength if appealed to.[42]

In spite of all efforts it was clear by the middle of December 1896, that £1,000 would not be collected. On 5 December only £392 13*s.* had been collected and *The Record* was already declaring that the fixing of a date was a mistake[43] while *The Standard* hoped that 'the Higher Education Scheme would not be abandoned and that if not in the form proposed by the Committee . . . some other form may be devised and carried out for this very commendable project.'

The scheme was sadly enough abandoned. The sinking man could not climb on to the raft; he drowned.

In the absence of anything else, attention was turned again to the Hussey Charity, which institution had previously been declared inferior. The *Standard* came out in its defence about a year after attacking it, and perhaps to save its own face, declared that 'it is likely that the [Hussey Charity] Institute suffers at present from the prejudice of its being originally a place solely for the education and boarding of "escaped slave-boys".' It now drew attention to its 'sustained fine reputation' and wished that the recent introduction of an industrial aspect be given more publicity. Not only that, but it was now open to 'free boys'. The second best had to be accepted: 'In the absence of what was proposed as "The Lagos Training College and Industrial Institute" the Hussey Charity supplied a long-felt want.'[44]

Why did the scheme fail? The first and most apparent reason was that the money was not forthcoming from the educated Africans in Lagos. Yet it seems surprising with a population which included wealthy figures like J. A. Otumba Payne,[45] who in addition to being the Chief Registrar and Taxing Master of the Supreme Court of Lagos was also such a wealthy businessman that he was able to visit Europe and South America as early as 1886; and R. B. Blaize, who in 1895, barely a year earlier, had donated £1,000 to the Anglican Native Pastorate for the foundation of an industrial school in Abeokuta.[46] Could it be that despite the apparent inadequacies of foreign education and all the outcry about the same, the populace still believed strongly in it? This may not be altogether too far-fetched, when one remembers that today in Nigeria with the greater availability of opportunities for education within the country, Nigerian parents, when money is available, will sometimes send their children to universities, secondary schools and even primary schools in England. There is no doubt that a period of education abroad, judiciously arranged for the more mature youth, would be useful. It appears, however, that the prestige value attaching to education in Europe was as high then as it still is today.[47]

Even if the money had been fully subscribed and the institution set up without the need for a government subsidy, there would still have been the most important question of finding native staff of the appropriate calibre. Even while the campaign for the Lagos Training College was still hot, at least one educational institution—the Collegiate Institute, a one-man effort by the Venerable Henry Johnson, M.A.—was closing down, for lack of adequate teaching staff.[48] What few native staff existed were hotly competed for by the educational institutions of the various missions.[49] Names of capable educated natives such as Henry Carr of Lagos and Anderson of Liberia were mentioned,[50] but the problem was not given the consideration it deserved. Although it was realised that the 'gravest of the difficulties we shall have to confront in the beginning will be that of finding natives competent to conduct such a college'[51], the contemporary closing of the Collegiate Institute was seen not as a cause for reflection, but as 'one more unexpected cause whereby necessity of a permanent untrammelled and unencumbered provision is emphasised for the education of the youth of the land'.[52] This was no doubt a reference to the 'trammelled' nature of missionary education, which dissipated the meagre staff resources among competing denominations.

In the covering letter which Governor Carter had despatched to the Secretary of State for the Colonies along with the correspondence between himself and Blyden on the Lagos Literary and Industrial Training Institute, the Governor had written that he was

> entirely in sympathy with Dr. Blyden's desire to provide suitable means of imparting a sound practical education to native youths among their own people and surroundings. . . . There is no doubt in my mind that the present system of leaving the whole training of young Africans in the hands of missionary bodies has produced very unsatisfactory results.

The schools would now appear to be at a standstill. . . . The difficulty appears to be the want of satisfactory teachers, and it is hardly to be expected that suitable men will be forthcoming at the small salaries which it is profitable to give them.

Sound industrial training is undoubtedly the most urgent need of the race and I would gladly see more attention devoted to this subject and less to the classics and the higher branches of mathematics which can be of little use to Africans for many years to come. Practical agriculture will do more for the development of the Yoruba country than a proficiency in the ancient languages or a knowledge of conic sections, and I desire cordially to second Dr. Blyden's proposal to start an institution established on a large plot of land, where experiments might be properly carried out.

Dr. Blyden is sanguine of success and I can only hope that some of the wealthier natives may take up the question with energy and determination and provide the necessary funds for the proper maintainance of a suitable institution. My mission is to suggest that the Lagos Government should give every reasonable facility in support of such a scheme and afford some financial assistance when it is ascertained beyond reasonable doubt that the natives are in earnest in their desire to give practical support to the commendable object which Dr. Blyden has in view.

Mr. Chamberlain, the Colonial Secretary, 'perused the correspondence with great interest' and approved the suggestion that the Lagos government had made regarding support and financial aid subject to the ascertaining of the genuine interest of the natives themselves.[53]

How sincere were the Governor and the British government in their declared conditional support for the scheme? Did the Governor and later the Secretary of State impose the condition of the subscription of the Africans only because they were aware that the Africans would not reach even their own target figure? Two factors need to be noted regarding the Governor's attitude to the financial aspects of the proposed scheme. The first was that he did not at any time say how much he thought the Africans ought to contribute to qualify for government aid. Whether or not this militated against the attainment of the target of £1,000 is difficult to say, but a stated contribution might have acted as an incentive. The second factor was that the Governor consistently rated the scheme more expensive than the Africans themselves thought. For instance, where the Africans thought scholarships should be worth £15 *per annum*, the Governor thought it would be £30. Was this due to a more realistic approach, or was it an attempt to dampen enthusiasm for the scheme?

The constitution of the proposed College placed power squarely in the hands of the Africans, although care was taken not to alienate European and therefore government interest. The Governor himself was, for instance, to be the President *ex-officio* of the College and three of the fifteen members of the council were to be Europeans. It would have been surprising if the government had invested money in a scheme in which it had next to no control. This is an added reason for doubting the sincerity of the Governor's support for the plan. Quite naturally the Governor drew attention to the existence of the government's own Hussey Charity. He then required reasons for improving the existing system, although he had agreed that foreign education was bad, and industrial education good, for indigenous youth.

When it is taken into account that the government decided to reorganise the Hussey Charity to introduce industrial education at about the same time as the Lagos Training College was being debated, it becomes difficult to accept that the Governor really wanted to support the plan.

It is possible that the natives of Lagos came to rely too heavily on the government's supposed benevolence because of an apparent change in the attitude of the British government towards their African colonies:

> Now that England is assuming such responsibilities in Africa and identifying herself with all the wide interests of the continent—political, industrial, and commercial—she cannot be indifferent to the social interest of the people. But at the bottom of the social interest lies the educational interest.
>
> In former times when England only touched the margin of the continent and deemed it her duty to have as little as possible to do with the life of the people; when the idea was, as Lord Shelbourne reminded his listeners the other day, to withdraw as soon as possible from West Africa, no interest was taken in the intellectual development of the people. But things are now changed. [53]

At another time and in another place Dr. James Africanus Horton had been led to demand a university by the declared intention of the British to withdraw from West Africa. [54]

What sort of institution was the paper model of the Lagos Training College and Industrial Institute? Blyden had, twenty-five years earlier, demanded a university for West Africa with no nonsense about industrial education. [55] All he appeared to have wanted then was to liberate the African mind from what he considered the adverse effects of missionary training. It is true that in 1896 he still believed that African education was very much dominated by European ideas; the educated African found himself, Blyden declared, 'alienated from himself and his countrymen. He is neither African in feeling nor in aim. He does not breathe African air through any of the lessons he has imbibed.' [56]

But Blyden's suggested remedy was not just a study of African languages, culture, geography, etc, [57] but a good grounding in the classical languages and in industrial work. Industrial work was thus the new feature of Blyden's educational ideas. It will be noticed that in the Lagos scheme little mention was made of the studies of African languages or culture. Rather the emphasis was on more vocational studies: botany, geology, mineralogy, and 'practical and scientific agriculture'. In this Blyden reflected the opinions held strongly by the educated gentlemen in Lagos and other parts of West Africa. The opinions in turn were the result of the educational theory held at the time in America, which advocated vocational education for the Negro. The chief propagator of this idea was Booker T. Washington. [58] Arguments such as those adduced by *The Record* reflected his influence, and indeed news of Washington appeared regularly in that paper. Blyden appears to have accepted over the years that industrial or vocational education was at least partly the solution for Africa's mis-education by Europeans.

The general similarity of the organisation of the proposed Industrial Institute to that of a university, and the mention of 'professors',[59] leave no doubt that a type of university institution was envisaged. Yet there were features which would make it different from what we call universities today. First, no mention of the name 'university' was made in all the discussion about the institute either in the press or in the Blyden–Carter correspondence. Second, Blyden himself says that higher mathematics would be taught. Subjects such as mineralogy, botany and geology, although included today in university courses, may be studied at much lower levels. The title of a course tells nothing of its content or depth.

The proposed Lagos Training College would have been at worst a high-powered secondary school, and at best, a highly vocational university—in archetype of the land-grant college of the United States.

Notes

[1] See Editorials on 'The Education of the People' and 'The Education Question' in *The Lagos Standard* of 20 May 1896. See also HAYFORD, *Ethiopia Unbound*, p. 192; KIMBLE, *Political History of Ghana*, pp. 84–85.

[2] *The Lagos Standard, loc. cit.*

[3] *Ibid.*, quoted from 79th Report of the American Colonization Society.

[4] 'Industrial Training for the African Essential for His Development', *Lagos Weekly Record*, 7 March 1896.

[5] For a most valuable account of the nationalist activities of Dr. Agbebi, see Akinsola Akinwowo, 'The Place of Mojola Agbebi in the African Nationalist Movements: 1890–1917', *Phylon*, Atlanta, 1966.

[6] *The Lagos Standard*, 20 February 1895.

[7] *Ibid.*, 3 July 1895.

[8] *Ibid.*, 29 April 1896.

[9] *Ibid.*

[10] *The Lagos Standard* Supplement, 31 July 1895.

[11] *The Lagos Standard*, 17 July 1895.

[12] *Ibid.* 31 July 1895.

[13] *Ibid.*

[14] *Ibid.*

[15] See issues of *The Sierra Leone Weekly News*, published 1895–97.

[16] Quoted in *The Lagos Standard*, 20 June 1896.

[17] *The Lagos Standard*, 18 April 1896.

[18] *The Lagos Weekly Record*, 16 May 1896.

[19] *The Lagos Standard*, 4 December 1895; *The Lagos Weekly Record* 21 March 1896.

[20] See Chapter 3.

[21] HUMPHREY J. FISHER, 'The Ahmadiya Movement in Nigeria', in *St Anthony's Papers No. 10: African Affairs*, London, 1961. 'Dr. Edward Blyden . . . was in Lagos several times in the 1890s. He at last persuaded the Lagos Muslims to establish their own school with Arabic, Yoruba, English and arithmetic', p. 62.

[22] *The Lagos Standard*, 4 December 1895; 20 May 1896.

[23] *The Lagos Training College and Industrial Institute, Correspondence between Edward*

W. Blyden, LL.D. and H. E. Sir Gilbert Carter, K.C.M.G., Governor and Commander-in-Chief of Lagos and its Protectorates, The Lagos Standard Office, Lagos, 1896.
[24] *Ibid.*, p. 2.
[25] *Ibid.*
[26] Dr. Hollis R. Lynch believes the book in question to be J. R. MAXWELL, *The Negro Question*, London, 1892.
[27] *The Lagos Training College Correspondenc*e, pp. 6–9.
[28] *Ibid.*, p. 7.
[29] It will appear that Blyden had a definite predeliction for the idyllic nature of the countryside as may be seen from his praise of the African countryside in *Liberia's Offering.*

A correspondent in *The Lagos Standard* of 6 May 1896 says this of Ebute Metta: 'From an undesirable islet [sic] presided over by indifferent rulers, Ebute Metta has been transformed . . . into a comparatively properous and law-abiding island. Furthermore it has become a more popular health resort than its great rival, the Beach . . . Hence a large proportion of those more or less physically handicapped avail themselves from time to time of the rural scenes and pleasures which it affords'.
[30] See also Inaugural Address as a Professor of Languages at Liberia College in E. W. BLYDEN, *Liberia's Offering*, London, 1862.
[31] *The Lagos Training College Correspondence*, pp. 10–12.
[32] The full name of the Institution was 'The Rebecca Hussey Charity School for Industrial and General Education'. It was named after Rebecca Hussey, daughter of a clergyman, who in 1713 directed in her will: 'I give and bequeath to the redemption of slaves, if it may be effected, or else to the easement of their slavery, £1,000: and would have those that are redeemed with this sum baptized as speedily as may be.' That year she died, but the will was discovered only in 1863, nearly one and half centuries after her death. By this time the money had accumulated to £23,481 14s. 4d. It was decided that the income from the funds should be shared equally between Lagos and the Island of St. Helena. In 1872 land was granted by the government for the founding of the Institute in Lagos. See HENRY CARR, *The Rebecca Hussey Charity School at Lagos for Industrial and General Education*, Lagos, 1899.
[33] CARR, *op. cit.*
[34] The meeting which was convened at the insistence of Dr. Blyden was held to determine 'the possibility of the educational Scheme proposed therein being made to assume practical shape in the Colony.' Those present were: Hon. C. J. George, Hon. J. J. Thomas, Rev. James Johnson, Ven. Archdeacon Henry Johnson, R. B. Blaize, J. S. Leigh, J. A. Otumba Payne, J. A. Savage, Dr. Mojola Agbebi, Dr. C. J. Lumpkin, H. A. Caulrick, G. A. Williams, E. Bickersteth, and John P. Jackson.
[35] The Prospectus Committee consisted of: J. W. Cole, R. B. Blaize, (Treasurer), J. S. Leigh, J. A. Otumba Payne (Treasurer), J. A. Savage, Dr. Mojola Agbebi, John P. Jackson (Secretary).
[36] Quoted in *The Lagos Standard*, 1 July 1896.
[37] *Ibid.*
[38] *Ibid.*
[39] *Ibid.*
[40] *The Lagos Standard*, 20 May 1896.
[41] *The Lagos Weekly Record*, 4 July 1896.
[42] *Ibid.*, 15 August 1896.
[43] *The Lagos Standard*, 5 July 1896.
[44] *The Lagos Weekly Record*, 5 December 1896; *The Lagos Standard*, 13 October 1896, See also Note 32.
[45] See T. O. ELIAS, 'Makers of Nigerian Law', *West Africa*, 19 Nov 1955 to 7 July 1956.
[46] See J. F. ADE AJAYI, 'The Development of Secondary Grammar Schools in Nigeria', *Journal of the Historical Society of Nigeria*, **4**, 1963.

[47] The Federal Military Government took steps (May 1966) to discourage this by making it illegal to transfer money to foreign countries for the education of Nigerians at the sub-university level (*Daily Times*, 1966).

[48] *The Lagos Standard*, 15 July 1896.

[49] *Ibid.*

[50] See Appendix to *The Lagos Training College Correspondence*.

[51] C.O. 147–110: Carter to Colonial Secretary. 13 August 1896; Correspondence minuted by J. H. Reed, also *The Lagos Weekly Record*, 4 July 1896.

[52] *The Lagos Standard*, 15 July 1896.

[53] *The Lagos Standard*, 20 May 1896.

[54] See HORTON, *West African Countries*, London, 1868.

[55] *The West African University*, Correspondence between E. W. Blyden and Hennessy. See Chapter 3.

[56] Blyden to Carter, 21 May 1896 in *The Lagos Training College* Correspondence, p. 6.

[57] ROBERT JULY, 'Nineteenth-Century Negritude: Edward W. Blyden', *Journal of African History*, 5, 1, 1964.

[58] See Booker T. Washington's autobiography, *Up from Slavery*, New York, 1901; and see below, ch. 14 paras. 4 and 5.

[59] See Blyden to Carter: 3 June 1896: 'It [the Executive Committee of five] is to meet monthly and to choose all teachers and professors to fix their salaries, to superintend, suspend and remove them, and conduct the financial and general affairs of the Institute; in short to perform all the functions of persons called Visitors in England;' in the The Lagos Training College Correspondence, p. 10.

5   The Yaba Higher College

It is necessary to precede this discussion of the earliest institution of higher learning in Nigeria with brief remarks on educational policy.

As has been shown in Chapter 2, western education first made contact with West Africans on a large scale through returned slaves or their descendants. The contact was brought about by Christian missionaries. For some eighty years after the establishment, in 1841, of what became the first permanent missionary establishment in Nigeria, the British government left education completely in the hands of the missionaries with no direct overall policy. It should be pointed out, however, that in Nigeria the local Colonial government did appoint an Inspectorate of Schools in 1901.

It should also be noted that there was sometimes a dichotomy between the policies enunciated by the British home government for its colonies and those actually carried out. The first clearly defined British government policy on education in the then African colonies was the Privy Council memorandum of 1847.[1] It was in fact prepared for the West Indies, although it was distributed to all the other colonies. The committee recommended four types of educational institutions.[2]

1. Elementary schools
2. Day schools of industry
3. Model farm schools
4. Normal schools.

Little action was taken in Nigeria on this memorandum.

Interest in education in her African colonies was forced on Britain by the report of the Phelps–Stokes[3] Commission in the U.S.A. The foundation, formerly primarily interested in Negroes in the U.S.A., decided to send out a commission to study the educational set-up in Africa. In 1923 an Advisory Committee on Education in Africa was set up by the Secretary of State for the Colonies. It is perhaps a measure of the British government's interest in education in her African colonies that, until the 1930s, part of the cost of running the Advisory Committee was met by funds from the Carnegie Corporation.[4] Indeed until the setting up of the 1923 Committee little concerted or sustained effort had been made either by the Colonial Office or the local colonial governments to control, direct, or provide education.[5]

The Advisory Committee on Education was indeed only an advisory body. Its functions as recommended by the 1923 Committee were:

1. To obtain, and in so far as may seem desirable, to publish information regarding the state and progress of education in the Colonies, protectorates and mandated territories in Africa.

2. To obtain information regarding the education of backward races and communities in other parts of the world.

3. To advise officers of education departments in African dependencies and missionary educators where they can best study particular problems and to put within reach of teachers the available experience and knowledge relating to their tasks.

4. To keep in touch with British schools and universities, with a view to keeping the claims of educational service in Africa before them and to assist them in recruiting.

5. In consultation with the Colonial governments, to help in thinking out the kind of education best adapted to the needs of the inhabitants of the African dependencies, and the best means of providing them.

6. To advise regarding the means of bringing about the most effective and harmonious co-operation between the state and private agencies in education.

7. To afford a means of consulting with foreign states for the furtherance of a common international policy and co-operation in matters of African education.

8. To advise the Colonial governments in any matters which may be specifically referred by them to the Committee.

Thus the Committee had no executive powers and merely provided a broad framework within which the various local Colonial governments functioned.

In March 1925 the Advisory Committee submitted to the Secretary of State, for transmission to the colonial governments of Africa, its first publication, *Education Policy in British Tropical Africa*. The memorandum dealt with broad principles, touching on such matters as the encouragement and control of voluntary (mainly missionary) educational effort, co-operation, adaptation to native life, religion, and women's education.

It suggested that depending on the peculiar circumstances of a given colony, the educational set-up should be organised thus:

1. Elementary education for both boys and girls, beginning with the education of young children

2. Secondary or intermediate education including more than one type of school and several types of curricula

3. Technical and vocational schools

4. Institutions some of which might later reach university rank and many of which might include in their curricula some branches of professional or

vocational training, e.g. training of teachers, training in medicine, training in agriculture
5. Adult education.

It is important to note at this stage that while the 1847 policy concerned itself primarily with elementary schools and the training of teachers, the 1925 memorandum mentioned the establishment of nuclei which might grow into universities.

The earliest educational institution anywhere approaching a university was the Yaba Higher College. How the building of the College itself fits into the recommendations of the 1925 Committee will be discussed below, but it will also lead to a greater appreciation of the position of the Higher College if we first discuss the other stages of the education system at the time of the initiation of the Higher College.

The background

The genius of the Higher College was Mr. E. R. J. Hussey, who became Director of Education in 1929. Hussey's proposals for education in the country were embodied in the *Memorandum on Educational Policy in Nigeria*, 1930.[6] Inevitably the document reflected the British policy of the time to keep the North separate from the South, for separate policies were planned for the two divisions of the country.

For the South, Mr. Hussey proposed three grades of educational institutions: elementary schools, middle schools, and the Higher College.[7] The elementary course would last four years. The middle schools would correspond to the top section of then existing primary classes [5 and 6] and forms 1 to 4 of secondary schools. English would be taught and used in these schools. In addition to mathematics and science, the history and geography of other countries would be taught.

There would also be some boarding schools which would provide instruction for the upper classes of the middle school course, with or without junior lower middle sections. The day and boarding schools of the missions would be adapted to fit into the scheme. Nevertheless, Mr. Hussey proposed that the government should have its own boarding schools and suggested that the Training Colleges at Ibadan and Umuahia be converted to middle schools. It was essential that there should be one government school on each side of the Niger, and the two schools in question, described as 'definitely of the public school type,' were to serve as models for other schools and to form an insurance for the supply of candidates to the Higher College if mission schools did not produce sufficient candidates.

If the government schools had not been in existence, Mr. Hussey would have asked the government to establish them, as it would have been, according to him, unreasonable to propose a scheme of higher education dependent entirely on mission institutions for candidates.

The Higher College in the South was to be established at Yaba, which was within easy reach of departmental activities. These were important for vocational training and students who had passed through the middle schools described above would be well-fitted to attend Yaba.[8]

In the North there was also to be a Higher College, but the problem was to decide between Katsina and Zaria. The former already had a highly reputable Training College, to which classes for the preliminary training of dispensers and male nurses were added in 1927, six years after its founding. Although Education Departmental Conferences had advocated for some time that this be converted to a Higher College giving vocational four-year courses in teaching, medical, and agricultural subjects, it had, according to Mr. Hussey, the disadvantages of not being easily accessible and also of being situated in the headquarters of a Muslim Emirate, which had had little contact with other people. Zaria on the other hand was not so handicapped, being close to medical, agricultural, teacher-training, and engineering establishments which could be used for instruction. Hussey suggested that Katsina might be used for the training of Moslem native judges (*kadis*).[10]

Reviewing the plans for the two territories, Mr. Hussey stated that there would be three grades of educational institutions—elementary, middle and higher. In elementary schools the syllabus in the two areas would be very similar, and indigenous languages would be taught—Hausa in the North, and Yoruba, Ibo and Efik in the South. The content of textbooks would in most cases be the same, but whereas English would not be taught in the Northern elementary schools, it would be introduced from class 2 upwards in the South. The middle schools would also differ in the respect that while in the North the middle classes would, at first, go up to class 4 only, classes 5 and 6 being taken as the preliminary of the Higher College course, in the South the middle schools would take the full course.

For the time being therefore, the Higher College in the South would be more advanced than that in the North, but only temporarily.

If at some future date it became desirable to amalgamate the two systems at the top of which would stand the central Nigerian University, there would be no technical difficulty in effecting the amalgamation.[11]

For the time being, according to Mr. Hussey, it was inevitable that the students in each area should advance at their own pace, in their own surroundings, and pass from their own Higher College into the public service of the country.[12]

It was planned that the proposed Higher College in Zaria should hold a maximum of 200 students. Yaba would take an ultimate maximum of 750, but would start with 240. In each case the first group of students could enter after one year's building programme had been completed and the scheme could be ready within two years.[13]

The motive behind the founding of the Higher Colleges was man-power needs coupled with reasons of economy. For according to Hussey:

> I have dwelt upon the vital necessity of providing an institution in Nigeria which can train men in the country to play an honourable part in its development. . . . A comparable study of staff lists for Nigeria and such countries as the Sudan, where higher training of the type contemplated at Yaba and Zaria has been in operation for many years, will show that a considerable reduction in European personnel is possible by this means, with a consequent saving of large sums of money on European salaries.
>
> No one who has travelled through the length and breath of Nigeria with its huge and increasing population can fail to be struck by its immense economic possibilities. Sound educational expansion among the masses of the people is an important factor in the realization of the latent possibilities and a demand for an increasing number of well-educated natives is a natural corollary of economic progress.[14]

The proposals were considered by a sub-committee appointed by the Advisory Committee on Education in the Colonies. At a meeting of that sub-committee on 29 May 1930 it was decided that the principles suggested by Mr. Hussey's memorandum should be the permanent form of organisation, from which there should be no departure in the future without careful consideration by both the government and missionary societies.[15] It is instructive to examine the composition of this sub-committee. Its chairman was the well-known Lord Lugard of Nigeria; the Committee itself included eminent educational authorities such as Sir Michael Sadler of Calcutta University Report fame, and Sir Percy Nunn. The findings of the sub-committee were unanimously approved at a meeting convened by Mr. Oldham, the Secretary of the International Mission Council, and attended by the headquarters staff of the various Protestant missions operating in Nigeria.

Despite approval of the proposals from these quarters the plans were not in fact executed as originally planned. First, the integration of the top classes of the primary schools was not universally accepted by voluntary agency schools.[16] Typical of this local opposition was the protest delegation sent by Herbert Macaulay's Nigerian National Democratic Party to complain that Mr. Hussey's new scheme would lower the standard of education all over the country.[17] As will be shown below, the portion of the policy concerning higher education was soon under fire.

A second departure from the plan concerned the colleges at Kaduna and Zaria. It was soon found that it was not practicable to develop two institutions 'to the full extent of a University College'; arrangements were therefore made for suitable Northern students to take advantage of the courses given at Yaba in the appropriate areas.[18]

Proposals for the Yaba Higher College

A detailed account of the nature of the courses at Yaba could not of course be stated in a document such as Hussey's *Memorandum*, which was concerned with principles. Suggestions of these came from speeches made by government officials, including Mr. Hussey. During the Legislative Council debate on the allocation of £25,000 for preliminary expenditure in connection with the foundation of Higher Colleges at Zaria and Yaba, Mr. Hussey made three important revelations about the Higher College. First, the aim of the Higher College was to provide well-trained assistants for various departments of government and private enterprise. Second, there would be a close liaison between prospective employing departments and the Education Department: there would be a section for the training of teachers of higher grade, and a commercial course. Third, the standard of the College would gradually rise and 'although no limit would be set to the scope of the institution, it may take a long time before it reaches the standard which must be its ultimate aim, that of a British University'.[19] The Governor also gave details of the College's courses. Instruction at the College initially would comprise civil engineering, medicine, agriculture and the training of teachers for more advanced work. The training would be of 'university or professional character', but would be so highly vocational that by itself it could not earn United Kingdom university or professional qualifications. However, 'as the level of attainment of the students who matriculate at Yaba rises in proportion to the improvement in the schools from which those students come, the standard of work at the college will rise to a corresponding degree, and we look forward to the time when it will be possible for men and women to obtain at Yaba external degrees of a British university.' But for this purpose it would probably be necessary to lengthen the course.[20]

The medical course, according to the Governor, would last for five years in the first instance, the first two years in premedical science, followed by training in the Medical School and hospitals, as in England. If successful, the student would be appointed to government service as an Assistant Medical Officer under obligation to serve for five years. The first two years of the five would be as House Officer. Thereafter if sufficiently promising he would return to Yaba for a year to acquire the College diploma and become a medical practitioner which would enable him to set up in private practice at the end of his obligation. Others would remain on the medical register as Medical Assistants.[21]

The teacher's course would last three years and would produce men specially trained to teach certain subjects.

The agricultural course at Yaba would be of two years, followed by another two at the experimental station at Ibadan. Similarly, courses in civil engineering would be completed after students had acquired practical experience working in the Public Works Department. Opportunity for further work at Yaba and of sitting for the external examinations of British universities would be available.[22]

F

Public response to Yaba Higher College

The medical course in the College began in 1930. Two years later, in February 1932, the other courses were started at a temporary[23] site with forty-one students. The College was, however, not formally opened until 9 January 1934. The opening immediately started a spate of public controversy and criticism. The heat generated by public discussion was so momentous that it prompted events which have profoundly affected not only the educational but also the Nigerian political situation for a long time.

When the 1929 *Memorandum* was first prepared it was not allowed to be discussed, either publicly or in the Legislative Council, until it had been approved by the Advisory Committee on Education in the Colonies. Despite the eminence of the members of the approving sub-committee, their recommendations did not reflect Nigerian public feelings. Discussion of the new policy after it had been approved in England was therefore appropriately described by the Second Member for Lagos in the Legislative Assembly, Dr. Eric Moore, as merely academic.[24] What discussion there was subsequently was on the whole limited to sections of the *Memorandum* other than those dealing with the Higher College. It was thought that the new educational system would lower standards and 'restrict elementary education.'[25] The concern in the Council at that time appeared twofold: first and over-riding was that regarding the expense, a natural preoccupation at the time of the great world economic depression. The other, less strongly expressed, was a vague feeling about the standard of the Higher College.[26]

The opening of the College and the subsequent announcement of its programme as already stated above signalled the beginning of the upsurge of public interest in it. Interest was aroused by an editorial which appeared in a leading newspaper four days after the opening ceremony of Yaba. It is so pertinent to subsequent events that it deserves quoting at some length:

> On Friday last His Excellency the Governor amidst great enthusiasm, performed the ceremony of formally opening the Higher College at Yaba, which may be described as the crowning result of the Hussey educational scheme about which so much has already been heard. The Higher College stands as a great landmark in the history and evolution of local educational effort and is an earnest expression of Government's desire to provide the best facilities for cultural development at the disposal of Nigerian youth. . . . Everybody appeared highly impressed with the elaborate programme outlined by the Governor, and there can be no doubt as to the great place the Higher College will take in Nigeria if it were possible for the aims of the College so gloriously portrayed to be carried fully out both in the spirit and in the letter. The more carefully the position is studied, however, the less confident we become of the likelihood of the aims being realized. The College as it is, we are afraid, is a grand idea, an imposing structure, resting on rather weak foundations. . . .
>
> We shall take Medicine for example. Have we got in the country men sufficiently qualified to lecture students in the several branches of a medical course up to a stand-

ard to qualify for a degree or diploma, such as would be recognized by the British Medical Board? . . . Mention was made [in the Governor's speech] of facilities to be afforded students wishing to take external degrees of British Universities. This seems to imply a change of faith in those responsible for recent educational policy, as in the past they had never concealed their complete disapproval of external examinations entering into the Nigerian scheme of education. It is well known, for instance, that the course of studies in the Government Middle Schools with the sole exception of King's College, is planned in such a manner as to exclude external examinations. And yet these are the schools which are intended to be feeders of the higher college students the public is told are to proceed to British University Degrees. Is it likely that boys can achieve all those aims of the College so rosily portrayed, without a thorough foundation and previous preparation at the Middle Schools? Unless the standard of these schools is high, it will be impossible to obtain a sufficiently high standard in the Higher College to justify the huge expenditure that is being incurred. . . .

As far as Nigeria is concerned nothing but the best is good enough for Nigeria. If we must have higher education we wish to declare emphatically that this country will not be satisfied with an inferior brand such as the present scheme seems to threaten. [27]

Two days later the Director of Education, Mr. E. R. J. Hussey, was assuring the public in an interview with the same newspaper that suitable lecturers and examiners for Yaba could be found in Nigeria, and that standards would be generally high.[28] But this did not satisfy the public, and meanwhile the discussion had shifted to the Legislative Council, where Dr. Henry Carr made his much publicised attack on the proposal.[29]

The main points of criticism at that time, besides those already mentioned, were as follows:

1. That Mr. Hussey was introducing the new education policy for no other reason than to establish a programme different from those of his predecessors. No account was taken of the suitability of the programme for the Nigerians. Thus continuity and permanence did not exist in the Nigerian educational scheme. The Hon. Eric Moore put it clearly:

In the year 1909 we had Mr. Rowden who was appointed Director of Education. He introduced a Code in 1910 abolishing the previous code. . . . Mr. Hyde Johnson was appointed Director of Education and he in 1923 introduced another code. . . . In 1926 Mr. Grier was seconded to the Education Office as Director of Education and introduced an education code. . . . The present Director [Mr. Hussey] was no sooner appointed than there was a rumour that there was to be a change in the educational policy of Government . . . This want of continuity does not make for progress in this Colony.[30]

It was felt that the Higher College was a white elephant added to an educational policy not much different from the previous one, except in so far as the College might provide 'a memorial of Mr. Hussey's Ministry of Education in Nigeria and no more.'[31] In some quarters it was considered that the College was no more than a bringing together of various government departmental training schemes launched ten years earlier.

2. That the public was not in fact allowed to know anything about the College until the whole educational policy of which it was part had been approved by the sub-committee of the Advisory Committee on Education

in the Colonies, was another cause for complaint. The matter appeared to have been settled by government officials and Christian missionaries (most of whom were non-Nigerians) operating both in Nigeria and in England. It appeared that even Mr. Carr, the only Nigerian on the twelve-man Board of Education,[32] was aware of the programme no earlier than the rest of the public. In short the public was not taken into confidence at any stage of the planning.[33]

3. When indeed the programme was launched, no one was sure of exactly what it was, what it was to do, and how it was to set about doing this; no syllabus was issued, no legal legislative basic existed to ensure its continuity. 'What,' asked a contemporary observer, 'is the Higher College? Is it an industrial school, a technical school or a school intended to give general post-secondary education to the youth of this country?[34]

4. What was disclosed of the College activities did not satisfy the aspirations of the Nigerians at that time. What, it was asked, was the value of a College which would cater only to supplying government service with young recruits instead of providing higher education for those who could pay for it? Would not the Yaba College duplicate training already being successfully offered by the various departments (Public Works, Marine, Railway, the Post and Telegrams and the Medical departments), since it did not appear that work of a quality higher than that of these departments would be offered at Yaba? It was a dangerous policy to produce a crop of mediocre men who in their circumscribed outlook might be capable only of supervised work.[35]

So high were public feelings at the time that a mass meeting was convened in the Glover Memorial Hall, Lagos, on Saturday, 17 March 1934 to protest against the Yaba Higher College. Among those present were Dr. Oguntola Sapara, the Hon. T. A. Doherty, Dr. M. R. Macaulay, Dr. K. Faderin, O. Alakija, E. A. Franklin, Tiyamiyu Savage, E. M. E. Agbebi, Dr. A. Maja, Dr. K. Abayomi, Jibril Martins, S. Edwin Cole, Mrs. Cole, the Rev. J. O. Lucas, Julius Ojo Cole and L. Emmanuel. The speakers were Dr. J. C. Vaughan (chairman), Ernest Ikoli, Dr. M. R. Macaulay, Dr. A. Maja, S. A. Akinsanya, V. A. Kayode and A. Onibuwe.[36]

At the end of the meeting, the following resolutions were passed:

1. That this meeting, representing the intelligentsia of Lagos, records its deep appreciation of the efforts of Government in recent years to extend educational facilities in Nigeria for the benefit of the people and more especially its programme for higher education, which is regarded as a great need at this stage in the history of the country's development.

2. They desire at the same time to make it very clear by stating most emphatically that the present movement is not one of opposition to the establishment of higher education at Yaba, or anywhere else in Nigeria, but that it is intended rather as a demonstration of protest against the manner of introduction and execution of the Yaba Higher College Scheme which the Hon. Mr. Carr described in a speech on the Education vote as 'shy and tentative', and to express their complete agreement with the remarks that,

although the broad principles are known, its details and implications were up to the present not understood.

3. That this meeting considered as most significant, in spite of the numerous public criticisms against this policy of reserve and absence of a clearly defined programme, that the government up to the present had not thought it expedient to issue a statement giving every detail of the Scheme for the information of the public.

4. That the conclusion which could be drawn from such an attitude is either that the Government themselves are not quite sure of their actual aims and intentions with regard to the working of the Scheme or that there was some motive behind this policy of studied silence.

5. That this meeting considers it necessary to point out that the public mind is considerably disturbed even by some features of the general outline of the Yaba Higher College Scheme as disclosed in the Governor's speech delivered at the inauguration ceremony on January 19th last.

6. Among the defects easily apparent in the speech is the obvious attempt to establish a system of isolation of Nigerian youths from the outside world and set up a false standard of values in the country both as regards general cultural endeavour and professional exercises. While it may be expedient and desirable that opportunity should be provided locally whereby a certain number of youths may be trained to acquire some measure of skill in the different professions to meet the immediate needs of certain services, it is considered inimical to the highest interest of Nigeria to flood the country with a class of mass-produced men whose standard of qualification must necessarily be deficient owing to the limited facilities available locally both as regards material and staff. The position with respect to the medical branch, involving as it does the question of life and death, occasions very grave public concern, especially as there is the tendency abroad to encourage the belief that the products under a system marked by such manifest disadvantages, which no effort, however heroic, would remove in even the next fifty years, would be as good as those who receive their training under infinitely more favourable conditions.

7. In view of the foregoing it is resolved that a memorandum embodying a comprehensive statement of the points raised in this resolution together with any proposals for a satisfactory and effective working of the scheme should be submitted to Government.[37]

This meeting was in fact the first meeting of what became first the Lagos Youth Movement and later the Nigerian Youth Movement (see Ch. 10). It was organised and attended mainly by Old Boys of King's College, Lagos[38] Nigeria's premier school at that time. It is easy enough to see why this was so. First, the new scheme placed the King's College in a strange situation. As it was designed, entry to the Higher College did not require work of a standard as high as that undertaken for the Cambridge School Certificate, which was offered by King's College. It meant that Old Boys of that school spent the first year or two at Yaba repeating some of the work they might have done earlier.[39] Those who could afford it of course proceeded to higher studies abroad; but most could not, and would not accept a second-best. Second, the government was unwilling either to sponsor students on scholarships abroad or to send them overseas after a Yaba course.[40]

A public issue as hotly debated as Yaba could not help but split the populace. It soon became apparent that the fight against Yaba was not fully supported by Herbert Macaulay's Nigerian National Democratic Party, a political party which up till then had been regarded as radical. It will be recalled that it was the very first to criticise the Hussey educational policy. In the Legislative Council, its elected members argued in support of Yaba. The Party newspaper, *The Lagos Daily News*, came out also in its favour.

> We entirely support the Elected Members of the Legislative Council in their approval of the Scheme and in their promise of [backing] for it; and we know as a matter of fact that through them the Honourable Mr. Hussey is assured of the support of the Nigerian National Democratic Party. . . . The mightiest critic is the public voice, and the general opinion of the public is that Mr. Hussey's Scheme should be given a fair chance through a number of years, [during which] they fully believe, it will achieve unmeasurable success and prove itself a blessing to Nigeria.[41]

A bitter attack was launched by the paper on any one who dared criticise the Higher College.

Mr. Henry Carr's criticisms, that of the 'shy and tentative' launching of the Yaba Scheme, and that humanities and religion should be taught to the science students, were scorned by *The Daily News* as 'the abortive debut of a political dog in the manger'. The meeting of the Lagos Youth Movement was described as that of a mere handful of gentlemen (515 in all), with the implication that they were uninfluential and of no consequence.[42]

Since the N.N.D.P. had failed to meet the aspirations of youth, the Movement gradually formed itself into a political party, the subsequent history of which will be discussed in Chapter 10. Suffice it to say that it changed its name to the Nigerian Youth Movement when in 1936 it was joined by H. O. Davies.

The protest against Yaba was not the first made on an educational issue. Five years earlier, in 1929, there had been a similar public outcry when the government attempted to replace the Oxford and Cambridge School Certificate with a local 'Nigerian High Standard Certificate,'[43] in much the same way as Yaba was to award its own local certificates. A decision was taken at a mass meeting to collect £10,000 for a 'National School'. About one-tenth of the target figure was actually collected and although advertisements for teachers actually appeared, the scheme never got under way.[44] One reason why the National School was not built was that the government dropped the proposed introduction of a local certificate.

The Yaba protests did not effect much change; instead Mr. Hussey, took every possible opportunity to reply to the criticisms.[45] Part of Mr. Hussey's adamant attitude may have been due to the successful introduction of a similar scheme in Uganda, where he had been the First Director of Education, before his transfer to Nigeria. But the situations in Uganda and Nigeria were vastly different. In Uganda, before his appointment, education had been completely in the hands of missionaries who cooperated and allocated government grants among themselves by the means of a locally-organised advisory committee. Mr. Hussey reorganised the Uganda system by placing the schools into various categories so as to provide an educational ladder at the top of which was to be the government-owned Makerere College.[46] Thus Yaba was to be Nigeria's Makerere, but the similarity goes no further than their both being at the top of their respective educational systems. For the educational conditions in Uganda were such that when Mr. Hussey became Director on 15 February 1925, Makerere was the only government-owned educational institution in the country. Mission schools were therefore reorganised and regraded to extend to junior secondary level. Makerere itself arranged for a three-year senior secondary school course leading to a matriculation examination.[47] Thereafter as soon as students of post-matriculation standard were ready, pre-matriculation courses were to be gradually transferred to mission schools and Makerere was to concentrate upon professional training up to the level of university intermediate examinations.[48] In Nigeria conditions were vastly different: there were schools, most notable of which was King's College, Lagos, which already did work of matriculation standard. Mission schools also did work of this nature. For example, when in 1933 Nigeria had eighteen passes at matriculation level, Igbobi College, Lagos, had six; St. Gregory's College, Lagos, and the Catholic Seminary at Oke Are, Ibadan, four passes each, while Hope Waddell recorded one.[49] These schools were all missionary-run. It would have been possible for Mr. Hussey to have set higher standards for Yaba if he had used King's College and the better missionary secondary schools as feeders to the new Higher College. Instead, these schools were by-passed and the Ibadan and Umuahia Teacher Training Colleges were converted, not to full secondary schools but to middle schools two forms lower than King's College and other secondary schools. The new middle schools were then to supply candidates for Yaba in much the same way as the junior schools of Uganda fed Makerere. It thus looks on the face of it as if Hussey had become a slave of his own planning.

It remains now to consider briefly how the Yaba College functioned during its early years and until its closing down in 1947. The description that follows was made at least ten years after the establishment of the college, at which time a certain amount of equilibrium had been attained. It will be seen that there was little deviation from the original plan drawn up by Mr. Hussey.

The Yaba College and the Advisory Committee on Education in Africa

It is possible to blame Mr. Hussey too heavily for the faults of Yaba College, the vocational nature of which was bitterly criticised by the

Table 2

Courses given at Yaba in 1944

Subject	No. of years of general course at Yaba	No. of years of subsequent professional course	Location of professional course
Agriculture	2	2	Ibadan
Forestry	2	2	Ibadan
Engineering	4	–	–
Medicine	1½	5	Lagos
Surveying	2	2	Oyo
Veterinary Science	1½	5½	Vom near Jos
Teacher Training	3	1	–

Source: *Report of the Commission on Higher Education in West Africa, 1945, p. 34.*

Lagos citizens of the thirties. The framework into which Yaba fitted was in fact formulated by the Advisory Committee on Education in Africa. The Committee itself was strongly influenced by the views of Negro advocates of vocational education for American Negroes.

The first memorandum of this Committee, *Education in British Tropical Africa*, 1925, emphasised that African education should be adapted to the mentality, aptitudes, occupations and traditions of the various peoples. As part of the general policy for the advancement of the people every department of government concerned with vocational teaching, including especially the departments of Health, Public Works, Railways, Agriculture, must co-operate closely in the educational policy.

As resources permitted, however, the door of advancement through higher education was to be opened for those who by character, ability and temperament showed themselves fitted to profit from such education. Thus although the policy made some concession to a gradual exposure of selected numbers of the population to an academic, literary, university education, it was clear where its sympathy lay. As Professor Brown of Ibadan puts it, British educational policy in the colonies involved a two-handed policy: on the right hand, there is the simple realistic education for the mass of the people and, on the left hand, a more advanced education for 'African leaders'. But following the practice of Jesse Jones and Booker T. Washington, the priority was given to the right hand.[50]

The composition of the committee itself could not have been better arranged to emphasise vocational education. It included Dr. Jesse Jones who had headed the Phelps-Stokes Commission to West Africa; that commission had strongly urged vocational education for Africa. There were also on the Advisory Committee J. H. Oldham, Secretary of the International Missionary Society, who was quoted as saying that 'education in Africa should mean agriculture'[51] Sir Michael Sadler, famous for his work on the re-adaptation of Indian education; and Sir James Currie, an authority of African Agriculture and head of Gordon College, Khartoum. The Secretary was Major H. Vischer, where Lugard's indirect rule was being carried out.

Courses offered at Yaba

As may be seen from Table 2, courses were offered for the production of teachers and various assistants. The teachers produced were drafted mainly to teach in mission schools, while the others filled vacancies in government departments, for which these candidates were in fact ear-marked. Candidates were selected by a competitive entrance examination and the numbers who passed depended on the available government jobs. In order to ensure that the market was not flooded, courses (except in medicine) were started in alternate years.[52] It was said in official circles that insufficient numbers of students capable of completing the course of study entered the College. But this may in fact be due to the unattractiveness of the conditions of service following successful completion of the course, rather than a lack of students of the right calibre. Between 1935 and 1943 thirty students left the College due to failure in the junior examination which was held at the end of the science courses, while twenty students who completed these courses failed their final examinations. Thus about 20 per cent of the students who passed the entrance examination failed to complete their studies. But one should note the remarks of Dr. Kenneth Mellanby that 'At the outset the standards [of Yaba] were not as high as in Britain, but as the schools improved and the entrants were better qualified the standards were raised. I believe that some of the examinations eventually became *more difficult than parallel examinations in Britain.'*[53]

Yaba students were not allowed to take external examinations so that the curricula might, in the words of the 1925 declaration of the Advisory Committee, be adapted to the mentality and aptitudes of the students. In other words, the courses were to suit the local environment. This was laudable. But the reward for this experience was a local diploma, which not being recognised outside Nigeria, caused a lot of frustration to the students who would have preferred certificates of international currency.[54] Nevertheless, although it was against official policy to do so, a number of students successfully took the external Intermediate B.A. and B.Sc. exams of the

University of London. Soon the College had to recognise this and geared
its teaching to the standards of London. Yet after this had happened it was
not uncommon for a student to pass the London Intermediate and fail the
local equivalent which came after a further term's work. This was an
additional reason for feeling that the standards of Yaba were unneccessarily
high.[55] Not only that, but the social status of those who studied similar
subjects abroad was higher than that of the Yaba's 'graduates'.

As one latter-day Nigerian sums up the Higher College,

> The gap between the academic attainments and status of those two groups of students
> [those qualified at Yaba and those qualified overseas] was astounding. What adds
> point to the comparison is that, by and large, those who succeeded in gaining entrance
> to Yaba were the more able of the secondary school products. But in addition to the
> abnormally long courses, there was a soul-destroying struggle for the survival of the
> fittest. It was axiomatic that some of the students should be weeded out at the end of
> every year. Of all the waste of the Colonial regime in Nigeria none was more pathetic
> than the spectacle of the erstwhile brilliant pupil, discarded after four or five years of
> gruelling toil at the Higher College, Yaba. Four or five years' work had gone down the
> drain, and a personality virtually wrecked: some committed suicide.[56]

Despite what may be said about Yaba all commentators agree that it was
a useful institution and did contribute to the satisfaction of the manpower
needs of the time. In 1944, ten years after its formal opening and three
years before it was finally closed, it had produced produced 58 teachers, 20
medical assistants, 15 assistant agricultural officers, 3 forest supervisors,
6 surveyors, 31 administrators in government and 9 in commerce.[57]

In December 1947 the Yaba Higher College closed down, thus ending a
turbulent career which might have led it to the dignity of being Nigeria's
first university. That honour was reserved for Ibadan.

Notes

[1] H. S. SCOTT, 'The development of Education of the African in relation to Western
contact', 'Education by the European', *The Yearbook of Education, 1938*, London, p. 708.
[2] *Ibid.*, p. 710.
[3] W. ORMSBY GORE, 'Education in the British Dependencies in Tropical Africa', *The
Yearbook of Education, 1932*, London, p. 748.
[4] H. S. SCOTT, 'Educational Policy in the British Colonial Empire', *Yearbook of
Education, 1937*, London, p. 414.
[5] W. ORMSBY GORE, *op. cit.*
[6] *Sessional Paper No. 31 of 1930*, Lagos, the Government Printer.
[7] *Ibid.*, pp. 16–19.
[8] *Ibid.*
[9] *Annual Report on Education Departments, North and South Provinces 1929*, Lagos, the
Government Printer, p. 11.
[10] *Sessional Paper No. 31*, pp. 11–12.
[11] *Ibid.*
[12] *Ibid.*
[13] *Ibid.*, p. 22.

[14] *Ibid.*, pp. 24–25.

[15] *Ibid.*, Appendix, p. 2.

[16] E. R. J. HUSSEY (Director of Education), Speech on 27 September 1930, *Legislative Council Debates, 8th Session, 1930*, Lagos, the Government Printer, pp. 29–31.

[17] 'Nigeria's New Education Scheme', editorial in *The Lagos Daily News*, 21 January 1930, p. 2.

[18] *Annual Report on the Education Department, 1935*, Lagos, the Government Printer, p. 8.

[19] *Legislative Council, Debates, loc. cit.*

[20] *Annual Report on the Education Department, 1933*, Lagos, the Government Printer, p. 8.

[21] *Ibid.*, p. 18.

[22] *Ibid.*, p. 19.

[23] *Annual Report on the Education Department, 1932*, p. 15.

[24] *Legislative Council Debates, 1930*, p. 59.

[25] *Ibid.*, pp. 59–70.

[26] *Ibid., passim*, esp. pp. 62, 70.

[27] Editorial on 'The Yaba Higher College', *Nigerian Daily Times*, 23 January 1934.

[28] *Nigerian Daily Times*, 25 January 1934.

[29] *Legislative Council Debates, 12th Session, 1934*, pp. 39–43.

[30] *Legislative Council Debates, op. cit.*, p. 60.

[31] 'Yaba College—Monument or Memorial', *Nigerian Daily Times*, 3 March 1934; also *Lagos Daily News*, 21 January 1930.

[32] The Board of Education was constituted under the 1926 Ordinance as follows:
Chairman: The Lieutenant-Governor, Southern Provinces;
Two official members: The Director of Education, The Deputy Director of Education;
Three other official members: The Secretary for Native Affairs, The Deputy Director, Medical Services, The Principal, Queen's College, Lagos: all appointed in 1930;
Unofficial members: Six, of whom four must be missionaries; in 1930 there were five missionaries and Mr. H. Carr.

[33] *Legislative Council Debates, 12th Session, 1934*, pp. 39–43.

[34] *Nigerian Daily Times*, 20 March 1934; also 3 March 1934.

[35] *Ibid.*, 3 March , 20 March, 24 March, 1934.

[36] *Ibid.*, 19 March 1934.

[37] *Ibid.*

[38] *The Lagos Daily News*, 17 April 1934.

[39] *The Nigerian Daily Times*, 24 March 1934.

[40] *Legislative Council Debates, 12th Session, 1934*, p. 16.

[41] *The Lagos Daily News*, 17 April 1934.

[42] *Ibid.*

[43] JAMES COLEMAN, *Nigeria, Background to Nationalism*, California, 1960, p. 217.

[44] 'What happened to the National School?' editorial in *Lagos Daily News*, 28 January, 1960, COLEMAN, *op. cit.*, p. 217; *Nigerian Daily Times*, 20 March 1934.

[45] See Mr. Hussey's speech at Igbobi College, Lagos on 28 April 1934, *Lagos Daily News*, 30 April 1934; also interview with the *West African Students' Union, West Africa* 6 October 1934, quoted in the *Lagos Daily News*, 26 October 1934.

[46] W. B. MUMFORD, 'Some growing points in African Higher Education', *Yearbook of Education, 1936*.

[47] *Annual Report of the Department of Education, 1925, Protectorate of Uganda*, Entebbe, p. 5.

[48] MUMFORD, *op. cit.*

[49] 'Our Schools and Colleges', *The Nigerian Daily Times*, 15 March 1934.

[50] *Report on Higher Education in West Africa*, H.M.S.O., 1935, pp. 34–37.

[51] Nyasaland Protectorate: *Report of the Native Education Conference held at Zouba,*

1927, p. 27, quoted in GODFREY N. BROWN, 'British Education Policy in West and Central Africa', *Journal of Modern Studies*, 2, p. 269.

[52] BROWN, *ibid.*, p. 370.

[53] KENNETH MELLANBY, *The Birth of Nigeria's University*, London, 1958, p. 46. Italics are the present author's.

[54] *Report on Higher Education in West Africa*, p. 37.

[55] MELLANBY, *op. cit.*, pp. 46–47.

[56] OTONTI NDUKA, *Western Education and the Nigerian Cultural Background*, Ibadan, 1964, p. 55.

[57] *Report on Higher Education in West Africa*, p. 36; see also O. IKEJIANI, (ed.), *Nigerian Education*, London, 1964, NDUKA, *op. cit.* p. 54; MELLANBY, *op. cit.*, p. 47.

6 The University College, Ibadan

As has been shown, educated English-speaking West Africans had for about a hundred years advocated the establishment of a university in West Africa. But up to the late 1940s the measures of success these advocates achieved were Fourah Bay College, Sierra Leone; Achimota College, Accra, Gold Coast; and the Higher College, Yaba. Fourah Bay College was owned and run by the Church Missionary Society and although it granted degrees in a few subjects, its primary aim was to prepare prospective candidates for the Ministry of the Church.[1] Achimota had a small 'university department' which prepared students mostly for the Intermediate examination of the Bachelor's degrees in Arts, Science and Engineering.[2] Yaba, as has been demonstrated in the previous chapter, was from the start very unsatisfactory and did little to improve its popularity. This chapter attempts mainly to discuss and analyse why the University College, Ibadan, was created when it was.

In 1933, the Advisory Committee on Education in the Colonies produced a Report on Higher Education[3] which began with the general theme of its 1925 predecessor, namely that education should be adapted to the environment and mentality of the people. It drew attention to the fact that the growing demand by Africans for higher education, was fulfilled for those able to afford it, in European and American universities. This was unsatisfactory because these universities were devised for their particular areas. The Committee therefore recommended that plans be made for the development of selected institutions to university standards.

It also suggested that these projected universities might be grouped together and associated for some time with London University, in much the same way as were Birmingham, Manchester, Leeds, Liverpool and Reading. It further suggested that arrangements be made to make it possible for exchange of staff between London University and the projected African colleges.

We thus see in this most far-sighted report the seeds of the Special Relationship arrangement between London and Ibadan, and also of the Inter-University Council for Higher Education in the Colonies. Discussions on the report went on among the colonial governments, but it was only in East Africa that it was acted upon immediately, for in 1936 a commission was set up on higher education. *The Report of the Commission on Higher Education in East Africa*,[4] published in 1937, was the first pronouncement of the British government on African higher education. But it was not until another decade that universities were established in the British tropical African dependencies.

Why, despite the demands for them, was not a government-sponsored institution of university standing founded earlier by the British government in West Africa? The answers appear to be many and interrelated and concern the local colonial governments, the natives of these colonies themselves and the government in Britain.

With regard to the British officials' opposition or indifference to higher education in West Africa and in Nigeria in particular, it is evident that there was a strong element of self-interest involved. As long as there were no Nigerians trained in the same or similar institutions as those which these local British officials attended there was no threat to their continued occupation of government posts. Only as late as 1937 was the policy of not granting government scholarships for university studies abroad abandoned in Nigeria.[5] Indeed even the establishment of the University College, Ibadan, was, according to the first Principal, Dr. Mellanby, not welcomed by most of the local colonial officials, who, though willing to help, seldom took the initiative to do so. Thus the University College was to some extent an imposition from above.[6]

In addition, the local governments in Nigeria and elsewhere in Africa were for a long time mainly interested in producing clerks and teachers[7] to man the various departments, and so long as this was so there was little need for university-trained Africans. It was sometimes suggested that there were not enough candidates for universities in West Africa,[8] but, as has been pointed out by Sir Eric Ashby, this was a misguided opinion, for many of the colonial officials had been to Oxford and Cambridge, universities which flourished long before a sound system of secondary schools was established in England.[9] In any case the demands were for one university in West Africa, and there would undoubtedly have been even in the 1920s enough candidates from all four colonies.

The other factor which militated against the establishment of universities in Africa was that the Africans themselves were either unwilling or unable to subscribe appreciably towards their founding. It will suffice to take three examples from Nigeria. When in 1896, as noted in Chapter 4, some educaated citizens of Lagos, under the leadership of Dr. Edward Blyden, decided on a target of £1,000 to found a Lagos Training and Industrial Institute, at the close of the dateline only about a third of this had been collected. Again, in 1929 when, in protest against the government plan to replace the Oxford and Cambridge School Certificate by a local Nigerian Certificate, it was decided that a national school should be built, only £1,600 of the proposed £10,000 was actually received. As Coleman points out, 'The failure of the national school campaign provoked endless self-criticism among Nigerians throughout the following two decades'[10] 1929–47). The third example occured during the early years of the University College, Ibadan. Dr. Kenneth Mellanby, the first Principal, gives an account of the efforts made at raising an endowment fund. He writes, 'Up to June, 1956 the endowment appeal only raised some £34,000, the greater part of which came from firms in Britain.' He then describes how some individuals used the appeal to make political capital for themselves without incurring expense.[11]

The aversion to public subscription had apparently been long known to officials of the Colonial Office in London. For instance, minutes dated 13 August 1896 appended to Blyden's request for the support of the Colonial Office in establishing the Lagos Training College (Chapter 4) read as follows:

> There is not much public spirit in the West African and Mr. Blyden will be a clever man if he can extract much in the way of subscriptions from his fellow countrymen, who moreover dislike anything in the shape of direct contribution.[12]

It is not surprising that armed with this knowledge, and also perhaps because British universities were for a long time supported by private endowments, colonial officials reacted to demands for universities in the spirit of the following extract:

> The educated African demands a University, and nothing could be more desirable than that African youths who wish to qualify for the professions, should be able to take their degrees locally. But its advocates and the native press which point to the present expense required for a 'four or seven years' stay in England' for professional qualification do not offer any suggestion as to how the endowment fund—without which of course, the founding of a university is impossible—could be raised. This absence of initiative and self-help among those who are foremost in demanding advanced institutions militates against the fruition of their desires.[13]

Nearer home, during the agitation for the improvement of Yaba, its founder, E. R. J. Hussey, had taunted Lagosians to create endowments:

> It is indeed a matter of surprise to me that Africans have not themselves founded some scholarships for this purpose [of sending the more brilliant students abroad]. British higher education depends very largely on endowment. Very few, if any, Nigerians have yet endowed Colleges or scholarships, and I suggest that a beginning be made in this direction and that those earnest young Lagosians who are apparently so interested in the subject should constitute a Committee for the purpose of collecting an endowment fund.[14]

The overriding factor which decided that the University Colleges of Ibadan, Legon and Makerere appeared when they did, was a marked change in the colonial policy of the British government, just before and during the Second World War.

Three broad stages may be discerned in the history of this policy. The first stage was that of exploitation, which lasted until late in the nineteenth century. The second was based on the principle that a colony should have only those amenities which it could afford. The demands of Horton, Blyden and the Lagos citizens fit into the first period; Yaba College was founded in the second.

The third began in the late 1930s and involved a recognition of responsibility for the development of the colonies and their resources.[15] The new policy was embodied in a white paper, *Statement of Policy on Colonial Development and Welfare*,[16] published in 1940. It claimed that the primary aim of colonial policy was to protect and advance the interests of the inhabitants of the colonies; but, for this, assistance from outside was necessary, as these colonies could not finance from their own resources the various activities which contributed to their well-being and development.[17]

The immediate cause of the publication of this policy was a Royal Commission[18] appointed in 1938 following riots in the West Indies. Before the Commission had produced its report, war broke out. 'While the Royal Commission have been investigating the situation in the West Indies,' said the White Paper,

> the Government has been examining the position in the colonial Empire generally. Conclusions in principle on the further development of colonial policy were reached some time ago, but it was thought desirable to await the result of the West Indian enquiry before taking final decisions. Though the unhappy intervention of war may inevitably affect the rate of advance, the Government propose to proceed with their policy of development as far and as fast as the exigencies of the times permit.[19]

Another reason for the publication of the policy at that time was gratitude to the colonial peoples for the spontaneity in which they had joined in the war effort. Said Mr. Malcolm MacDonald, in the House of Commons:

> In these sombre days our anxieties and our hopes are fully shared by the peoples of the colonies [who are] distant peoples, alien to us in race. [But] every single Colonial territory has voluntarily associated itself with us, every one of them has asked in what way it could help best the Allied war effort.[20]

It may be added that the colonies had little choice, by their very position, but to act as they did. According to him, however,

> the proposals for assistance towards Colonial development which are contained in this Bill were not devised after the War began. They are not a bribe or a reward for the Colonies' support in this crisis. For many months before that the details of these proposals were already worked out in the Colonial Office. They are a part of the normal peace-time development of our Colonial policy, and if we had not been engaged in war, the Government would still have been introducing this legislation in the present Session of Parliament.[21]

An important, if not the most important cause, was the growing criticism of the British colonial policy within Britain itself.[22] The Colonial Welfare and Development Bill was introduced:

> to make provision for promoting the development of the resources of colonies, protectorates, protected states and mandated territories and the welfare of their peoples and relieving colonial and other Governments from liability in respect of certain loans.[23]

The need for help to the colonies had been recognised ten years earlier and a bill of the same title was in fact passed. But that was in the second of the three eras of colonial policy outlined above. The purpose of the 1929 Bill was not to help the colonial peoples for their own sake, but 'in order to stimulate that development mostly to bring additional work to idle hands in this country [i.e. Britain]. It was part of our scheme to solve our own [British] unemployment problem.'[24]

In terms of money the new Bill introduced legislation to enable help of up to an annual maximum of £5 million to be given to the colonies, five times the amount allowed in the 1929 Bill.[25]

Furthermore, 'development' was interpreted in the broadest sense to mean 'everything which ministers to physical, mental or moral development'.[26] Education was obviously a mainstay of any such programme and it was logical that it should soon be mentioned if there were a serious intention to implement the development bill. This was indeed the case, for as the Secretary of State for the Colonies said three years later:

> It is quite clear that if our goal of colonial government is to be achieved, colonial universities and colleges will have to play an immense part in that development . . . They will, first of all, have to meet the enormously increased need for trained professionals which increased social and economic services will necessitate . . . I am accordingly setting up a Commission of Enquiry [under Mr. Justice Sir Cyril Asquith].

Thus came into being the Commission on Higher Education in the Colonies, whose *Report* was to have such a far-reaching effect in deciding the future of Ibadan and the other 'Asquith University Colleges,' Legon, Makerere and the West Indies.

At the same time the Elliot Commission was set up to study the same topic in West Africa. The Colonial Secretary gave three reasons for this. First, there were several existing centres of education in West Africa; these centres had different standards and did different types of work, and the various West African dependencies were widely separated one from the other. Furthermore there were great contrasts in the social, economic, and political development of these territories, not only from one to the other, but even within the same territory between the coastal and inland areas. Finally, although not fought there, the war had had an immense impact on West Africa.[28]

It is interesting to look at other possible reasons for the special West African Commission. The most important of these was probably pressure from the West Africans themselves. Horton and Blyden, and Hayford and his West African Congress, had all in the past asked for a university in West Africa. Azikiwe had recently published his *Renascent Africa* (1937), and protests and criticisms of Yaba were still current. The Lagos Youth Movement was consolidating itself into a political party, the Nigerian Youth Movement. This then was a time of vigorous nationalist activity in Nigeria and other West African colonies. Indeed it was inevitable that

G

special notice should have been taken on the nationalist and other aspirations of West Africa, for on 13 November 1940, a Member of Parliament asked the Under-Secretary of State for the Colonies 'whether he will consider in relation to existing plans of Colonial development a ten-year programme of social, political and economic development specifically applicable to West Africa and to commence immediately the war ends; and whether he will secure the advice to this end, of the native representatives, social and educational workers and administrators in West Africa'[29]

The British Governors in West Africa were at last forced to concede something to these long-standing demands. In August 1939, they at last agreed at their Conference that the establishment of a West African university was an 'ideal' at which they should aim and 'recommended to the Secretary of State the early appointment of a Commission to examine the details of a co-ordinated scheme of higher educational development in West Africa, the Governors' recommendations on higher education were examined and endorsed by the Sub-Committee on Higher Education of the Advisory Committee on Education in the Colonies.[30]

It was indeed West Africa's turn to have a Commission: although West Africa was more advanced in the acquisition of western education[31] than the eastern part of the continent, a Commission had examined higher education in East Africa in 1937.

Thus two Commissions[32] were set up simultaneously: the first to examine higher education in the colonies generally and the second higher education in West Africa. Much has been written about these Commissions and only some of their recommendations need to be dealt with. Both reported in 1945, two years after they were set up.

The recommendations of the Asquith Commission were necessarily of a general nature since they dealt with the colonies in general. Some of these are given below:[33]

1. That in the interest of higher education in the colonies universities should be established at an early date to serve those areas where they do not exist.

2. That these universities should begin as university colleges, and in the interim before attaining full university status, the colleges should enter into special relationship with London University. This would ensure that while the standard of London University was maintained, the syllabus was adapted to local conditions.

3. That an Inter-University Council for Higher Education should be created, through which co-operation in respect to staffing, etc., between the British universities and the new colonial universities could be achieved.

4. That an appropriate part of the funds available under the Colonial Development and Welfare Act should be specifically assigned as provision for the establishment of universities in the colonies.

5. That these colleges should be residential and cater to both men and women.

6. That among vocational studies attention should be paid to teacher training.

The Elliot Commission which reported on West Africa disagreed among themselves on certain issues. The majority report submitted that:[34]

1. Three university colleges be set up immediately in West Africa: one at Ibadan, one at Achimota in the Gold Coast (Ghana), and that Fourah Bay College in Sierra Leone be developed on a new site and that it should also serve Gambia.

2. The university colleges in Nigeria and the Gold Coast should include the faculties of arts and science.

3. In Nigeria professional schools of medicine, agriculture, forestry and animal health as well a teacher training course should be instituted.

4. In the Gold Coast an institute of education should be set up to carry out research and conduct training courses for teachers.

5. The university college in Sierra Leone should include courses in arts and science up to the Intermediate level and teacher training course. With this it was hoped that there would be an arts degree course intended mainly for theological students and financed by the Church Missionary Society, the authorities of the college.

6. Each university should have the closest possible contact with British universities through the Inter-University Council already recommended by the Asquith Commission.

7. That a Council should control the functions of non-academic administration, and an Academic Board (to be known as the Senate on assumption of autonomy), the academic functions of each new college.

8. That examinations taken in West Africa should be equal in standard to those taken in British universities, through association with London University, but that Fourah Bay might prefer a Durham University liaison.

9. That at first the greater share of the expenditure should be met from the Colonial Development and Welfare funds.

The main point of the minority *Report* was that it recommended only one West African University College, at Ibadan, and also 'territorial colleges' in the Gold Coast, Sierra Leone, Gambia and one east of the Niger. These territorial colleges were to be feeders to the main institution in Ibadan and should provide Intermediate courses. Wholly new university-type institutions should be established in the future in areas which did not have them, when recommended by the Inter-University Council.[35] The minority *Report* was based on the belief that too few students were available to fill the three institutions recommended by the majority.

Both *Reports* stressed the urgency of the matter and that work should start as soon as possible.

Soon after the submission of the Asquith and Elliot *Reports*, a change of government occurred and the Labour Party came to power. The British government of the day not unnaturally accepted the minority *Report*, since Mr. Arthur Creech Jones, one of the signatories, had meanwhile become Under-Secretary of State for the Colonies. This decision, announced about a year after the submission of the reports, immediately raised protests in Sierra Leone, and most especially in the Gold Coast. In the Gold Coast the Legislative Council set up a committee to consider ways of starting a university.[36] Gold Coast indignation and protests were natural to a country with the first, if short-lived, school in West Africa and with a much longer government interest in education, including higher education, than any other in West Africa. It had been the Gold Coast's good fortune to have as Governor Sir Gordon Guggisberg, who in the 1920s established Achimota as a 'stepping-stone' towards a university.

It will be recalled that the Asquith Commission had recommended the setting up of an Inter-University Council for Higher Education in the Colonies. The Secretary of State in accepting this recommendation wished the Council to strengthen co-operation between the universities of the United Kingdom and the existing universities in the colonial territories, to foster the development of higher colleges in the colonies and their advance to full university status. In particular it was recommended that visits be made to the colonies as often as necessary to give the Council first-hand experience of the development and needs of higher education. The representatives of the universities of the United Kingdom and the Colonies meeting in March 1946 constituted themselves, together with the Educational Advisor to the Secretary of State, into the Inter-University Council for Higher Education in the Colonies. (Its name was changed in 1952 to the Inter-University Council for Higher Education Overseas.[37])

This Council then sent out a delegation under Sir William Hamilton-Fyfe in December 1946 to report on the situation in West Africa, following the outburst of protests in the Gold Coast. The delegation's main problem was to decide whether there should be one or more universities. It found that the Gold Coast Legislative Council Committee had stated that the Gold Coast could and would provide money for the capital and recurrent expenditures for the establishment of a university college in the Gold Coast. That being so, the delegation recommended that a large proportion of the money available for higher education in West Africa be devoted to the development of Ibadan. On the strength of the delegation's report, Mr. Creech Jones reversed the earlier decision and in August 1947 approved the establishment of two colleges, one in the Gold Coast and the other in Nigeria.[38]

It is perhaps fortunate for Nigeria that because of her size both sections of the Elliot Commission had recommended a university there. Had the Secretary of State accepted a minority report which recommended the erection of the mother university in the Gold Coast rather than in Nigeria,

it is doubtful, in view of previous experience, if Nigerians would have protested their willingness and ability to financially support a university of
their own.

The demand of the Gold Coasters for their own university is a testimony
to the altered loyalty which had taken place in West Africa. Horton (1868),
Blyden (1872) and Hayford (1911) had each in turn called for *one* university for Western Africa, and as late as 1920, Hayford's West African
National Congress was asking for one West African University. By 1945
the colonial territories had become more inward-looking and regarded
themselves as comprising separate units, rather than as primarily West
African, in a larger sense.

It is also interesting that Kumasi was proposed by the Fyfe delegation as
the site for the university which was eventually installed at Legon. Its
argument was that it was necessary to choose an unsophisticated,
un-Europeanised area—this was much the same argument as that put
forward by Hayford in his *Ethiopia Unbound* in 1911 (see Chapter 3).

The appointment of the first Principal of the University College, Ibadan,
Dr. Kenneth Mellanby, was announced on 8 May 1947. The initial financial
support came, as recommended by the Asquith Commission, from the
Colonial and Welfare Development Funds. The amount so granted was
one and a half million pounds. About 1952 the British government added
another £200,000 and the Nigeria government £300,000.[39]

Lectures began in January 1948 in the temporary site at Eleyele, Ibadan,
in disused army huts. The first batch of 104 students came from the defunct
Yaba Higher College; of these students thirty-eight and seventeen were to
take the Intermediate examinations in science and arts respectively in June
that year. The others were teacher-training or survey students and did not
proceed to degree courses. In October of the same year, 148 more students
were admitted.[40] There were four faculties: Agriculture, Arts, Medicine
and Science.

Public reaction to the University College, Ibadan

For some time, especially before 1960, the University College, Ibadan,
continued to be attacked publicly, relieved occasionally by a kind word from
a Nigerian. In his book, *Nigeria's University College*,[41] Dr. Mellanby has
given an account of this onslaught when it was at its most fierce, in the
early days of the College. So vehement was the attack that the Inter-
University Council Visitation of 1952 remarked that 'At present the College does not have full public confidence,' although as Mellanby points out
'All Nigerian leaders were undoubtedly enthusiastic supporters of the idea
of the University College, and the Legislative Council was willing to vote a
larger proportion of the national income for this purpose than has any
other country in the world.'[42]

A number of allegations were made against the College and its authorities in the early years (1948–53). First there was alleged 'racial discrimination' in the appointment of staff, in that expatriate teachers (mainly British) were paid more than their Nigerian counterparts, and were generally better treated. As a result of this supposed discrimination, staff were said to have resigned in great numbers. Dr. Mellanby has given a lucid description of these events in his book; Dr. Ikejiani, a Nigerian member of staff who resigned in 1950, has presented his case from one Nigerian's point of view.[43] Both accounts are interesting reading. Second, it was believed in Nigerian circles that the College was unduly strict in its standards in order to frustrate Nigerians. Dr. Mellanby explains that this was because of the erroneous impression then current that the possession of a matriculation certificate was an automatic guarantee of ability to benefit from university education.

The widespread distrust of the College stemmed from the fact that it had been set up by the colonial government, and politics of the time were marked by a general distrust of this authority. The fact that a great majority of the lecturers were British served only to confirm this distrust, although few qualified Nigerians were then available. It must be remembered too that Yaba was still fresh in the memory of Nigerians, and it was not uncommon for Nigerians to couch all their distrust of the new College in such a phrase as 'just another Yaba'.[44]

Often the criticisms of Nigerians were ill-founded and attacks were made to keep in the favour of public sentiment or for personal gains. But there were many constructive criticisms on which the authorities might have acted more promptly had there been felt any urgent need to identify the College with Nigerians' aspirations. Two examples, both concerning the curriculum of the College, exemplify this. The first was a call for the establishment of a Faculty of Education, made on several occasions by Mr. E. E. Esua,[45] the General Secretary of the Nigerian Union of Teachers, in which he was supported by editorials in local newspapers.[46] In reply to this demand, the Registrar, Mr. A. W. Husband, issued the following public statement:

> The feasibility of founding a Faculty or Department [of Education] has been actively in the minds of the College authorities. It is not possible properly to plan such a Faculty until the permanent structure of the education system of the country is outlined. . . . [Further] it might appear that the University should concentrate on research into teaching methods, leaving the actual training of teachers to other institutions.[47]

The College's argument was strange. It ignored the great emphasis laid on teacher training by the Asquith and Elliot Commissions. One need only ask whether the inclusion of teacher training need necessarily await the permanence of the *structure* of an educational system, as if education systems anywhere are ever permanent, and, again whether the University of London and others had not been training teachers from various countries other than their own. However, the College established an Education Faculty in 1956, to serve the needs of a country whose regions had indeed differing and changing systems.

The second demand was for the establishment of a Faculty of Law:

> When this country becomes self-governing, [a 1953 editorial in a local newspaper told the College] English Law would be to Nigeria what Roman Law is to Great Britain today. It would therefore be a mistake to think that the English legal system would continue to operate in this country indefinitely and our future lawyers would continue to devote all their time as [they do] now, to specializing in English Law. There is thus an urgent need at the moment for some effort to be made towards codifying Nigerian Laws in order that freedom for Nigeria, when it comes, might not find us without a fully-developed legal system of our own.[48]

No action was taken on this appeal.

In 1951, following the introduction of a new Constitution, party political activities had become more intense and better organised. The parties sustained a continuous attack on what they regarded as symbols of the colonial regime and inevitably they aroused the feelings of their members regarding Nigeria's only university institution.

One such attack was embodied in a speech by Dr. Nnamdi Azikiwe, leader of the National Council of Nigerian Citizens (N.C.N.C.), in the House of Representatives in August 1954, when he described the University College as a 'million-dollar baby' who received a kiss worth this amount each time the baby cried. The College administration was accused of financial irresponsibility. The points which emerge from the speech are as follows:

1. FINANCE

(*a*) That annual first class passages for the European members of the University should be discontinued.

(*b*) That 'those who control the finance of the College must be told in plain language that the taxpayers of this country can no longer afford to pay super-scale salaries to the senior staff [members]'.

(*c*) External students should not be barred from the university.

(*d*) Pre-fabricated houses should be built for junior and senior staff.

(*e*) The university should submit its annual report to the House of Representatives until it could 'demonstrate its financial responsibility'.[49]

2. CURRICULA

(*a*) While respecting the principle of academic freedom, 'we expect the University to relate its curricula to the immediate needs of the country.'

(*b*) Instead of creating separate faculties for Education and Economics, these should be included with other subjects in the Liberal Arts curriculum.

But far the most constructive and lucid discussion of the University College by a Nigerian political party was the exposition set forth in the Action Group Policy Paper on *Higher Education in Nigeria*, published in 1958.[50] According to the Party there were then four serious defects in the policy for higher education in Nigeria;

1 RIGID EXCLUSIVENESS OF THE EDUCATION

The exclusiveness resulted from the fact that the University College was completely residential. The Paper contended that the number of new students admitted to the College annually was decided neither by the quantity nor the quality of the available student material, nor even by the country's needs, but 'purely and simply by the factor of sleeping accommodation available in the exclusive residential halls in the College'. Lecture rooms and laboratories were therefore under-used.

> But suppose the University College had been made only partially residential, and that students were allowed by the Constitution of the College to make private arrangements for their lodgings around the College campus and attend lectures, as is done in all the British provincial universities; that would certainly have resulted in filling the lecture rooms and laboratories to capacity and automatically have reduced the recurrent expenditure of the College per student.

It blamed the adoption of the residential system on the recommendation of the Elliot Commission, whose members had been to Oxford or Cambridge. The Paper argued that Nigeria was unfortunate in the higher education policy formulated for her by the Commission. A hundred years earlier, in 1853, a similar report had been made on Indian higher education, at a time when London University had just come into being and academic liberalism inspired all official planning. The Indian universities founded at that time did not follow the Oxford and Cambridge pattern but were for some time practically examining bodies, in the same way as London. The Paper suggested automatic admission for all those students who had a Grade I plus a third of those who had Grade II in the School Certificate Examination.

2 WRONG ACADEMIC ORIENTATION

By academic orientation the Paper meant 'the allocation of priorities to certain faculties at the expense of others and the emphasis placed on certain courses in relation to others.'

The Paper stated that courses were available at the Ibadan University College in arts, pure science, agricultural science and medicine. But no Faculties of Law, Economics or Engineering existed; neither were there courses in geology, archeology, anthropology, sociology, forestry, public administration, or philosophy. It had taken the College eight years to introduce studies in Education, and while from its inception, it had provided courses in Christian Religious Knowledge, none had been available in Islamic and Arabic Studies.

The need for the Faculties of Law, Economics and Engineering could be seen from the fact that in 1956 there were in Britain 447, 196, and 343 Nigerian students studying these subjects respectively. On the other hand there were only eight Nigerian students in Theology in that year. The Paper concluded:

A Department of Religious Studies is, of course, a desirable thing to have in Nigeria but the point at issue is: should it be given priority over departments of Engineering, Economics and Law? . . . This clearly provides one illustration of how divergent the academic orientation of the Nigerian Institution for higher learning is from national needs.

In the sciences, too much emphasis was placed on the production of pure scientists rather than of applied scientists such as engineers, geologists, agriculturists, and medical men. Britain, whose example Nigeria followed, had become out of date in its production of twice as many pure as applied scientists. In Western Germany and the U.S.S.R., on the other hand, the reverse was the case. Nigeria, a developing country, needed to copy the two latter countries, rather than Britain.

Little emphasis was placed on the study of foreign languages in the University College, Ibadan, whereas in most continental European countries foreign languages were required for all degree students.

3 THE POOR RELATIONSHIP BETWEEN TECHNOLOGICAL AND UNIVERSITY EDUCATION

Not only were facilities for technological education poor, but the Nigerian conception of this kind of education was unorthodox. In Britain, colleges of technology were founded and developed as institutions of higher education complementary to universities and not operated in competition with them, as was the case in Nigeria (see chapter 7).

4 THE DEFECT OF AN ANTI-NATIONALIST BIAS OF THE POLICY-MAKING AUTHORITIES

This was discussed under three headings:

(a) *Higher education as a unifying factor*

The Action Group Paper accused the University College, Ibadan, of having missed a wonderful opportunity for forging greater unity between Northern and Southern Nigeria. For, of the 746 students there in 1957/58 only about fifteen were Northerners. Thus a region with more than half the population of the country had only two per cent of the students of the country's only university. Such a state of things could not but have serious consequences for the unity of the country. As graduates of the College would eventually become leaders in various spheres in the country, Northern leaders would have justifiable fears that the higher posts of their civil administration might eventually be manned by Southerners. It was indeed common knowledge that Northerners already entertained this fear, and hence offered appointments to expatriates rather than to Southerners. A consequence of the imbalance was the Northerners' establishment of their own separate institution with lower minimum standards, for the production of trained personnel with less than university degree qualifications. The reason for this situation was the comparative paucity of secondary schools in the North.

The Paper suggested that the University College might have provided special intensive courses for fifty Northerners a year to bring them to the required minimum level before admitting them to compete with their Southern counterparts in the University courses.

(b) The myth of academic autonomy

The Paper complained that the University authorities always retorted that the College was an 'autonomous institution' when constructive suggestions were made by non-University bodies about how the place might be improved, and that the College could not accept 'dictation'. It was mythical to talk of autonomy and nonsense to suppose that an institution within a state could be absolutely autonomous and independent. It was recognised all over the world that institutions of higher learning were meant to reflect, and did in fact reflect, the national aspirations of the countries in which they were situated. Even within countries, regional interests were considered in courses given in universities: Liverpool University, a port of entry for many tropical diseases, had a School of Tropical Medicine; Manchester, in an area where textiles were important, had a course in textile chemistry, etc.

The Paper concluded that it was not the University itself, but the community it served which should determine the orientation of the curricula. It blamed the state of affairs partly on the attachment of the College to the 'apron-strings' of the University of London. Once Ibadan was free from London it would be easy to re-orientate the courses and curricula to meet Nigerian needs.

(c) Staffing

This was influenced by colonialist considerations, so that for many years to come, many of the departments would continue to be manned by expatriate Europeans, who at the time out-numbered the Nigerians by seven to one. The Paper re-iterated the Party leader's (Chief Obafemi Awolowo's) earlier pronouncement that 'Our political independence would be a sham and at best incomplete if the control of much of our intellectual life remained in foreign hands, and the policy of our premier University College is decisively influenced by bodies established outside the country.'

In the light of the analysis given above, the Paper concluded, it was obvious that the state of higher education in Nigeria was far from satisfactory. It was also clear that a solution would have to be imposed from outside; the only outside body competent to take such action judged desirable from the national viewpoint was the government of the Federation. The Action Group, however, did not win the Federal Elections of December 1959, as it had hoped, and therefore could not impose any solution.

Opportune as the Action Group Paper was, some of its criticisms were ill-founded and some suggested remedies quite impracticable. For instance, to have made the University partly residential in order to increase numbers and hence to avoid 'exclusiveness' was almost impossible in the Ibadan of the fifties. Not only were suitable houses for students not available near the campus, but bus services were few and irregular. Similarly, to have offered automatic admission to all students with Grade I in the School Certificate and a third of those with Grade II would have been costly in the sense that a considerable amount of weeding out might have been necessary.

The College reacted to these criticisms by the introduction of new courses; it increased the number of Nigerians in the predominantly ex-patriate Senate and promoted (although belatedly) a number of well-qualified Nigerians. It is of course true that some of the changes may have been planned before 1958, but the Paper undoubtedly hastened them. It is perhaps fortunate for Ibadan that the Action Group was not in a position to impose its ideas from outside. This would have resulted in a protest against an infringement of academic freedom from the predominantly expatriate staff and Ibadan's lustre might unfortunately have been tarnished at a time when its academic reputation was attaining its peak.

In 1962 the University College became the autonomous University of Ibadan, with powers to award no longer London degrees, but its own.

The Ashby Committee had been appointed in 1959 to examine higher education and it recommended the founding of new universities. In the meantime the University of Nigeria, Nsukka was incubating. The new Universities of Ahmadu Bello, Ife, Lagos and Nsukka, were founded after Nigeria's independence. In general they reflected the initiative of Nigerians, for the new institutions took into account some of the alleged failings of Ibadan.

Notes

[1] *Report of the Commission on Higher Education in West Africa, 1945*, passim. Cmd. 6655 —H.M.S.O., 1945.
[2] *Ibid.*, p. 44.
[3] A.C.E.C. 44–33 (December, 1933); see W. B. MUMFORD, 'Some growing points in African Higher Education', *Yearbook of Education, 1936*, pp. 249–769; LORD HAILEY, *African Survey*, Oxford, 1957, pp. 1231–2.
[4] *Report of the Commission on Higher Education in East Africa, Col. No. 142*, Entebbe, 1937.
[5] J. COLEMAN, *Nigeria: Background to Nationalism*, California, 1960, p. 124.
[6] KENNETH MELLANBY, *The Birth of Nigeria's University*, London, 1958, p. 103.
[7] F. LUGARD in his *Dual Mandate in Tropical Africa*, Oxford, 1929, p. 355, writes:
   If the institutions for higher learning are at present few and far between in British Tropical Africa, we must not forget that the problem hitherto has been to keep abreast of the demands of Government and Commerce, and to supply requirements for teaching staff.
[8] e.g. I. B. GREAVES, 'The education front in British Tropical Africa', *Yearbook of Education, 1940*, p. 491; also LUGARD, *op. cit.*
[9] ERIC ASHBY, *African Universities and Western Tradition*, Oxford, 1964, p. 15; also

A. M. CARR-SAUNDERS, *New Universities Overseas*, London, 1961, pp. 30–33.

[10] COLEMAN, *op. cit.*, pp. 217, p. 459.

[11] MELLANBY, *op. cit.*, p. 109.

[12] C.O. 147/110. Minutes by J. J. R. 13 August 1896.

[13] LUGARD, *op. cit.*, p. 455.

[14] *The Lagos Daily News*, 30 April 1934.

[15] H. S. SCOTT, 'Educational Policy and Problems in the African Colonies', *Yearbook of Education, 1940*, p. 473.

[16] *Statement of Policy on Colonial Development and Welfare*, Cmd. 6175, H.M.S.O., 1940.

[17] *Ibid.*, pp. 3–4.

[18] *West India Royal Commission, 1938–1939*, Cmd. 6174, H.M.S.O., 1940.

[19] *Policy on Colonial Development*, *op. cit.*, pp. 3–4.

[20] Mr. Malcolm MacDonald (Minister of Health), *Parliamentary Debates, House of Commons*, Vol. 361, 15 May 1940, pp. 42–43.

[21] *Ibid.*

[22] *Parliamentary Debates, 1939–40*, Vol. 360, p. 914.

[23] *Policy on Colonial Development*, *op. cit.*, p. 1.

[24] *Parliamentary Debates, 1939–40*, Vol. 361, p. 45.

[25] *Policy on Colonial Development*, *op. cit.*, p. 6.

[26] *Parliamentary Debates, 1939–40*, Vol. 361, p. 45.

[27] *Parliamentary Debates, 1943*, Vol. 363, p. 52.

[28] *Ibid.*, p. 55.

[29] *Parliamentary Debates, 1939–40*, Vol. 365, p. 1709.

[30] Governor's Address on 14 April 1920, *Legislative Council Debates*, Lagos, p. 11; *Overseas Education*, 1940.

[31] CARR-SAUNDERS, *New Universities Overseas*, London, 1961, pp. 30–32.

[32] *Report of the Commission on Higher Education in the Colonies*, Cmd. 6647, H.M.S.O., 1945. *Report of the Commission on Higher Education in West Africa*, *op. cit.*

[33] *Higher Education in the Colonies*, *op. cit.*, pp. 103–14.

[34] *Higher Education in West Africa*, *op. cit.*, p.p 123–4.

[35] *Ibid.*, pp. 175–6.

[36] J. T. SAUNDERS, *University College, Ibadan*, Cambridge, 1960, p. 24.

[37] *Inter-University Council for Higher Education Overseas*, Cmnd. 9515. H.M.S.O. London, 1946/54. Originally instituted to assist higher education in the Commonwealth countries of Africa, the Far East and the West Indies, in recent times non-Commonwealth countries such as Ethiopia, Sudan and Jordan have benefited from its services. As constituted in October 1966, the Council consisted of a nominee each from each of the United Kingdom universities (normally the Vice-Chancellor), the Educational Adviser to the Ministry of Overseas Development, and members co-opted for their special knowledge of overseas affairs. By far the most important aspect of the Council's work is in the field of staff recruitment, and by December 1965 it had advertised 5,670 vacancies and recommended over 4,000 appointments. See brochure issued by the Council in October 1966.

[38] SAUNDERS, *op. cit.*, pp. 34–38.

[39] MELLANBY, *op. cit.*, p. 106.

[40] *Ibid.*, pp. 137–8.

[41] *Ibid.*, Chapter 13, *passim*.

[42] *Ibid.*, p. 241.

[43] OKECHUKWU IKEJIANI, (ed). *Nigerian Education*, London, 1964, pp. 147–8.

[44] MELLANBY, *op. cit.*, p. 24.

[45] *The Daily Service*, Lagos, 22 May 1952; *West African Pilot*, 22 January 1953.

[46] For example see editorial in *West African Pilot*, 26 October 1953.

[47] *The Daily Service*, 28 July 1952, p. 3.
[48] The *West African Pilot*, 22 October 1953, p. 2.
[49] *Debates: House of Representatives, August 1954*, Lagos, p. 265.
[50] *The Action Group Paper on Higher Education in Nigeria, The Daily Service*, Lagos, 5 and 6 September 1958.

7 The Nigerian College of Arts, Science and Technology

This institution does not fall properly into the category with which this book is concerned, but as will be demonstrated, the Nigerian Colleges [there were branches at Zaria (North), Ibadan (West), and Enugu (East)] formed the nuclei of future new universities. It is therefore desirable that something should be said, however briefly, of these Colleges and their origins.

The origin of the Colleges may be traced to the *Report on a Technical College Organisation for Nigeria*[1] produced in 1950 by W. H. Thorp, Chief Inspector of Technical Education, Nigeria, and F. J. Harlow, Principal, Chelsea Polytechnic, London. The two-man team had been appointed by the government:

1. To make an assessment of the need for establishing a college, or colleges, of higher technical education with provision for training for the social services.

2. To advise on the organisation and location of those colleges.

3. To indicate how the new college organisation and the institutions for technical education provided under the Ten Year Development Plan can be integrated into a complete technical education structure.

The team toured extensively round the country and, presenting their proposition as shown below, they found no opposition to their allegations that:

1. Technical education is of primary importance in a country which is thirsting for economic and social development.

2. The aim of technical education must be to provide for the requirements of industry, commerce, and society, and to adjust itself to the changing needs of the territory. The curricula and organisation must be adapted to meet national and local demands and must not adhere to fixed and immutable forms.

3. Large numbers of men and women engaged in industry and commerce and in professional and ancillary occupations lack the specialised knowledge and training which would allow them to be efficient in their vocations and fit them to accept greater responsibility. For them, courses must be arranged so that they can improve their knowledge and efficiency while continuing in employment.

4. Special attention must be paid to the training of teachers, particularly

for secondary schools and technical institutions and for institutions engaged in the training of primary school teachers; also for persons engaged in social activities such as youth and community centre work, or in community development generally.[2]

The team suggested that a large proportion of the work of the proposed Nigerian College should be conducted under the 'sandwich system', which consists of an alternation of the college courses with spells of 'training within industry' or training in departmental schools. It did not, however, rule out the possibility of a limited number of full-time courses.

Furthermore, Nigerian secondary schools suffered from a lack of Sixth-form courses. In the meantime, therefore, full-time courses to Higher School Certificate level and of one or two years' duration might well find a place in the Nigerian College.[3]

It was further recommended that the College should have a semi-autonomous constitution in which the Principal and College Council would be responsible for everything except the broadest outline of financial and general policy and that the three branches should be under unified control with the Ibadan branch as headquarters.

The entrance standard should, in general, be that of School Certificate or something comparable, with the proviso that experience of life and industry might compensate in some way for lack of formal education.[4]

Early in the team's investigation it became apparent that an undesirable overlap might occur between the Technical College courses and those of the University College, Ibadan. A meeting was therefore convened on 22 December 1948 between Dr. Mellanby, Principal of the University College, and the Heads of the Government Technical Department. It was agreed that the 'University College would be responsible for continuous courses of instruction leading chiefly to administrative, specialist and research posts. The Technical College would on the other hand deal mainly with "sandwich" courses [from which] would come the field and executive officers of the Departments.'[5]

In 1952/53 the Zaria and Ibadan branches of the College (see Table 3) opened. Zaria was chosen as the headquarters rather than Ibadan because remarks made by the Northern Region members of the Nigerian Parliament suggested that Ibadan had been receiving too many favours.[6] The Enugu branch did not open until 1955/56. The courses and intake of students planned for the College are shown in Table 4.

The Mission of the International Bank for Reconstruction and Development which sent a committee to review the economic development of the country submitted in its report in 1954 three suggestions concerning the Nigerian College.[7]

First it suggested that the Schools of Agriculture owned by the Northern and Western Regional Governments and situated at Zaria and Ibadan respectively should be merged with the branches of the Nigerian College in those towns. Enugu was too far from Umuahia to make this feasible. The advantage expected was better library and teaching facilities for both sections. The amalgamation was especially proposed for three-year post-secondary agricultural diploma courses.

Second, pharmacy should be taught at all three branches. Where other programmes of training existed in regional government departments these should also be merged with the appropriate branches.

Third, the Mission believed that courses in bookkeeping and accounting at the Nigerian College should be substantially expanded and that courses should be given at each centre. The plan at the time called for a maximum of thirty students, at Ibadan only, a much lower figure than the country needed.

An important recommendation of the Mission was that the structure of the College should be reconsidered, with the College separated into three distinct parts, responsibility for each part being with the respective Regional Government. It recognised, however, that it would be unwise for the Federal Government to divest itself of all interest in the College, particularly as regards the maintenance of uniform standards. It was therefore suggested that a portion, perhaps half or two-thirds of the College's running expenses be met by the Federal Government, and that these funds should be administered by the Federal Inspectorate of Education, which should also be empowered to require the maintenance of minimum standards.

We see in these suggestions the germs of the Ashby recommendations which are discussed in Chapter 12, including his National Universities Commission. The Mission's reason for making their recommendations are illuminating:

> We doubt whether, as a federally-operated institution, it is capable of adjusting its activities in each region to the diverse educational activity of each. Moreover, we think that difficulties of transportation and communication between Ibadan, Enugu and Zaria make it impractical for a centralized administration to attempt to cope with the many day-to-day administrative and organizational problems. On the other hand a regionalized college is more likely to attract the local interest needed to enable it to serve as the local point for educational, technical and cultural growth in each region.[8]

The Mission's recommendation with respect to part-ownership by the regional governments was not accepted. But a compromise was arrived at: while the Federal Government supplied all the funds, local interests (e.g. mining at Enugu) were reflected in the location of courses. In addition the governing boards of the branches were chosen from among indigenes of the Region in which each branch was located.[9]

The College gave three types of courses: Intermediate Courses (i.e. G.C.E. Advanced Level Courses), Professional Courses and In-Service Courses (see Table 4).

The Nigerian College was 'dismembered' by Ashby's recommendation that its three branches should form the nuclei of universities owned by the governments of the three Regions of Nigeria. Why did this happen only some ten years after its establishment? It is sufficient here to record that during the ten years or so of its existence the Nigerian College was the 'Cinderella' of higher education in Nigeria, always living in the shadow (in a literal sense at Ibadan) of the much more popular and more widely recognised University College, Ibadan.

Table 3

Growth of the Student Body at the Nigerian College.

	ENUGU	IBADAN	ZARIA	TOTAL
1952·3	–	8	31	39
1953·4	–	113	29	142
1954·5	–	162	92	254
1955·6	32	190	191	413
1956·7	99	232	220	551
1957·8	148	291	273	712
1958·9	204	336	335	875
1959·60	241	424	423	1088

Source: *Nigerian College of Arts, Science and Technology Calendar, 1960/61*

Table 4

Nigerian College: Planned Courses and Enrolment, 1953

	Maximum number of students
ZARIA:	
Civil Engineering	100
Sub-Professional Engineers	60
United Kingdom Teacher Training College Certificate	75
Physical Education Specialists	20
Art Teachers	15

H

Table 4—*cont*.

Architectural Assistants	30
Agriculture and Veterinary Assistants Course	30
Higher School Certificate for Northern Students	40
Secretarial Course for Northern Students	20
Local Government Course	30
Total	420

IBADAN:

Matric. (Old Inter.) Arts or Higher School Certificate	40
Matric. (Old Inter.) Science or Higher School Certificate	40
Laboratory Technicians	20
Science for Agriculture and Forestry	30
United Kingdom Teacher Training College Certificate	75
Local Government	40
Bookkeeping and Accountancy	30
Total	275

ENUGU:

Matric. (Old Inter.) Arts or Higher School Certificate	40
Matric. (Old Inter.) Science or Higher School Certificate	40
Science for Agriculture	30
Local Government	40
Secretarial Work	30
Mining Engineering	30
Surveying	30
Total	240

Source: *Proposals for the Future Financing of the Nigerian College of Arts, Science and Technology*, Sessional Paper No. 10, Government Printer, Lagos, 1953.

Table 5

Courses given at the three branches of the Nigerian College of Arts, Science and Technology 1960/61

Course	Duration (years)	Qualification obtained	Branch where given: Zaria	Ibadan	Enugu
A. Intermediate Courses	2	G.C.E. 'A' Level (London University) in Arts or Science	√	√	√
B. Professional Courses					
1. Engineering (civil, mechanical and electrical)	3	B.Sc. (Eng.) of London University (by special relationship)	√		
2. Land Surveying	3½	1st and Intermediate examinations of the Royal Institution of Chartered Surveyors in the Land Surveying Division			√
3. Estate Management	2	1st examination of the Royal Institution of Chartered Surveyors in Valuation, Housing Management, etc.			√
4. Architecture	5	Final examination of the Royal Institute of British Architects	√		√
5. Education		Teacher's Certificate (Nigeria College) with reference to: *(a) Secondary schools *(b) Teacher training supervision †(c) Physical Education	√ √ √		
6. Fine Art	4	Diploma (Nigeria College) in Fine Art or Commercial Design	√		
7. Pharmacy	3	‡ Diploma of the Pharmacy Board of Nigeria *and* Diploma (Nigerian College) in Pharmacy		√	
8. Accountancy	5 in College and 3 in employer's office	Qualifying examination of the Association of Certified and Corporate Accountants (England)	√	√	[cont.

* Awarded in consultation with University of London Institute of Education
† Awarded in consultation with University of London and Leeds Institutes of Education
‡ Approved by a delegation of the Pharmaceutical Society of Gt. Britain

Table 5—*cont.*

Course	Duration (years)	Qualification obtained	Branch where given: Zaria Ibadan Enugu		
9. Administrative Secretaries	4 with a period of training in offices after two years	Final examination of the Chartered Institute of Secretaries (England)			√
10. Government and Administration	2	§Diploma (Nigerian College) in Public Administration			√
C. In-Service Courses 1. Accountancy	1	Students nominated by government and commercial departments			√

Source: *Nigerian College of Arts, Science and Technology, Calendar 1960–61*, pp. 36–54

§ Moderated and approved by Examiners appointed by the University of Exeter

The origins of the College might, in a way, be seen to lie in the minority *Report* of the Elliot Commission, discussed in the previous chapter. That section of the *Report* had argued that rather than have three university institutions in Nigeria, Gold Coast and Sierra Leone, there should be only one, which should be situated in Ibadan. However, there would develop territorial Colleges, of which there would be three at the outset. Achimota in the Gold Coast, Fourah Bay in Sierra Leone and a new college to serve Nigeria east of the Niger. The three chief functions of each college would be to provide academic courses to the intermediate level; to train teachers for the primary and secondary schools, and social welfare workers; and to act as the main centre from which the extra-mural activities throughout each territory would be organised. It will be recalled that the majority report was eventually implemented in so far as two university colleges were founded. But the Gold Coast's university was almost entirely supported by the country itself and not through the Colonial Welfare and Development Fund. (By 1961, The University College, Ibadan had received about £2¼ million from the higher education vote of this fund, while the University College of Ghana had received less than £½ million).[10] Thus although the majority opinion was acceptable in terms of finance, the minority view was not rejected.

The minority proposal for territorial colleges was further considered by the delegation of the Inter-University Council on Higher Education sent out under Sir William Hamilton Fyfe in December 1946. But the delegation recommended that substituted for the territorial colleges as organs of higher education should be 'regional colleges', the number of which was not specified. The delegation saw them as adaptable organs of higher education which would satisfy government and other vocational needs as they arose.[11]

They would serve temporarily to fulfil the need for sixth forms, this need disappearing with an improved educational system. They could also provide training for those with a practical rather than an academic bent. Organisationally, they would not be autonomous in the same sense as a university but should, under the government, fit into the general education system.[12] Thus the delegation suggested the establishment of colleges on the general lines of institutions known then as 'polytechnics' in the United Kingdom.[13]

As has been seen, the Harlow–Thorp team was set up by the Nigerian government to review technical education. It was this team which discarded the name 'Regional College', as this 'might be credited with a connotation which its authors [the Fyfe delegation] never intended'. The Inter-University Council Delegation had no intention of inspiring the foundation of colleges financed from regional allocation of funds, each catering exclusively for the inhabitants of a political district. The Harlow-Thorp team therefore suggested the whole organisation be called 'the Nigerian College of Arts, Science and Technology'.[14]

The Nigerian College did not provide courses of a technical nature in subjects such as printing, cookery, and photography, journalism, and bookbinding.[15] In short, the College in many ways competed with, rather than complemented, the University.

The reason for this is historical. When Western education was first introduced it was mainly literary; although attempts were subsequently made to bring the vocational subjects into school curricula, these had met with little success.[16] Literary tradition and the university degree had become symbols of prestige, and technology, agriculture and other more practical undertakings, especially at the sub-professional level, had not been very popular. Training therefore, such as might usefully have been incorporated into the Nigerian College especially at the sub-professional levels had not been attractive to Nigerians. The College found itself limited by these circumstances.

The recruitment of staff for the Nigerian College did not help either. Its first Principal, Mr. W. H. Thorp, had been for many years connected with education in Nigeria and as Chief Inspector of Technical Education had reported with Dr. Harlow on the founding of the College. He was therefore considered a most suitable choice for the position. In 1954 Mr. Thorp retired and Dr. C. A. Hart was appointed. There can be little doubt at all about Dr. Hart's academic distinction. During the 1939–45 war he was engaged in research and development work which led to the application of radar navigation to precise mapping. After the war he became the first Professor of Civil Engineering (Surveying and Photogrammetry) in the University of London and was actively concerned with research in geodesy.

From 1949–53, he was Vice-Chancellor of India's first technical university at Roorkee, Uttar Pradesh.[17] There can be no question that the high academic standing of the Head of an institution could be a great asset. But in the case of the Nigerian College it is doubtful if it was wise to employ for a college designed for non-university courses, one who had been not only a Professor but Head of a technical university. Similarly the list of other staff members shows an impressive collection of men who should have been in universities. Many of them had had active research interests with which they were continuing while in the College.[18]

By 1960 the Nigerian College had in fact become a university in all but name: it was limited mainly by the fact that it did not grant degrees. In this anomalous position the Nigerian College was ripe for its eventual fate, and it was left to Ashby to deal it the death blow. The Ashby Commission was convinced that technical institutes were the appropriate places for technical education and that the most efficient development would be to have some half-dozen large institutes in centres of population, rather than a proliferation of small ones.[19]

The Commission recorded its views about the Nigerian College thus:

> It [the Nigerian College] has played a valuable part in an expanding system of education, especially inasmuch as it has provided courses in subjects inappropriate to University College, Ibadan, and has compensated for the shortage of sixth forms by providing courses for the G.C.E. Advanced level. But as the numbers of sixth forms increase and as universities on the one hand and the technical institutes on the other assume responsibility for many of the subjects the Nigerian College was designed to teach, its purpose needs to be re-defined. We are of the opinion that the branches of the College should be integrated as quickly as possible into the university system of Nigeria. As parts of universities they have a great contribution to make to the educational system. We confess that we cannot see them having an equally great contribution to make if they retain their present identity. Accordingly we recommend that arrangements be made as soon as possible to rescind the Act incorporating the Nigerian College of Arts, Science and Technology and to integrate its three branches into three different universities.[20]

The subsequent dissolution of the Nigerian College is a significant though easily overlooked event in Nigerian higher education. In the first place the conversion to university courses of some subjects the Nigerian College was *designed* to teach is a recognition and an acceptance of the prestige value of a degree as opposed to equivalent non-university qualification. But more importantly it represented a departure from the established British practice of relegating vocational courses to technical colleges or to training 'on the job' and was a significant change in the educational atmosphere. There can be no doubt that this was influenced by the presence, for the first time on a Commission specifically studying higher education in Nigeria, of Americans who favour the system in the United States where degrees are awarded in colleges for many professional courses.

Notes

[1] *Report on a Technical College Organization for Nigeria, 1950*, Sessional Paper No. 11 of 1950, the Government Printer, Lagos.

[2] *Ibid.*, p. 1.

[3] *Ibid.*, p. 2.

[4] *Ibid.*, p. 9.

[5] *Ibid.*, pp. 18–19.

[6] J. T. SAUNDERS, *University College, Ibadan,* Cambridge, 1960, p. 47.

[7] *The Economic Development of Nigeria, Report of the International Bank for Reconstruction and Development*, Federal Government Printer, Lagos, 1954, pp. 386–8.

[8] *Ibid.*, p. 388.

[9] See *The Nigerian College of Arts, Science and Technology Calendar, 1960–61*.

[10] A. M. CARR-SAUNDERS, *New Universities Overseas*, London, 1961, p. 98.

[11] SAUNDERS, *op. cit.*, pp. 42–44.

[12] *Ibid.*

[13] *Nigerian College Calendar, 1960–61*, p. 1.

[14] *Report on a Technical College Organization for Nigeria, 1950*, p. 1.

[15] *Higher Education in Nigeria, Action Group Policy Paper, Daily Service*, Lagos, 5 and 6 September 1958.

[16] See, however, F. F. ADE AJAYI, 'The development of Secondary Grammar Schools in Nigeria', *Journal of the Historical Society of Nigeria*, 4, 1964, p. 512: The missionaries did try to introduce vocational education, but failed. First, they were not rich enough to meet the demands of technical education; second, their african staff were not all for it; third, the Colonial government gave little thought to industrial or technological education.'

[17] *Nigerian College Calendar, 1960–61*, p. 2.

[18] *Ibid.*, pp. 11–19.

[19] *Investment in Education*, Government Printer, Lagos, 1960, p. 18.

[20] *Ibid.*, p. 28.

8 Dr. Nnamdi Azikiwe and the University of Nigeria

On 7 October 1960 the University of Nigeria, Nsukka, admitted its first students. But the University's story goes back much further, and the man who provided the historical link between the aspirations of past generations and the founding of the first Nigerian-initiated university is Dr. Nnamdi Azikiwe. The purpose of this chapter is to record and analyse the role he played in the development of the University of Nigeria.

According to Dr. Azikiwe[1] the concept of the University of Nigeria had its origin in the *Report* of the International Bank, which stated that the University College, Ibadan, the only university in Nigeria at the time, needed not only to produce many more graduates, but also to diversify its courses.[2]

> The mission believes that the establishment of the University College [Ibadan] was a very important step forward. . . . But this achievement must be taken as a starting point. Nigeria's needs call for many times the trained manpower the University can supply as presently planned. To make one comparison, India has one student at the College level to every 1,400 of population, while Nigeria has less than one to 70,000. Thus if Nigeria is to reach the level of India there will be 20,000 students instead of the present 400 . . .
>
> Besides expanding its present enrolment, the University College should undertake to broaden the courses offered as speedily as possible. The mission believes that the programme of the University should be related rather more directly to the economy of the Nigerian people than it has been so far.

Following this, an Economic Mission to Europe was undertaken from 5 May to 11 July 1954, soon after the assumption of office by the government of the then Eastern Nigeria, headed by Dr. Azikiwe. The objects of the mission were defined as follows:

1. To attract investors to Eastern Nigeria for the purpose of economic development.

2. To make contacts for the expansion of our trade, commerce and industries.

3. To seek co-operation for training and recruiting technicians.

4. To make arrangements for facilitating vocational higher education in Eastern Nigeria.[3]

This mission consisted of Dr. Azikiwe and Mr. (later Sir) L. P. Ojukwu, a Lagos-based businessman of Eastern Nigeria origin. The mission's report touched on such matters as the attraction of investors, expansion of trade, training of technicians, vocational education in secondary schools and university education. In discussing vocational university education it took note of certain recommendations made by the Phelps-Stokes Fund, the ideas of the great broadminded Governor of the Gold Coast, Sir G. Guggisberg, and others.[4] Finally the Commission recommended the founding of a university.

> In order that the foundation of Nigerian leadership shall be securely laid, to the end that this country shall cease to imitate the excrescences of a civilization which is not rooted in African life, we recommend that a full-fledged university should be established in this Region without further delay. Such a higher institution of learning should not only be cultural, according to the classical concept of universities, but it should also be vocational in its objective and Nigerian in its content.[5]

The Commission recommended that the University should start with six faculties: Arts, Science, Law, Theology, Engineering and Medicine, and that the curricula should be related to the day-to-day life of the people. The University should be so organised as to relate its mission to the social and economic needs of the Region. Towards these ends the Commission recommended the following Institutes, which in its view, were necessary for the professional and technical education of men and women of the Region for the difficult years ahead:

> Agriculture, Architecture, Diplomacy, Domestic Science, Dramatics, Education, Finance, Fine Arts, Fishery, Forestry, Journalism, Librarianship, Music, Pharmacy, Physical Education, Public Administration, Public Health, Secretarial Studies, Social Work, Surveying and Veterinary Science.[6]

The commissioners hoped that if these Institutes were so organised as to operate with the six Faculties, then the Region would embark upon a real renaissance in the field of professional and technical education on the lines of the land-grant colleges of the United States.[7]

The Commission also felt it was of the utmost importance that students should be inculcated with the idea of the dignity of labour, and that by hard work, sacrifice and self-determination a poor student could obtain vocational higher education. To this end therefore:

> We strongly support the encouragement of prospective Nigerian students to the University, who must work in order to be able to meet their university expenses, to do so in earnest, because the experience gained thereby will stand them in good stead in the struggle for survival in life. By making sacrifices, being thrifty, and working hard, such types of students will cultivate self-reliance and confidence. Many elements which, ordinarily, would have discouraged the average student and possibly cause him to be a failure in life, are usually encountered by such working student with remarkable fortitude and determination to rely on his own resources to succeed no matter the handicaps. Later in life he can always recount the turning point with pride.[8]

In conclusion the Commission hoped that the training in self-help and the experience in self-reliance would make students of the proposed University more confident of themselves and enable them 'to puncture the myth of the proverbial lack of initiative and drive on the part of the Nigerian worker'.[9]

Thus Dr. Azikiwe presented the official viewpoint of the University's origin: that it was born out of the recommendations of the International Bank Mission of 1953 and the Economic Rehabilitation Commission of Eastern Region of 1954. Even if one were to forget for a moment that Dr. Azikiwe was himself one of the two Eastern Nigeria Commissioners, as will be shown below, he played on important role in creating the University of Nigeria. Attention has been drawn in Chapter 3 to his role in creating in the minds of his contemporaries the demand for a university in Africa through the medium of his *Renascent Africa*.[10] As has been mentioned, he wanted a university which would help correct what he called the mis-education of Nigerians by Europeans.

His thoughts on the founding of a 'University of Nigeria' had, however, been formulated as far back as the early thirties (1933) when he was about to return home after eight years' stay in the United States. Dr. Azikiwe relates in *My Odyssey*[11] how he tried unsuccessfully to obtain employment first in the government service and later in the missionary education systems. He was convinced that he was rejected because of prejudice, 'personal and racial' against him, and that

> Christian Missions look with disfavour [on] the appointment of Africans to respon-sible educational and evangelical posts or the elevation of Africans to a position which would not remind them of their subordinate status as a race and as Christians.'[12]

Bearing all these factors in mind, therefore, he

> decided that I should return to Africa and establish a school of my own which should be a nucleus for a 'University of Nigeria'.[13]

He had two plans. First, he would establish a 'University of Liberia' in Monrovia for the benefit of all Africa, if he was able to convince influential Americans to supply him with the necessary capital. If money collected were not enough he would establish a 'University of Nigeria' and rely on the patriotism of Nigerians to 'consummate the scheme'.[14] In making 'elaborate preparations for the University' he decided that it was not possible to 'found a University in West Africa where several faculties could be incorporated'. He therefore decided the University would have the following Faculties: Liberal Arts, Education, Music, Medicine, Pharmacy, Engineering, Commerce, Agriculture, Technology, Journalism, Law, Dentistry, Graduate Studies.[15]

The degrees and diplomas to be awarded were as follows:

> The 'University of Nigeria' I soliloquised, should thus be able to confer the following degrees locally: B.A., B.Sc., B.Ed., B.Agric., B.Comm., LL.B., B.Phar., B.Litt., B.Th.,

M.A., M.Sc., M.Ed., M.Agric., M.Comm., LL.M., M.Phar., M.Litt., M.Th., Ph.D. The following Diplomas were to be granted to those who could not gain degrees: in Theology, Education, Agriculture, Technology, Engineering, Music, Journalism, Law, Science.[16]

To raise the necessary capital to establish this University ('either in Liberia or in Nigeria') he decided to use the example of Wilberforce University, of Xenia, Ohio, which had opened a 'Wilberforce University Roll of Honour' into which the name of any donor of not less than one dollar had his name and biography inscribed:

> I mused that if twenty million Nigerians would subscribe one shilling per capita, on the average, then one million pounds would be available as a permanent endowment for the University which I pictured . . . and with interest of at least 5 per cent the University should have an income of about £50,000 annually, for ever, to be administered by a self-perpetuating Board of Trustees.[17]

He decided, however, to appeal to Americans and thus to raise £50,000. His letter, written with 'the desire to revolutionize African intellectual life' deserves to be quoted in full as it gives a clearer picture of Azikiwe's dreams:

> My dear Friend:
> May I enlist your support in the cause of African education.
> For eight years (i.e. 1925–1933) have I laboured and struggled in the United States in education for service to those who are not as privileged as I have been.
> My tutelage is invaluable and I feel that no greater service could I render to African youth than to share with them the joys of my new life in the West.
> Towards the realization of my aims and dreams, it is proposed to establish an institution in West Africa for the intellectual and manual education of Africans, male and female.
> Unfortunately, the education of Africans has been regarded as a problem.
> This is due to the fact that the type of training which the average African receives tends to alienate him from his indigenous environment.
> Invariably he becomes a misfit.
> He despises African institutions and glorifies the social and material cultures of other peoples.
> There is need in West Africa for an educational centre which would select the more constructive concepts of the West to modify the outlook of the African, and [which is] based on African culture and social organization.
> Therefore, it is planned to establish an institution whose fees would be reduced to the minimum in order to popularize education in West Africa.
> It will begin as an elementary school gradually to develop into university status.
> In order to carry out this programme it is necessary to raise a working capital. The other funds will be contributed by Native Africans and interested friends.
> This appeal comes to you as a friend of popular education. Will you be kind enough to contribute whatever you may feel convenient to offer, to aid this ambitious plan of the African to educate himself in Africa?
> For reference, I suggest Rev. Dr. W. H. Johnson, M.A., Ph.D., D.D., President of Lincoln University, Pennsylvania.
> Respectfully yours, Ben. N. Azikiwe, Instructor in Political Science, Lincoln University, Pennsylvania, U.S.A.[18]

This appeal yielded less than £40 within six months. He was painfully discouraged and he refunded the money to the donors, but he did not give up; instead he 'began to make other plans for my return to Africa, bearing in mind *my pet scheme for the founding of a University someday'*.[19]

The immediate cause of Azikiwe's desire to found a university was thus inability to obtain employment in educational institutions of his time, due to prejudice. But this only crystallised and brought into sharp focus the early nationalist aspirations of which he was certainly aware. As already indicated in Chapter 3, Blyden was one of the earliest West Africans to declare the education of nineteenth-century Africans as unsuitable for the African environment, and a group of Lagos citizens headed by Blyden had indeed made moves to establish a university for that very reason. Following Blyden, Hayford had advocated this in his *Ethiopia Unbound*. The National Congress of West Africa had also demanded a university organised on 'such lines as would preserve in the students a sense of African Nationality'.[20] That the National Congress resolution influenced Dr. Azikiwe he himself admitted at the first meeting of the Provisional Council of the University of Nigeria on 3 March 1960, when as Chairman of that Council he outlined the following as one feature which animated the founding of the University:

> Its [the University's] intent to preserve the dignity of the African as expressed by the National Congress of British West Africa when the struggle for national self-determination was at its earliest beginning.[21]

The idea of starting an elementary and a secondary school, both of which would feed the University, was not new either. The National Congress had made similar suggestions.[22] Indeed Achimota in the Gold Coast was already implementing such a programme when in 1933 Azikiwe conceived the plan.[23]

The name, 'University of Nigeria,' had been suggested as far back as 1919, a year before the National Congress Resolution, in an Editorial of *The Lagos Weekly Record*. The theme of this article was that a university should be developed in Nigeria 'from where all that [is] best in human thought [is] diffused throughout the country'.[24] This *The Record* claimed, was the original idea of universities—and it was in this respect that the universities of Europe have contributed so much to the progress of the world. Indeed according to the editorial the history of the progress of Europe in ethical, political and religious ideas was the history of her universities. The motivation for advocating a university for Nigeria was not to bring into being a corporation of colleges with powers to grant degrees; rather the concern was to create a centre of thought for healthy ideas.

> Our greatest drawback in Nigeria, and perhaps in West Africa generally, is the absence of such centres of thought—without them there can be no cohesion in the body politic and no strong public opinion, but with them the lost balance in native Society would soon be restored.

A university in Nigeria need not be a place where compulsory Latin and Greek are taught. It need be a place where . . . more attention is paid to the study of local affairs. With the existence of a centre of learning in Nigeria, it would be possible to give the world our collected thoughts about things and at the same time to gather information and bring to light several things which the foreigner [no matter how pains-taking] would be unable to probe into. We have a great deal to teach the world about our customs, our religious ideas, our secret cults and the uses of our herbs.[25]

The idea of a university, Nigerian in content, had thus been mooted long before 1960. It was, however, transformed and brought into reality through the perseverance of Dr. Azikiwe.

The consolidation of the proposals for the University took form in the *University of Nigeria Law, 1955*, enacted when Dr. Azikiwe was Premier of Eastern Nigeria.

The Cook-Hannay-Taggart Commission

Discussions and correspondence soon followed between Dr. Azikiwe, in his capacity as Premier of Eastern Nigeria, and the Eastern Nigeria Ministry of Education, on the one hand; and the Inter-University Council for Higher Education Overseas, London (I.U.C.), with the International Co-operation Administration of the United States (I.C.A.) on the other. The result was that on 30 August 1957 the Permanent Secretary of the Ministry of Education wrote to the I.U.C. and I.C.A. requesting them to send experts to advise the government of Eastern Nigeria on the establishment of a University of Nigeria in Eastern Nigeria. Following this, visits were made to Eastern Nigeria in April–May 1958 by Dr. J. W. Cook, the Vice-Chancellor of the University of Exeter, England; Dr. John A. Hannay, President of Michigan State University; and Dr. Glen L. Taggart, Dean of International Programmes, Michigan State University, U.S.A.

After discussions with Dr. Azikiwe and educational and religious leaders in Eastern Nigeria, visits to the proposed site at Nsukka and to a number of the larger towns, the Commission agreed that the establishment of a university in Eastern Nigeria was desirable, although they noted many problems had to be solved. In arriving at its decision it considered the following:[26]

1. The educational attitude of the people of the Eastern Region, who the Commissioners believed were highly desirous of education. It noted however, that the motivation for such education appeared to be the desire to gain a degree and obtain prestige-winning employment, rather than a desire to use education to solve problems and improve economic and social conditions. It hoped that the University might help to correct this attitude.

2. Availability of qualified students: scarcity of prospective entrants would not be a problem as there was likely to be an increasing stream of pupils qualified to enter the University.

3. Financial support: half a million pounds would be set aside annually from the Marketing Board funds. This along with possible revenue from the developing oil industry would be a source of finance.

4. The availability of staff: the Commission thought that this was the most important problem. It felt that eventually the University would be manned by Nigerian scholars and recommended that suitable Nigerians with Bachelor's or Master's Degrees be trained to take up positions on the staff.

Other matters considered included employment opportunities for the graduates, the site of the University and the area from which to draw students.

The Commission recommended the establishment of a Provisional Council, and set out a number of academic areas in which the new University could adventure, including the sciences (social, biological and physical) agriculture, engineering, home economics, business and public service, education, humanities and theology.

That Dr. Azikiwe's philosophy for the University was accepted by the Commissioners may be seen from this quotation from their report:

> In order that Nigerians will effectively perform roles of leadership which they are increasingly assuming and will assume several years hence with the coming of independence, there is interest in the country for founding a university, and subsequently a broader educational system, rooted in African life, and [drawing] fully upon the educational philosophies of other cultures; . . . not [as] an imitation but rather a full adaptation to the needs of the indigenous culture.[27]

Notes

[1] NNAMDI AZIKIWE: 'Origins of the University of Nigeria', in *The University of Nigeria Appraises Itself*, a collection of four speeches delivered at the University 'Alma Mater Night', 9 June 1963, published by the University of Nigeria, p. 1.

[2] *The Economic Development of Nigeria*, (Report of a Mission organised by the International Bank for Reconstruction and Development,) Lagos, 1954, pp. 383–4.

[3] NNAMDI AZIKWE and L. P. OJUKWU, *Economic Rehabilitation of Eastern Nigeria*, (Report of the Economic Mission to Europe and North America), Enugu, 1955, p. 3.

[4] *Ibid.*, pp. 32–33.

[5] *Ibid.*, p. 34.

[6] *Ibid.*, p. 34; see also Appendix 10, pp. 68–70, for the detailed scheme of the University of Nigeria.

[7] *Ibid.*, p. 34.

[8] *Ibid.*, pp. 35–36.

[9] *Ibid.*, p. 36.

[10] For instance see K. O. MBADIWE, *British and Axis Aims in Nigeria*, New York, 1942, pp. 178–9: 'Since there are no universities in the British Colonies of West Africa the few who can afford it proceed abroad [to Britain] to get their higher education. This is another form of [British] economic exploitation. The fees and living costs are fabulously high. . . . Since there are no higher institutes of learning at home, it is impossible to carry on research on spheres of African life'.

Speaking of Dr. Azikiwe, p. 183, he says: 'Africa has caught the spirit of fire. There is no stopping. Professor Nnamdi Azikiwe led the way, and others are following.'

[11] A series of autobiographical sketches published by Azikiwe in 1938–39 in his *West African Pilot;* bound mimeographed copy, (320 pp.), in the University of Nigeria Library under the title of the original series.

[12] AZIKIWE, *My Odyssey*, pp. 181–6, especially p. 185.

[13] *Ibid.*

[14] *Ibid.*

[15] *Ibid.* It does appear unusually strange for Dr. Azikiwe to regard the range of Faculties mentioned as constituting less than he would have recommended had he hoped for more money. Most of the largest universities have these Faculties or fewer. The really crucial point is the size of the staff in each Faculty.

[16] *Ibid.*, pp. 186–7.

[17] *Ibid.*, pp. 187–8.

[18] *Ibid.*, pp. 188–9.

[19] *Ibid.* (Italics mine.)

[20] NATIONAL CONGRESS OF WEST AFRICA, 1920, *Resolutions*, p. 2.

[21] AZIKIWE: 'Origins of the University of Nigeria', *op. cit.*, p. 7.

[22] NATIONAL CONGRESS OF WEST AFRICA, *op. cit.*

[23] See C. K. WILLIAMS, *Achimota: The Early Years, 1924–1948*, London, *passim.*

[24] 'A University for Nigeria', editorial in *The Lagos Weekly Record*, 20 September 1919.

[25] *Ibid.*

[26] UNIVERSITY OF NIGERIA, *Eastern Region Official Document No. 4 of 1958*, Enugu, 7 pp.

[27] *Ibid.*, pp. 1, 2.

9 Manpower Needs: The Ashby Universities
(Lagos and Ahmadu Bello)

The motives for the demand for universities in Nigeria have been twofold. The first was nationalism, i.e. the desire to counter the denigration of the Negro race, as observed earlier in the endeavours of Horton, Blyden, Hayford and Azikiwe. The demand received its crowning glory in the founding of the University of Nigeria. The motto of that University, 'To Restore the Dignity of Man', may be seen as the epitome of the yearnings of West Africans for over a century and might indeed be interpreted 'To Restore the Dignity of the Negro'. It seems an interesting coincidence that the University should have opened its door to students in 1960, the year in which the country after which it is named became independent of Britain.

The other impetus for the demand (and creation) of universities was increasing man-power needs. With the possible exception of Horton, this factor does not seem to have been important to the other West African nationalists. As seen from the Elliot and Asquith Commissions, the necessity for manpower was the impelling motive of the British colonial administration in attempts to found institutions of higher learning in West Africa.[1] It was not until Independence or shortly before it that high-level manpower considerations became an important factor in the thinking of university planners.[3] According to Professor Harbison the requirements are basically threefold. First, to expand activities in sympathy with economic growth; second, to replace expatriates, and third, to replace normal attrition due to retirement, emigration, death, etc.[3]

In April 1959, with just over a year to Independence, a Commission was appointed to conduct an investigation into Nigeria's need in the field of post-School Certificate and Higher Education over the following twenty years, under the chairmanship of Sir Eric Ashby, Master of Clare College, Cambridge. In a Special Report prepared for the Commission, Professor Harbison classified high-level manpower according to educational qualifications into Senior and Intermediate categories. The Senior category comprised persons in occupations normally requiring a university degree or its equivalent, i.e. engineers and scientists, agriculturalists, doctors, veterinarians, graduate teachers, lawyers, diplomats, journalists and writers, and persons in higher managerial and administrative posts, both public and private. The Intermediate category comprised persons in occupations normally requiring one to three years of education beyond School Certificate, i.e. engineering technicians, nurses, supervisory personnel, et cetera.[5]

It is instructive to record some of Professor Harbison's comments on Nigeria's future man-power needs:

> As an emerging independent nation, Nigeria is faced with the task of maintaining, and if possible, accelerating the pace of economic growth. . . . In comparison with many other newly-developing countries, Nigeria's rate of growth is fairly high, yet her living standards are still very low. In 1957 the income per head was about £30. Among the 100 countries and territories which today may be classified as economically under-developed, Nigeria ranks in the poorest 20 per cent. Thus rapid growth is required to raise living standards even to a level equivalent to the average of the world's presently underdeveloped countries.

Of all the resources required for economic development, top-level manpower requires the longest time for creation. Modern dams, power stations, textile factories or steel mills can be constructed within a few years. But it takes between ten and fifteen years to train the managers, the administrators and the engineers to operate them. Schools and colleges can be erected in a matter of months; but it takes decades to produce high-level teachers and professors.[6]

According to Professor Harbison, the requirements for future growth were first a very substantial increase in the productivity of agriculture, forestry, and animal husbandry; second, development of mineral resources, particularly petroleum; third, development of all forms of transport; fourth, substantial industrial growth, and last, a continued increase in trade and industry.[7]

Harbison estimated that 31,200 would be needed in the senior manpower category in the ten-year period, 1960/70. Of these about 20,000 should have a university education or its equivalent; the annual output rate of graduates should therefore be 2,000. Table 6 lists Professor Harbison's breakdown of the speculative 1960/70 needs. At the time the report was prepared (1959), fewer than 300 graduated annually (mainly from the country's only University College at Ibadan). An estimated 800 would return from training overseas with university degrees. This would still leave a shortage of about 1,000 per year. The Report suggested that technical and scientific education should be given priority in university programmes.[9]

Professor Harbison stressed that his report could be only speculative because statistical information for a proper survey was lacking.[11] The manpower needs depended on the rate of economic growth envisaged. If the rate of growth desired was to be at least as high as that before Independence (i.e. about four per cent annually),[12] then the figures suggested were the *probable minimum 'inputs' of high-level manpower*.[13]

I

Table 6

Manpower Needs, 1960/70[10]

Graduate teachers	8,500
Engineers	5,000
Agricultural, forestry and fishery specialists	1,200
Veterinarians	800
Doctors	2,000
Scientists (for research institutes)	500
Others	2,000

To achieve this minimum of 2,000 graduates per annum, the Ashby Commission argued that at least 7,500 student places would be needed in Nigerian universities; the figure took account of students in longer-duration courses. But this figure was only a a modest 'first objective' to be achieved before 1970, and would still fall below the number of graduates per thousand of population in Ghana and Egypt (1959). The Commission was certain that in 1970/80 the population of students should considerably exceed 10,000.[14]

There were two possible ways of raising student numbers to the required level. The first was to increase the number of students in the university-type institutions. The second was to increase the number of universities themselves. The Ashby Commission recommended expansion of student numbers primarily by the creation of more universities. It rejected the concentration of all the extra students in the existing institutions in tacit acknowledgment of the inter-regional rivalries, although it also felt that the universities could be useful tools for forging national unity.

> The distances in Nigeria, the variety of people which comprise her population, and, above all, the need for diversity in higher education, all point to the need for at least one university in each Region . . . But the borders between Regions must never become barriers to the migration of brains. Nigeria's intellectual life, and her economy, will suffer unless there is free migration of both staff and students from one Region to another. . . . One of the purposes of education in this country is to promote cohesion between her Regions. Universities should be a powerful instrument for this purpose and it is their duty to respond.[15]

The Commission then recommended the creation of two more new universities. At the time the Commission was appointed, the University of Nigeria, Nsukka, was already being planned, and shortly after the publication of the Commission's Report it was opened. With the two proposed universities at Lagos and Zaria, plus those at Ibadan and the University of Nigeria, Nsukka, there were to be four universities in all.

Recommendations on new universities

WESTERN NIGERIA
1. The Ibadan branch of the Nigerian College of Arts, Science and Technology to be transferred to the University of Ibadan.
2. Transfer of the engineering courses at Zaria to the proposed University of Northern Nigeria.
3. Simultaneously Ibadan should expand its activities in the fields of medicine and agriculture, and student numbers be enlarged to spread the overhead costs of running the University.[16]

NORTHERN NIGERIA
1. A university with its headquarters in Zaria in the Nigerian College buildings, which after taking over the engineering course of the old College, should be one of the national centres in this field of studies.
2. A link should be established with the Samaru Agricultural Institute, the Institute of Administration, Zaria, the Veterinary Research Institute at Vom, and the Ahmadu Bello College, Kano.[17]

EASTERN NIGERIA
1. The University of Nigeria, Nsukka, to form the centre of the institution.
2. Buildings and equipment of the old Nigerian College at Enugu should be absorbed into the University of Nigeria.[18]

LAGOS
1. A non-residential university comprising initially (*a*) a School of Commerce and Business Administration, offering both day and evening courses, to serve as the nation's centre in commercial subjects; and (*b*) a School of Economics and Social Science, offering day and night courses.
2. A Department for correspondence courses leading to university degrees.[19]

Ahmadu Bello University

Following a request from the government of the Northern Region of Nigeria transmitted through the Federal Government to the Secretary of State for Commonwealth Relations, a delegation was sent by the Inter-University Council for Higher Education Overseas (I.U.C.) 'to advise on the scope of the proposed University, the adaptation of existing institutions (including their curricula) which would be absorbed into the new University and the modification of legislation affecting them'. The delegation was headed by Sir Alexander Carr-Saunders, former head of the London School of Economics. Other members included Mr. J. L. Reddaway,

Lecturer in Engineering and Fellow of Emmanuel College, Cambridge; Professor R. B. Serjeant, Professor of Modern Arabic, School of Oriental and African Studies, London; and Professor E. G. White, Professor of Veterinary Preventive Medicine, Liverpool University. Mr. I. C. M. Maxwell, Secretary of the I.U.C., accompanied the delegation. The delegation visited Northern Nigeria in April 1961 and issued its recommendations that month.[20]

The delegation said it was aware that primary and secondary education needed to be developed in Northern Nigeria, but it did not think that the foundation of a university should wait on further progress in school education. Rather it thought educational advance should proceed on all fronts at the same time; the university would in fact stimulate all forms of educational progress in the Region, besides providing much-needed manpower. It stressed the need for extra-mural studies, and the need to investigate and do research into local problems.

Like Mr. Hussey's Memorandum of 1929 (see Chapter 5), this predominantly British delegation stressed the uniqueness of the Northern Region. 'The Northern Region has its own cultural traditions which distinguish it from the other regions; care for these traditions should be a main function of the University'.[21]

It did not think a separate School of African Studies was necessary, but a Board of African Studies to which staff in the various departments concerned would be assigned was suggested. It proposed a Centre for Higher Muslim Studies.[22]

The same month a law establishing a Provisional Council was passed by the Legislature of Northern Nigeria and Sir Kashim Ibrahim was appointed Chairman of this body at its formation in November 1961. Sir Kashim (then Hon. Shetimma Kashim) was a member of the Ashby Commission. The law establishing the University was passed in June 1962. It came into effect on 4 October that year and lectures started about a week later, on 10 October.[23]

The administrative headquarters and most of the teaching departments are located on the site of the Zaria Branch of the disbanded Nigerian College. In keeping with the recommendations of the Ashby Commission, the assets of the Nigerian College were transferred to the new University. The Abdullahi Bayero College in Kano (formerly Ahmadu Bello College) was also incorporated. Two previously existing Northern Nigeria government institutions are also included in the University, but they are semi-autonomous. These two are the Institute of Administration, Zaria, and the Research and Special Services of the Ministry of Agriculture (now the Institute for Agricultural Research and Special Services).

THE ABDULLAHI BAYERO COLLEGE, KANO

The College was founded in October 1960, prior to the establishment of the University and incorporated into the University in October 1962. It has (1965/66) the Faculty of Arabic and Islamic studies and offers Degree courses in Arabic, Islamic institutions, English, history, and subsidiary French.[24]

THE INSTITUTE OF ADMINISTRATION, ZARIA
Under the Ahmadu Bello Law of 1962 this Institute, founded in 1954, enjoys a semi-autonomous status within the University. It contains two full departments of the University, Law and Administration, and offers Ahmadu Bello Degrees or Diplomas in these subjects. It also gives in-service courses for employees of the government and Native Administration leading to the Diploma or Certificate of the Institute in Local Government, Education Administration, Business Administration, et cetera.[25]

THE INSTITUTE FOR AGRICULTURAL RESEARCH AND SPECIAL SERVICES
This Institute is situated at Samaru, about eight miles from Zaria. It has three subsidiary research stations, one at Shika, one at Mokwa, 240 miles south-west of Samaru, and one at Kano.

The Institute conducts research into agronomy, field crops, animal husbandry and various other problems of agriculture.[26]

The main campus at Zaria, the Abdullahi Bayero College, Kano, and the University courses at the Institute of Administration are financed equally by the Federal and the Regional government with respect to capital and recurrent expenditure. The Institute for Agricultural Research and the in-service courses of the Institute of Administration are financed by the Northern Regional government.[27]

The University of Lagos

The Federal Government accepted the recommendation of the Ashby Commission to build a university at Lagos[28] and sought the aid of UNESCO. In June 1961, The UNESCO Advisory Committee for the Establishment of the University of Lagos was appointed. The Committee's terms of reference were:[29]

1. To assist the Federal Government in defining the status, scope and nature of the proposed University of Lagos and its relationships with other institutions of higher education in the country, with particular reference to the findings of the Commission on Post-School Certificate and Higher Education and to the decisions taken by the Federal Government thereon, and in the light of the economic and social development of the country;
2. To prepare detailed recommendations in regard to the organization, administration

and financing of the University, as well as to the range and organization of the disciplines and research programmes required;

3. To formulate a plan of development for the University with detailed estimates as to requirements for facilities and equipment for the training and recruiting of staff and for the selection and admission of students;

4. To examine areas for and the resources of external aid for the development of the University, and to prepare requests to the United Nations Special Fund and any other agency or bodies for this purpose.

The composition of the Commission is interesting, as for the first time advisers on matters of education were drawn from outside the United Kingdom or the U.S.A. The breadth given to the report owing to the diversity of the background of the members of the Commission will be discussed in a later chapter, but the Commissioners may now be listed:[30]

UNESCO Members

Mr. J. Capelle (France), Directeur Général de L'Organisation et des Programmes Scolaires, Ministère de l'Education Nationale (Chairman of Commission).

Professor K. I. Ivanov (U.S.S.R.), Pro-Rector of the University of Moscow.

Dr. A. H. Garretson (U.S.A.), Professor of Law and Director of the Institute of International Law, New York University School of Law.

Dr. E. H. Van Delden (U.S.A.), Professor of Management, Graduate School of Business Management, New York University.

Dr. C. Wayne Hall (Canada), Professor of Education, McGill University.

Mr. D. B. Welbourn (U.K.), Faculty of Engineering, University of Cambridge.

Members nominated by the Federal Government of Nigeria

Dr. G. B. A. Coker, Justice of the High Court of Lagos.

Dr. Eni Njoku, Dean of the Faculty of Science, University College, Ibadan.

Mr. H. Orishejolomi Thomas, Senior Lecturer in Surgery, University College, Ibadan.

Ex-officio member of the Commission

Mr. T. Wilson, UNESCO Chief of Mission in Nigeria.

The Commission's recommendations fall under three main headings:

1. That a University of Lagos be established in Lagos in 1962.

2. That the National Universities Commission be constituted as soon as possible to co-ordinate the development of higher education through the allocation of federal funds.

3. That with respect to the establishment of the University of Lagos certain aspects of Nigerian education be taken into consideration. These facts included the necessity of rapidly increasing the number of qualified teachers at all levels of education; the need for the expansion of Sixth Form work; the utilisation of all existing facilities for day and evening work; the desirability of re-arranging the Nigerian educational year to include an additional term in June, July, and August; the desirability of introducing African material into the curriculum at all levels of education.[31]

On the University itself, it made *inter alia* the following recommendations:

1. That the University should open with the Faculties of Medicine, Law and Commerce, but that Faculties of Arts, Science and Education should also be opened in 1962 if adequate temporary quarters could be obtained.
2. That the Faculty of Engineering be opened only when permanent buildings become available in 1964, and that this year might also be the opening date for Arts, Science and Education.
3. That an Institute of African Studies be established and courses given in the University should not only be of a high standard but should also be adapted to meet the special interests and needs of Nigeria.
4. That evening classes be developed in all Faculties, especially those of Law and Commerce.[32]

Location

On the question of location, compromise was arrived at between the Ashby recommendation that, the university be estalished in the city of Lagos and other factors. These factors were the necessity to acquire extensive land for residential purposes and for laboratories, class rooms, et cetera. There was also the need to make it possible to house together and therefore to integrate as much as possible students from different parts of the country. It was therefore decided to recommend the establishment of a campus at the then undeveloped edge of the Federal territory, to be constructed by October 1964 and to establish an Island of Lagos 'centre' to be opened in 1962.[33]

The *Report* of the UNESCO Committee was submitted in September 1961, and in April 1962 the *University of Lagos Law* was passed by the Federal Parliament, and both the Provisional Council and the Medical School Council were inaugurated.[34]

The first academic year of the University commenced in October 1962 in temporary premises in Suru-Lere with day courses in the Faculty of Business and Social Studies, the Faculty of Law, and the Medical School. In January 1963, evening courses in the Faculty of Law began. In the second academic year the Faculty of Business and Social Studies began its evening classes (2 October 1964). The third academic year saw the opening of four new Faculties—Arts, Education, Engineering and Science.[35]

At the beginning of the 1965/66 year the University moved to its permanent premises in North-East Yaba.[36]

Notes

[1] An exception to the colonial administrators was Sir Gordon Guggisberg, who advocated higher education for the Gold Coast for reasons other than man-power requirements. See C. K. Williams, *Achimota, The Early Years*, London, 1962.
[2] Even after Independence the universities were still being looked to to 'liberate' the Nigerian mind. See for example ENI NJOKU:

'It is not often realized by non-Africans that the present content of higher education in Africa involves a very great deal of cultural aggressiveness from outside Africa. [The Nigerian student finds that] all the significant ideas and discoveries appear to have been by people outside his own culture. His very academic success in the study of [his subject] cannot but engender in him a feeling of insecurity, of the inadequacy of his own culture and certain enslavement to Western Culture.

Our universities are trying to remedy this by the emphasis placed on African studies and the Africanization of courses. . . . The aim is not singly *chauvinism* or a return to the old cultural pattern . . . because that also has its own bondage. What is required is a true renaissance which will liberate educated men and women from both enslavements, a flowering of the spirit which will draw from deep indigenous roots as well as from the current world heritage of ideas and produce Africans who can contribute with confidence to the world stock of knowledge.

9th Congress of the Universities of the Commonwealth, 1963, Proceedings, p. 68.

[3] FREDERICK HARBISON, 'The African University and Human Resource Development', *Journal of Modern African Studies*, **3**, 1, 1965 pp. 53–63; especially 55–56.

[4] *Investment in Education*, The Report of the Commission on Post-School Certificate and Higher Education in Nigeria (under the Chairmanship of Sir Eric Ashby), Lagos, 1960.

[5] *Ibid.*, pp. 51–52; HARBISON, *op. cit.*, p. 55.

[6] *Ibid.*, p. 50–51.

[7] *Ibid.*, p. 51.

[8] *Ibid.*, p. 63.

[9] *Ibid.*, p. 64.

[10] *Ibid.*, p. 63.

[11] *The Ashby Report* (pp. 67–72; 47) recommended the setting up of an Inter-Regional Manpower Board. The National Economic Council considered and approved this recommendation in December 1960. In May 1962 Dr. T. M. Yesufu, a Senior Labour Officer in the Federal Ministry of Labour, was appointed Secretary to the Board and charged with responsibility for establishing the necessary machinery for implementing the relevant recommendations of the Ashby Commission. *Annual Report of National Manpower Board 1st December 1962–31st March 1964*, Lagos, 1965, p. 3. See also *Sessional Paper No. 3* of 1961, Lagos, and *Government Notice No. 334*, published in the *Federation of Nigeria Gazette* of 15 February 1963. The National Manpower Board has been active in collecting manpower data and up till the time of writing (April 1966), has produced three detailed studies: *Manpower Situation in Nigeria* (*Preliminary Report*), Lagos, 1963; *National High-level Manpower 1963–70*, Lagos, 1964; *A study of Nigeria's Professional man-power in selected Occupations, 1964*, Lagos, 1965.

[12] HARBISON, *op. cit.*, p. 50.

[13] *Ibid.*, p. 53.

[14] Two years after the publication of the *Ashby Report*, the National Universities Commission was recommending 10,000 full-time students by 1967–68, a reduction of 2,500 on the submissions put before it by the universities. The Federal government in accepting this recommendation also drew attention to the presence of part-time students and stated that the number of these in all universities should not exceed 500. *University Development in Nigeria*, Report of the National Universities Commission, Lagos, 1963, pp. 20–21. *Decisions of the Government of the Federal Republic of Nigeria on the Report of the National Universities Commission, Sessional Paper No. 4* of 1964, Lagos, 1964, p. 5.

[15] *Investment in Education, op. cit.*, p. 25.

[16] *Ibid.*, p. 28.

[17] *Ibid.*, p. 27.

[18] *Ibid.*, p. 26.

[19] *Ibid.*, p. 28

[20] *University of Northern Nigeria*, Report of the Inter-University Council Delegation, April 1961.

[21] *Ibid.*, p. 8.

[22] *Ibid.*, p. 10.

[23] *Ahmadu Bello University Calendar 1965–66*, p. 10.

[24] *Ibid.*, p. 79.

[25] *Ibid.*, p. 76.

[26] *Ibid.*, pp. 79–84.

[27] *Ibid.*, p. 11.

[28] *Educational Development, 1961–70, Sessional Paper, No. 3*, Lagos, 1961, p. 7.

[29] *Report of the UNESCO Advisory Commission for the Establishment of the University of Lagos*, UNESCO, Paris, 1961.

[30] *Ibid.*, p. 5.

[31] *Ibid.*, p. 13.

[32] *Ibid.*, p. 12.

[33] *Ibid.*, p. 18.

[34] *University of Lagos Calendar, 1965–66*, pp. 9–11.

[35] *Ibid.*

[36] *Ibid.*

10   The University of Ife: a Study in Regional Rivalry

It will be recalled that the Ashby Commission had recognised the strong regional loyalties in Nigeria and had therefore recommended that there should be four universities, one in each Region and the fourth in Lagos. While agreeing that there would be need for a second university in each Region during the following twenty years, the Commission did not feel able to recommend that Federal aid should be given for the time being to more than one in each Region and to Lagos.[1] In this the Commission seemed to underrate the strength, pride, and autonomy of each individual Regional government. For the country as a whole, the Ashby Report's recommendation of Federal aid for only one university in each Region was perhaps a sound decision, but Regional governments had Regional interests to satisfy.

While the final drafts of the *Report* were being prepared the Western Regional Minister of Education informed the Commission that the Western Region government had some time earlier decided to establish a university in that Region with regional funds. The Commission was not told where the university would be situated or what form it would take and therefore could not discuss this proposal.[2]

Subsequently a member of the Commission, Dr. Sanya Onabamiro,[3] of Western Nigerian origin, who became Minister of Education in that region, before the Commission had concluded its work, submitted a reservation recommending seven rather than four universities, three of which were to be sponsored by the three Regional governments:

> I do not agree that four universities financed by the Federal Government will adequately meet the needs of Nigeria during the next ten years. I favour the creation of an additional Regional University in each Region which will bring the total to seven. In my view the University of Nigeria at Nsukka and the proposed Ahmadu Bello University at Kano should be allowed to develop into full universities owned respectively by the Eastern and Northern Regional Governments but with Federal financial support if required. The University which the Western Regional Government proposes to build somewhere in the Region should fall into the same category.[4]

What Dr. Onabamiro was suggesting was not clear from his reservation. Presumably he meant that there should be four Federal government universities, one in each Region and one in Lagos, the new Federal universities in the Regions being developed from the Enugu and Zaria branches of the Federal-owned Nigerian College. These two, along with his three proposed Regional universities and the already existing Ibadan University would bring the number to six. The seventh university was therefore the proposed one at Lagos. What was not clear was the fate of the Nigerian College at Ibadan. Was it to be absorbed by the University College, Ibadan, or was it to form part of the proposed new Western Regional University?

The aim of Dr. Onabamiro's suggestion was to give the Western Region control over one university, in the same way that the other two Regions were to do, under the Ashby recommendation. There was to continue to exist in the Western Region, according to Ashby, only the University College, Ibadan, but that was to be Federally-owned.

Dr. Onabamiro's suggestion is not surprising in view of his close association with the Action Group, the party in power in Western Nigeria during the Commission's meeting. It would have been out of character if the Action Group had accepted a proposition which would have relegated it to the position of not having control of a university in that Region. The Action Group, under Chief Awolowo's leadership, had presented the public image of a highly disciplined and well-organised party and the government it formed in the West had led the other Regions in the introduction of many modern amenities such as free primary education, radio and television services, et cetera, and it was generally regarded as most progressive.

The Ashby Commission, while not encouraging the founding of a Western Regional University, concluded in its *Report* however, that 'If the proposed university applies for Federal aid, we would expect its application to be dealt with by the National Universities Commission.'[5]

Subsequently a *White paper*[6] was published by the Western Nigeria Government on the establishment of a university in Western Nigeria 'to explain the purpose of such an Institution and indicate the steps which are being taken towards its establishment'.[7] It emphasised that the proposed university would in no way be exclusive to the Western Region and would open its doors not only to students from all parts of the Federation, but also from the rest of the world.[8] The white paper reviewed the progress of education in the Region, stating that students of university calibre were being produced in its secondary schools, but that there was only one university in the country. There was thus a need for more institutions of higher learning, for which reason the East and North were planning to build universities of their own. The Ashby Commission had suggested an annual output of 2,000 graduates in the next ten years. Since

> the Western Region is, up to now, in advance of others in producing students suitable for admission into the Universities, then it follows that liberal provision should be available in this Region for providing a substantial quota of the required number of University graduates.

The irony of the situation, according to the *White Paper*, was that while the

Ashby Commission recommended the up-grading of the Enugu Branch of the Nigerian College of Arts, Science and Technology to the status of a university in conjunction with the Institution at Nsukka, and also the up-grading of the Zaria Branch of the Nigerian College, it had not done similarly for Ibadan:

> The outcome [of this recommendation] might well be that the Eastern Region will have a new University institution at Enugu and its own Regional University, as well as continue to enjoy its quota of admissions into the University College, Ibadan. The Northern Region might also have a new University at Zaria and its Regional University College in Kano, the Ahmadu Bello College, as well as continue to enjoy its own quota of admissions into the University College, Ibadan, with the consolation, of course, that students from this Region might also be admitted into the Federal Institutions in other parts of the Country.[9]

According to the *White Paper*:

> This Government has seriously considered the present position and the new situation that might arise, and regards it as its duty to take the proper measures to safeguard the interests of the people of Western Nigeria in the provision of facilities for higher education. It is in order to meet the challenge of the situation that the Government has decided to build a new University, initially from regional funds, somewhere in Western Nigeria.[10]

The *White Paper* must be seen as a political justification for the government's decision to own a university like its other counterparts. It will appear that some facts were deliberately given a slant towards this end. For instance the Ashby Commission recommended that Nsukka and Ahmadu Bello should merge with the branches of the Nigerian College nearest to them and not that each Nigerian College should form a separate university. On the other hand the Western government may have felt that each of the colleges in each Region was the possible nucleus of a separate university at some time in the future—in which case the *White Paper* should have mentioned four universities in the North and two in the East. It should be noted that the University College, Ibadan, had not been known to reserve 'quotas of admission' for people from different regions of the country. The first criterion for admission there had always been academic merit.

The *White Paper* also announced the government's intention to establish two committees:[11] (*a*) The University Planning Committee, comprising 'persons who are qualified to advise on the intricate planning of a University,' and (*b*) A University Parliamentary Committee drawn from both sides of the House of Assembly and also from the House of Chiefs. The latter committee was to be advisory to the Minister of Education and would *inter alia* consider the views of the general public on the question of provision of higher education in the Region.

The Planning Committee comprised an impressive list of the foremost intellectuals and public men of Western Nigerian origin, including university lecturers, civil servants, schoolmasters, and so on, totalling fifty-nine in all.[12] After giving a 'general background', its *Report* dealt with Faculties, organisation and staffing of the University, residence of students, higher education for women, and finance. For the present only certain portions of the general background section will be discussed.

While recognising the world repute which universities such as Legon, Ibadan and Makerere had acquired through their association with London University, they made the following criticisms of these Universities.

1. Specialisation took place at the expense of general education. Apart from beginning too early, specialisation in the African universities of the time assumed a background of general education which was absent. European universities, on which these were modelled, trained specialists, who would need great adjustment to become the politicians, civil servants, educationalists and others in the key positions in which the country needed them.

2. Too few students were trained.

3. The methods of preparing students for degrees were too conventional and needed to include evening courses, sandwich and correspondence courses.

4. Modifications to suit local needs should be introduced in the study of medicine, veterinary science and engineering.

5. Too much administrative burden was placed on professors and Heads of departments.

The Committee enunciated principles[13] on which the new University should be based, some of which follow:

(*a*) The University should make it a point to improve the general education of its students. In devising courses in the humane and social studies for scientists and in science for students of arts and social studies, the object should be not the mastering of a smattering of techniques of several disciplines but training to recognise how the different branches of knowledge are significantly related and what their import is for human life in general and for Africa in particular. We recommend that the Faculty should draw on the experience of Harvard, Keele, and other universities in the field of general education.

(*b*) Nigeria needs a large number of graduates with general degrees and a smaller number with honours degrees. Therefore in order to meet the manpower needs of the country, the University should strike a judicious balance between facilities for general degrees and facilities for honours degrees. To this end we recommend that every student begin by taking a general degree after which, provided he is fit to do so, he may proceed to the honours degree.

(*c*) African studies (sociology, history, etc.) should form an integral part of the education of every university student. Research into African problems should be given priority in every department.

(*d*) University buildings, academic robes, and organisation should reflect African cultural traditions.

(*e*) Subject to location, the University should give evening courses and sandwich courses leading to degrees.

(*f*) The content of professional courses should be more closely related to the country's needs and experience drawn from the United States in the training of doctors and other professionals.

(*g*) The aim of the University should be to produce graduates who will be able to adjust themselves to life in the communities in which they may be called upon to serve, and for this reason students should be able to clean their own rooms, serve at meals, etc.

(*h*) Teaching departments should include arts, science, agriculture, engineering, law, medicine (pre-clinical) and social studies during the first quinquennium, while medicine (clinical) and veterinary medicine should be developed in the second quinquennium.

(*i*) Professors and Heads of departments should be spared as much as possible from administration.

(*j*) The University should be named after the town of its location.

In October 1962, the University, named the University of Ife, opened at the site of the Ibadan Branch of the disbanded Nigerian College with five Faculties—Agriculture, Arts, Economics and Social Studies, Law and Science.[14]

The University now has an Institute of African Studies, and an Institute of Administration, which was founded in 1963–64. Evening courses in Law also started in 1963–64.[15]

Notes

[1] *Investment in Education*, Report of the Commission on Post-School Certificate and Higher Education in Nigeria, Lagos, 1960, p. 29.

[2] *Ibid.*

[3] Formerly Senior Research Fellow, University of Ibadan.

[4] *Investment in Education*, *op. cit.*, p. 48.

[5] *Ibid.*, p. 122.

[6] *White Paper on the Establishment of a University in Western Nigeria*, Western Nigeria Legislature Sessional Paper No. 12 of 1960, Ibadan, 1960.

[7] *Ibid.*, p. 1.

[8] *Ibid.*

[9] *Ibid.*, pp. 2–3.

[10] *Ibid.*, p. 3. (Italics mine.)

[11] *Ibid.*, p. 4.

[12] See Appendix 'B', *Report of the Committee on the Proposed University in Western Nigeria*, mimeographed, Ibadan, n.d.

[13] Report of the Committee on the Proposed University in Western Nigeria, Ibadan, mimeographed, n.d., pp. 6–8.

[14] Early in 1966 plans started on the permanent site at Ile-Ife, about fifty miles from Ibadan.

[15] *University of Ife Calendar, 1965–66*, p. v.

11   Academic Freedom, Autonomy and Politics in Nigerian Universities: Three Cases

We have adopted in this book the definition of a university as being a community of senior and junior scholars or learners, i.e. a community of teachers and students, bound together by a common purpose of learning.

Academic freedom is that freedom claimed by students and teachers to enable them to effectively carry out their roles of teaching, learning, and practice of the arts and research.[1] It is thus the freedom of the student within his field of study.[2]

The concept that the scholar should be free to learn and teach what he pleases derives from Europe. First, there was the philosophy of intellectual freedom, which originated in Greece, arose again in Europe under the impact of the Renaissance, and came to maturity in the Age of Reason. Second, there was the idea of autonomy for communities of scholars which arose in the universities of Europe.[3] The modern conception of academic freedom was, however, formulated in nineteenth-century Germany. There grew up the idea that a university was a place where scholars were to pursue truth as well as to formulate and transmit it to students, who at the same time learn to search for truth for themselves. It was held that knowledge grew as an individual made deductions for himself, and a free interplay of ideas was the means of purifying it. Intellectual discipline over the members of the university community was excluded lest it distort their search.[4]

There were two aspects of this freedom. *Lernfreiheit* and *Lehrfreiheit*. By *Lernfreiheit* (freedom of learning) the German academician meant that university students should be able to take whatever courses they liked, when and where they liked, with no formal attendance requirements or examinations until the final degree examination. This system was deemed essential for the training of mature scholars and professional men in contrast to the rigid school-type discipline of the preparatory Gymnasium. By *Lehrfreiheit* (freedom of teaching) was meant the freedom of the German university professor to investigate any and all problems in the course of his research and to reveal his findings, whatever they might be, in teaching and in published works.[5] Usually nowadays academic freedom, especially in the British Commonwealth countries, does not include *Lernfreiheit* or student freedom. The tradition of student freedom is, however, strong on the continent of Europe where, especially in Germany, students may transfer from one university to another and stay nearly as long as they wish. There is evidence though that the traditional concept of *Lernfreiheit* is altering even in these countries. In the United States the idea of student freedom, which came from Germany, was incorporated into the elective system,[6] i.e. that in which, in the extreme case, students might choose any subject.

The most pertinent point for discussion here is thus the academic freedom of the teachers or faculty. Academic freedom in this sense is a right claimed by the properly appointed educator, as teacher and as investigator, to interpret his findings and to communicate his conclusions without being subjected to any interference, molestation, or penalisation because these conclusions are unacceptable to some constituted authority within or beyond the institution. In practical terms, in order that their freedom should be safeguarded, university teachers need supplementary protection. In the United Kingdom and North America this supplementary protection includes the absence of conditions of appointment or controls over the promotion of educators, so designed or operated as to give preference, irrespective of professional qualifications, to those whose views on any issues—social, economic, political, religious, or other—are more congenial to the administrative or other authorities.[7] Similarly, exclusion from participation in academic affairs on grounds of race or tribe might be considered a violation of academic freedom. In other words, the institutional choice of those who shall participate in higher education as well as the field of study or research are the preserve of academics themselves and anything which inhibits these functions would be considered to have violated academic freedom.

In the final analysis academic freedom hinges on the protection of the university teacher from dismissal should his views and actions become displeasing to the authorities of his university. In the United States, the academic is legally protected when he is given 'tenure' after a period of probation. In the United Kingdom and many countries of the British Commonwealth academic freedom does not depend on legal protection but on those intangible and peculiarly British attributes, tradition and public opinion.[8]

There are, however, responsibilities attached to this freedom. The first is that the freedom of the university teacher cannot exceed the freedom of the other citizens of the country or state in which the university is located.[9] Second, it is obvious that because of the special position of the university teacher, especially in communities where his profession is new, his conduct outside his immediate academic duties ought to take into account the general social, political and other factors of his environment. To conclude these preliminary remarks it is necessary to examine briefly the term autonomy. Sir Eric Ashby and Dr. Mary Anderson attempted to remove some of the 'confusion about what the expressions [autonomy and academic freedom really] mean and how they are related to each other'. According to the authors, the terms

> are sometimes regarded as synonymous though it is a commonplace of history that an autonomous university can deny academic freedom to some of its members (as Oxford did in the early nineteenth century) and a university which is not autonomous can safeguard academic freedom (as Prussian universities did in Humboldt's time).[10]

Yet they admit a little later that

> As to autonomy, the truth, though it is often blurred by rhetoric, is that nowadays no university can expect to be *completely* [their italics] self-governing in the sense that an independent state or a municipality is self-governing.[11]

This indeed is the crux of the matter: most universities now are run mainly on funds subscribed by some outside body, usually a government or state, occasionally a religious body or even the alumni of the university. In all cases those who pay the piper dictate the tune either directly or indirectly (as is the case of the University Grants Commission of the United Kingdom). The authors were apparently thinking of conditions pertaining to Great Britain, where 'academic freedom and university autonomy are more effectively protected by unwritten conventions than by charters and statutes'. It is known that in the United States academic freedom is safeguarded *legally*. From this author's point of view, autonomy in the modern university is non-existent except as a corollary of academic freedom. Where for instance there exists academic freedom as defined earlier, then the faculty is able to administer the courses as it considers fit, to choose who should teach, to choose the area of research, et cetera. It is in the actual act of deciding what, how, when and whom to teach that autonomy lies. The atmosphere in which this is possible is one in which academic freedom exists.

With these remarks let us now examine three cases of events in Nigerian universities which have been interpreted as infringements of academic freedom. The cases in question are: (1) the Oyenuga affair at the University of Ife, Ibadan; (2) the Lindsay episode at the University of Nigeria, Nsukka, and (3) the Njoku crisis at the University of Lagos.

First, a detailed account of each event will be given, in so far as these are relevant to the subsequent discussions in this chapter. Second, an analysis of the causes and the courses of the crises will be made; and finally I will attempt to determine how far, if at all, academic freedom was violated.

The Oyenuga affair at the University of Ife

Professor V. A. Oyenuga was Professor and Dean of the Faculty of Agriculture at the University of Ife from its inception in 1962. On 3 February 1964, Professor Oyenuga was dismissed after he had refused to accept an

K

ultimatum either to apologise within seven days for insubordination or to resign his appointment.

An early indication that trouble was brewing at Ife occurred in May 1963[11a] when the Western Nigeria Government changed the composition of the Council of the University of Ife. Later that year, on 20 November, the Minister of Chieftaincy Affairs, Chief R. A. Akinyemi, said that his Government (of Western Nigeria) was considering the possibility of closing down the University of Ife. The statement was made during the inaugural meeting of the Management Committee of the Ibadan Southern District Council. Chief Akinyemi blamed the University for not 'keeping pace' with her sister institutions in the country and alleged that it had failed to discharge the purpose for which it had been set up because some of the lecturers were engaging in active politics instead of devoting themselves to conscientious teaching.[12] These lecturers were seeking to propagate communism and to sabotage the efforts of the government.[13] The Minister was a member of the National Council of Nigerian Citizens (N.C.N.C.). Two days after Chief Akinyemi's pronouncement the United Peoples Party (U.P.P.), the other party in the coalition government, came out in his support:

> Chief Akinyemi was not only speaking his mind on this issue, he was also speaking for millions of tax payers in Western Nigeria who pay to get the Ife University going. The University has been placed in a very difficult position today because of the activities on the part of the Action Group lecturers and fellow-travellers who inhabit the campus. These A. G. lecturers, instead of devoting their efforts for [that] which they are paid, waste their time planning to discredit the government. The time has come when the Government of Western Nigeria in the name of its people should make up its mind and clear the Augean stables of the University of Ife . . . The promotions of some of the professors and lecturers made entirely on Action Group political considerations should be annulled.

The threat of closure because of activities of the faculty was unusual in the history of universities in Nigeria. Closure as a result of student activities had occurred. In 1957 the University of Ibadan (then University College) had been closed because students tore down fences built round their halls of residence. Similarly the new University of Nigeria had been closed in 1962 following a students' riot because of alleged bad feeding, et cetera. But staff matters had never been the cause of closure. One Nigerian newspaper commented on the situation thus:

> Some politicians have recently had cause to lay serious charges against the University of Ife and their lecturers. Happily the Western Nigeria Government do not share the views of these politicians. But these complaints must be examined and shown for what they are worth, otherwise the reputation of Ife University may be tarnished if it is made the target of political mudslinging. . . .
> The present complaints about the University stem from the fact that the political beliefs of some of the Ife lecturers differ radically from those of members of the present Western Nigeria Government. But that in itself does not warrant the threat of closing a university, just like a rural local council.

It has been alleged that some of the lecturers are 'sabotaging the efforts of the government'. It is further claimed that they are using the University as a forum for the propagation of communism.

These are serious charges which should not be made lightly. There are ample provisions in the criminal code to deal with any individual who does anything illegal against our Government. And it is debatable whether communism in any way inhabits the true functions of a university.

If the University has not made any significant progress since its inception that may be due to reasons other than the political beliefs of a few lecturers.

It is an obvious fact that Ife has been making do with the facilities which it inherited from the old Ibadan Branch of the Nigerian College of Arts, Science and Technology.

Since its inception Ife University has suffered from two great misfortunes. First, it has not been able to secure funds necessary for its expansion. Second, university policy and policy-makers have changed as often as the vagaries of political fortunes....

Some of the most enlightened and articulate Nigerians are found among our university lecturers. And we cannot expect them to hold no opinions about the politics of their country.[14]

Meanwhile the students had protested to the Premier of Western Nigeria affirming confidence in their teachers. On the same day as the editorial appeared, he issued a statement in which he denied any plan to close the University and blamed a few lecturers for its bad name. These few, according to the Premier, were 'political braggarts masquerading as intellectuals', and 'synthetic intellectuals' who had abused and debased the sacred name of academic freedom and had turned the University into a seat for subversion.

On 19 December 1963, about a month after Chief Akinyemi's warning, Dr. S. O. Biobaku, Pro-Vice-Chancellor, deputising for the Vice-Chancellor who was outside the country, told a Special Congregation of the University that the University authorities had only one policy and that was to support the government of the day, to which the University looked up for sustenance. 'This is [our] credo and if anyone disagrees with this fundamental policy, the remedy lies entirely in his hands—to resign.'

The Provisional Council, according to Dr. Biobaku, had gone thoroughly into the question of the rules governing expression of views in public on topical issues by members of the staff of the University. The regulations provided a clear statement of the right of the individual member of staff to express his views within the limit that he should not thereby endanger the very existence of the University. He stated 'categorically' that the Council would enforce the regulations most emphatically and that the Vice-Chancellor, or in his absence, himself, would not fail in his duty to call to order any of their colleagues who ran counter to them, and if he persisted, to recommend disciplinary action to the Council.

He denied that the authorities of the University had received, or expected to receive, any instructions from the Regional government to sack any member of the staff, since the law establishing the University firmly placed responsibility for appointing and disciplining staff on that Council.[15]

Within twenty-four hours after the meeting, one lecturer, Wole Soyinka, lecturer in English, writer, poet and playwright, gave notice of resignation, and another, Dr. S. A. Aluko, Senior Lecturer and acting Head of Economics, formally joined the Action Group and was accepted. One member of the University's governing council also resigned.[16]

A week later (27 December), the local press carried the news that the Provisional Council was recommending disciplinary action against Dr. Oyenuga, Professor of Agriculture, because of his refusal to apologise to the Vice-Chancellor for a letter in which he protested against being queried about a trip he had made to Germany in June that year. Dr. Oyenuga said he had gone to Germany to read a paper on nutrition, during a time when the University was on holiday. Dr. Oyenuga was charged with 'bare-faced disobedience' to the Vice-Chancellor and the Council. In reply to the query about his absence in June Dr. Oyenuga had written:

> Even assuming that I had broken a regulation laid down by either or both of these authorities, and you wish, as the administrator executing these regulations, to invite my attention to them, I would not normally have expected such to come in the form of a query. A query, I will respectfully point out, is reminiscent of civil service methods and, as far as I am aware, alien to a university environment. During the whole period of my academic career, I have never had any single instance, even as a junior member of the academic staff, of being queried.
>
> I should, with respect, be most interested to know how often during your thirteen years of service as Professor of Preventive and Social Medicine in the University College, Ibadan, you received queries from any of the three principals with whom you work in that University.
>
> It is only since I got to this University, as a colleague of yours, that the strange method of issuing queries even to professors and Heads of departments and to the Dean of a Faculty has been introduced by you. I mention the point in the last paragraph because I am most anxious that those of us from Western Nigeria, who have found ourselves saddled with the serious responsibility, opportunity and privilege of building a university institution, should be fairly conscious of this responsibility and should try to create the correct university environment in this institution, the only condition under which the University can be correctly and properly developed.
>
> I should most respectfully and seriously like to appeal to you that we should address ourselves to this serious responsibility of building the University of Ife. Other universities in other parts of the country are making progress. I am not sure that we at Ife can claim to be doing the same. I should like to give an example. The students of this University are assembling on 25 September 1963. Amongst them is a batch of second-year Part II agricultural students. Up to the moment of writing, we have not laid the foundation of the building indispensable to the teaching of their laboratory work in all subjects of agriculture as from 1 October 1963. There is no equipment for these laboratories. There are no teachers to teach these students except three of us to teach three out of the fourteen subjects that have to be taught from 1 October 1963.
>
> The reason for this state of affairs is due to the lack of co-operation I have consistently received from you since I submitted these requirements in December 1962 and January 1963.
>
> You did not find it fit, for instance, to authorise the advertisement of the posts for the teachers who should start teaching from 1 October 1963, until July 1964. Similarly for the construction of the laboratory buildings. It is for these purposes—to teach and

to carry out research—that the university is mainly established. I respectfully suggest that to these essential and fundamental duties, and not to bickerings and queries, we must now address ourselves.[17]

On 3 February 1964, Professor Oyenuga was dismissed after he had refused to accept an ultimatum to apologise within seven days or to resign his appointment. On the same day, four lecturers, Dr. S. A. Aluko, Dr. Olu Odumosu, Dr. Boye Fayemi, and Mr. Chambers resigned in protest against the dismissal. Their resignations were accepted and became effective immediately. A day later all the students of the University kept away from classes. Four more lecturers—three expatriate and one Nigerian —also resigned.[18]

Subsequently Dr. Oyenuga, Dr. Odumosu, Dr. Fayemi, Dr. Aluko, and Mr. S. A. George were awarded a total of £5,212 damages and 550 guineas costs against the Provisional Council of the University of Ife by an Ibadan High Court judge. The damages were in respect of salaries and emoluments due to them as a result of their resignations and for salaries and emoluments due in lieu of notice following the termination of the appointment of Dr. Oyenuga. The Judge held Dr. Oyenuga's appointment had been wrongly terminated.[19]

The implications of this judgement in the history of academic freedom in Nigeria will be discussed later.

The Lindsay episode at the University of Nigeria, Nsukka

Professor J. K. Lindsay had been educated in the Universities of Dublin, Edinburgh and London. Before joining the staff of the University of Nigeria, Nsukka, Eastern Nigeria, he had held appointments in universities in the United States, Canada and West Indies. In 1961 Professor Lindsay, an Irishman, was appointed to an Nsukka professorship and held the post until his appointment was terminated at the end of August 1964, following a misunderstanding between him and the University authorities. Professor Lindsay has published the correspondence, *University of Nigeria—Lindsay Correspondence*,[20] between him and the University during the period immediately preceding termination.

It appears that the matter was triggered by a memorandum which the Professor had circulated to members of Senate consisting mainly of the Professors, Heads of Departments and some senior members of the teaching staff. In it he had criticised the admission of students to study archaeology (which was part of the History Department) before the Department was ready to offer it. He also criticised the University for bad planning in general.

Professor Lindsay's memorandum claimed that the Department of History and Archaeology was not consulted before applications were

issued in the press inviting candidates for the Honours Degree in Archaeology. Despite protests from the Department, students were in fact
admitted. According to Professor Lindsay there were two reasons why the
course should not be started at that time. First, the University had been
niggardly in distributing funds; second and more important, there was a
world shortage of competent archaeologists. All the University wanted
was to impress the outside world.

> . . . Even if the University were suddenly to become as generous to archaeology as
> hitherto it had been niggardly . . . there would remain the more difficult problem of
> staff shortage. . . . It is true that the insertion of archaeology helps to make more
> impressive the list of courses in public advertisements and to narrow the foolish
> rivalry between this University and sister institutions. To retain it now that the
> implications have been made abundantly clear and to enrol students in the subject
> would be to flout ethical decencies in a way which would cause the professionals of
> Madison Avenue to hesitate.

But archaeology was not, according to him, the only area of 'misguided
decision'. Others included the setting up of a Department of Fisheries some
two hundred and fifty miles from the sea, the setting up of a School of
Forestry and a School of post-graduate Librarianship. To sum up:

> the University has been grandiose and naïve in important areas of planning and has
> been indifferent to, or unaware of, the cost in money and reputation for itself and of
> the consequences for the students.[21]

The Vice-Chancellor, Dr. G. M. Johnson, reacted immediately by suspending Professor Lindsay with powers conferred on him by the University of
Nigeria Law. Dr. Johnson accused Lindsay of abusing the privileges of
being a professor, of being a member of staff in the History and
Archaeology Department, a member of Senate. The fourth charge accused
Professor Lindsay of making erroneous statements and intemperate
criticisms of the authorities of the University, including its Council.[22]

Professor Lindsay of course denied these charges and claimed 'good faith
and the best interests of the University at heart'.[23] After he defended himself before the University Council itself, his suspension was lifted, for
reasons which were not specified.[24] According to the Secretary to Council,
that body 'felt itself disappointed in your attitude when you appeared
before Council and did not show any signs of repentance. . . . The errors
and false information contained in your memorandum to Senate were
discussed and you were referred to the Official Documents of the University.'

Finally Professor Lindsay was warned 'that should another situation
occur in the future, Council would justifiably feel itself obliged to terminate
your appointment'.

Professor Lindsay was not repentant. In a letter to the Council, he
claimed that that body would be 'astonishingly misinformed' about the
affairs of the University if the Council expected him to repent for the

statements in the memorandum. He felt that his memorandum to the Senate was reasonably accurate, since he consulted opinion outside his own field in making statements about forestry, fisheries, and so on.

He then went on to make other criticisms which he said he had left out in the Senate memorandum—including poor landscaping on the campus, the building of a stadium, and 'maladministration'.

Meanwhile matters were complicated by a wrangle which had developed between Lindsay and the Secretary to the Council as to whether or not the former was the Head of the Department as well as Professor in the Department of History and Archaeology. For in the meantime a Nigerian had been appointed Head of the History and Archaeology Department.[25]

Despite a further letter from the Council,[26] Professor Lindsay insisted that he was Head of the Department of History and Archaeology. This was the final straw. On 31 August 1964, the Council terminated Lindsay's appointment as a Professor in the Department of History and member of the academic staff of the University, giving him six months' salary in lieu of notice in accordance with the University policy of the time.[27] Professor Lindsay did not take legal action although he complained that constructive criticism given in the course of his duty had been ruthlessly crushed.[28]

The Njoku crisis at the University of Lagos

Professor Eni Njoku, a Nigerian, was Professor of Botany at the University of Ibadan before he became first Vice-Chancellor of the new University of Lagos in October 1962. It will be remembered from Chapter 9 that he had served on the UNESCO Commission that recommended the setting up of the University of Lagos. His initial appointment was for three years. The Law under which the University functioned was the University of Lagos Act, 1962. In 1964 a Draft Bill was prepared in collaboration with the Council and the Senate, and was due to have been passed in the Nigerian Parliament in December of that year, but political disturbances held up the work of Parliament. Part of the Draft Bill reads as follows:

> The first Vice-Chancellor shall be Eni Njoku, Bachelor of Arts, Master of Science, Doctor of Philosophy.

On 1 March 1965, Nigeria's national newspapers carried the news that Dr. Sabiru Biobaku, then Pro-Vice-Chancellor of the University of Ife, had been appointed to succeed Professor Njoku whose appointment would end on 31 May 1965.[29]

This was surprising news for two reasons. First, Dr. Biobaku had only shortly before that accepted, and at the time of the announcement had not yet rejected, the post of Vice-Chancellor of the new University in Zambia. Second, Professor Njoku had not only been mentioned as Vice-Chancellor in the new Bill but had actually been proposed by a majority of the Senate.

On the day of the announcement some of the students barricaded the entrance to the University and locked the doors to the buildings for three days until 4 March, when an order suspending all (except the medical) students until further notice was passed by the Provisional Council.[30]

The Senior Staff Association of the University (except those in the medical school) passed a resolution protesting against the change of Vice-Chancellor: forty-one voted for the resolution, four against, and six abstained. Later, two members of the Senior Staff, on behalf of themselves and forty-three others, dissociated themselves from the above resolution. They assured Dr. Biobaku of their support and loyalty. Similarly a split occurred in the student body. This new group accused their counterparts who were barricading the University of 'being motivated by tribal sentiments engineered and actively supported by a political party'.[31]

It was immediately clear that even if the matter was not originally politico-tribal, it had become so, the Yorubas supporting Dr. Biobaku and the Ibos Professor Eni Njoku. For instance on 1 March when the change of Vice-Chancellorship was first announced, *The West African Pilot*, organ of the National Council of Nigerian Citizens (N.C.N.C.) headed the news with 'Another shock for the Ibos: Njoku forced out of Varsity job'. Similarly the Action Group, a predominantly Yoruba Party, sent a lengthy message of congratulations to Dr. Biobaku.[32]

At the University of Ibadan, the Association of University Teachers 'expressed distress at the recent conflict over the appointment of a new Vice-Chancellor for the University of Lagos' and asserted that

the standards by which competence for office are assessed must be exclusively those of academic and administrative ability and personal character; political and tribal considerations should not enter . . . the teaching and administrative staffs of the country's universities [should] renew their solidarity in the pursuit of learning in order to maintain their high name and reputation before the nation and before the academic community of the world at large.[33]

The next day a counter-statement was issued purporting that the previous day's announcement did not represent the views of the entire Academic Staff of the University of Ibadan:

In so far as the statement of the Ibadan University AUT imputes tribal and political motives to the recent happenings in the University of Lagos, without being in full possession of the facts, as they themselves admit, we wish completely to dissociate ourselves from this view.

It was signed by three lecturers on behalf of forty-six others. Again the split was on tribal lines.

At the University of Ife, where Dr. Biobaku was the Pro-Vice-Chancellor, the Association of University teachers announced full backing of his appointment. There was no split.[35] Similarly there was unanimous agreement when the Association of University Teachers at Nsukka 'condemned the injection of politics, remotely or otherwise, into the working of universities in Nigeria' and appealed to the Councils of Nigerian Universities to re-examine the relationship between them and the Senates of their respective universities 'with a view to ensuring better working relationships between the academic and the administrative bodies'.[36] Ife and Nsukka are owned by the Western and Eastern Regional Governments respectively. The Nigerian staff at Ife are predominantly Yoruba while those at Nsukka are predominantly Ibo (1967).

This split on a tribal basis was described as 'domestic affairs of Nigeria' by a well-known Nigerian, Chief H. O. Davies, when he attacked certain expatriate members of the Lagos University Staff who apparently supported Professor Njoku. According to Chief Davies, 'Nigeria will not tolerate any expatriates who attempt, by aiding tribal imperialism, to impose their will on our country'.[37]

The Ibo State Union soon waded into the controversy when it called on the Prime Minister to 'use his good offices to rescind the discriminatory decision of the Lagos University Provisional Council and reinstate Dr. Eni Njoku as the Vice-Chancellor of Lagos University in the interest of peace and unity'.[38]

An 'Organization for Nigerian Unity' asked, in congratulating Dr. Biobaku, 'Does the appointment of a man from a particular tribe detract from the merit of the appointment . . . ? There are two Federal government sponsored universities in Nigeria: the Universities of Ibadan and Lagos; must both by all means be headed by members of one tribe?'[39] (Dr. Dike, an Ibo, was head of Ibadan at the time.)

No wonder that the Secretary of the Lagos Association of University Teachers soon resigned from his post because it had 'degenerated into irreconcilable triplets, that is Ibo, expatriate and non-Ibo-non-expatriate'.[40]

Appeals both public and private were made to the Prime Minister of the Federation to intervene. But he did not. Government statements were made by the Minister of Education. On the first occasion, 9 April 1965, he attacked 'one expatriate individual, headstrong, tactless, and cantankerous, (who) has fouled the fountain at our institution of higher learning, and spread the spirit of rebellion not only among the expatriates but also among a section of the students.'

The Council, having suspended the students, decided that those of them who re-applied would be re-admitted on 5 April. This was later postponed until 7 June, after the Senate had decided that the atmosphere was not suitable for teaching. The Deans passed on the Senate's instructions to their staff, but the Chairman of the Council circulated a counter letter directing the staff to ignore those instructions.

The University opened as planned on 7 June, but closed again on the 8th after further disturbances. The Council then closed the University till further notice.

In mid-June 1965, five Deans who were under contract were dismissed.

Thereafter, one Dean who was on permanent appointment and thirty-other members of the academic staff handed in their resignations. Twelve others, seconded from overseas universities or international organisations, announced that they were asking their sponsors to withdraw them. In all, fifty-one senior members of staff resigned, asked for recall or were dismissed.[41]

The political bases of the crises

Although the crises described above occurred at different universities at different times and under widely different conditions, it is possible to trace a relationship between them by examining certain aspects of politics in Nigeria beginning from earlier periods. It will be necessary to have a brief look at the political parties and some of their activities.

The earliest political organisation in Nigeria in modern times appears to be the People's Union, formed in 1908. Its origins are associated with a People's Petition signed by the leading citizens of Lagos under the leadership of two doctors, Dr. Randle and Dr. Obassa.[42] Earlier there had been two protests: the first in 1895 was against a house and land tax proposed by the Governor, the second in 1907 against the Land Acquisition Ordinance whereby land in Lagos Island was acquired by the government for the provision of official residences.[43] The protests were an outcome of growing distrust of the British by the Lagosians. The latter felt that some of the measures against which they protested were designed to favour Europeans. This discrimination extended not only to social and financial benefits, but also to political affairs, for the Lagosians, like their counterparts in other British West African Colonies, were denied participation in government.

In 1920 (see Chapter 3), educated West Africans met in Accra under the leadership of J. E. Casely Hayford for the first conference of the National Congress of West Africa. They demanded *inter alia* 'an effective voice in their [British West African Colonies'] affairs both in the Legislative and Municipal Government'. It will be recalled that this conference also called for the establishment of a university. Partly as a result of the activities of the West African Congress a new constitution was introduced in 1922 which permitted a measure of elected African membership in the Legislative Council.[44] Two new political parties were ushered in a year later: the Nigerian National Democratic Party, led by Herbert Macaulay, and the Union of Young Nigerians, led by Ayo Williams. The defunct People's Union was also revived.[45]

At this stage it is necessary to state that the major preoccupation of political parties at the time under review was distrust and suspicion of the British colonial government. This was to grow from the early 1930s and consolidate itself within the post-World War II political parties, the organisational basis of the nationalism evident in this period.

The Union of Young Nigerians[46] died after successive failures at the elections, but the flame that it lit flickered on until it blazed in the 1950s into the Action Group (see Figure, p. 152). The Union was formed by Lagos elements younger than Macaulay and Randle. It channelled its antagonism towards the Colonial regime into educational questions and its leaders spear-headed the 1929 agitations against the proposed Nigerian School Certificate. In 1934 its elements reorganised themselves into the Lagos Youth Movement which was formed primarily to protest against the Yaba Higher College (see Ch. 5). With the arrival of Chief H. O. Davies, the Movement altered its name in 1936 to the Nigerian Youth Movement (N.Y.M.) and became thenceforth the gathering point for 'anti-imperialist' nationalism. According to Chief Awolowo, who was for many years connected with it:

> The Nigerian Youth Movement was the first nationalist organisation ever to make real efforts to bring within its fold all the nationalists and politically conscious elements in Nigeria. It was a vigilant, dynamic, and selfless nationalist organisation. It lived up to and worked for its declared objectives and ideals, and spared no pains in fighting to uphold them. . . . It provided a unique platform for the unification of all the diverse ethnic groups that constitute Nigeria, and a forum where all conscientious and right-thinking Nigerian patriots and nationalists could unfold their ideas.[47]

In 1937, Dr. Azikiwe arrived in Nigeria and joined the Movement. According to Chief Awolowo, Dr. Azikiwe brought with him a propaganda technique which was new in politics and journalism in Nigeria and which further boosted the popularity of the Nigerian Youth Movement and disarranged its opponents. Thus, activated by Dr. Azikiwe's presence, the Party won a number of elections, beating the longer-established NNDP.[48] (It is necessary from this point to append Macaulay's name after his party's to distinguish it from the much later party of the same name founded by Akintola in 1963.) According to Chief Awolowo, despite Dr. Azikiwe's constructive contributions to the Movement, it was Dr. Azikiwe himself who 'delivered a succession of blows—now subtle, then hard and heavy, but always accurate and harmful—which, aggravated by a series of bunglings and mismanagements on the part of some of its leaders, brought about the fall and the ruin of the N.Y.M.'[49]

To shorten a story whose detail will be found elsewhere,[50] Dr. Azikiwe resigned from the Executive Committee of the N.Y.M. in 1939 and from the Party itself in 1941.[51]

Ostensibly, Azikiwe's reason for breaking with the N.Y.M. derived from the fact that Akinsanya, one of the founders of the Party, was dropped in favour of Ernest Ikoli in the nominations to fill a vacant seat in the Lagos Town Council. Apparently Azikiwe resented this treatment because he believed that Akinsanya was discriminated against because he was an

Ijebu, and they were unpopular among Lagosians. But various other reasons have been put forward. The first is that Azikiwe did not welcome the competition implied by the adoption of *The Service* as the N.Y.M.'s official organ. Prior to that, Dr. Azikiwe's *West African Pilot*, which had been so helpful to the N.Y.M.'s cause, had fulfilled the function. Another suggestion is that Azikiwe's personality does not permit his playing second fiddle and that he could not remain for long in a party where all he got was membership of the Executive Committee.[52]

The third suggestion for Azikiwe's break with the N.Y.M. is believed to be connected with the leadership of the Party, which was mainly in the hands of Yorubas. In this connection, it is pertinent to quote Chief Awolowo once again:

> The fact that in the leadership of the Nigerian Youth Movement there were more Yorubas than those belonging to other ethnic groups was an accident; and it was in fact not noticed until 1941. . . . It was only to be expected that in the pre-War Lagos community, where there were only few non-Yorubas who cared to take part in politics, that those Yoruba professionals and merchants with an almost obsessional urge for politics should predominate in the ruling hierarchy of the Nigerian Youth Movement.[53]

That up to about the Second World War the Yorubas dominated what there was of the political life of the country was indeed an accident. Owing to its geographical position, Yorubaland had had closer contact with Europe than other parts of Nigeria, excepting perhaps the Oil Rivers. As far back as the nineteenth century children from the wealthier Yoruba families had been sent to England for their education. Many of the Christianised descendants of slaves who returned from Sierra Leone in the nineteenth century were also Yorubas. This earlier contact is reflected in the names associated with the political parties and the pioneers of the professions such as medicine, law and engineering in Nigeria, which are predominantly Yoruba. At Fourah Bay College, nearer home, most students came from Nigeria, and of these the majority were from Western Nigeria. According to Hair:

> The earliest Nigerians [in Fourah Bay College] came from Lagos and Abeokuta, the latter town the contemporary C.M.S. headquarters in Nigeria. As the missions extended their activities, students came to the College from new areas. At the beginning of the present century a few students arrived from Eastern Nigeria, the scene of Bishop Crowther's later missionary labours. But up to the present day [then 1950] most of the Nigerian students came from Western Nigeria.[54]

There was thus a great gap between the Yorubas and other Nigerian peoples in Lagos. Even outside Lagos, the Yorubas controlled the highest posts in the civil service and commercial houses.[55]

To illustrate this, in 1937 at the reception organised by the Ibos for the newly-returned Dr. Nnamdi Azikiwe there were no Ibos of sufficient professional, social, or educational standing to take the Chair, which was therefore occupied by Magistrate Jibowu, a Yoruba. The Ibos realised that their social position was due to lack of education, and partly as a result of this,

> the Ibo embraced Western education with great enthusiasm and determination. Christian missions were welcomed, and were encouraged to set up schools in Iboland. Village improvement unions sponsored scholarships and Ibo students flocked to secondary schools in what is now the Western Region. By the late 1930s the Ibo were more heavily represented than any other tribe or nationality in Yaba Higher College and in most Nigerian Secondary Schools. Thenceforward the number of Ibos appointed to the African Civil Service and as clerks in business firms increased at a faster rate than that of any other group. By 1945 the gap between Yorubas and Ibos had virtually closed. Increasing numbers of Ibo barristers and doctors began to arrive from England.[57]

This sudden rise of the Ibos from subordinate positions in the large towns, especially Lagos of the early 1920s, to positions where, following the arrival of Dr. Azikiwe and their whole-hearted embracing of Western education, they became a powerful group, is a factor which lies at the root of subsequent Ibo-Yoruba rivalries. At the centre of this is the figure of Dr. Azikiwe. It offers an explanation for certain developments in Nigerian politics and for the crisis in Lagos University. As Professor Coleman puts it:

> Perhaps the most provocative features of the Ibo entrance into Nigerian politics were the political activities and journalistic enterprise of Nnamdi Azikiwe. Some Yoruba and Hausa leaders resented Azikiwe and his associates because they felt he threatened their positions and challenged their own aspirations for leadership.[58]

An important factor in the Ibo drive for advancement was the formation of the Ibo State Union, which developed from the several associations in villages and towns all over Nigeria. The Ibos in Lagos, for instance, had formed themselves in 1933 into an Ibo Co-operative Society. Initially the main aim of the Ibo State Union was educational advancement—building of secondary schools.[59]

When Dr. Azikiwe broke with the N.Y.M. in 1941 he took with him the bulk of the non-Yoruba elements in the Movement, thus leaving the leadership once again in Yoruba hands.

In 1944, at the instigation of the Nigerian Union of Students (mainly old boys of King's College, Lagos), a Nigerian National Council was formed with Herbert Macaulay as President and Azikiwe as Secretary. Membership was organisational, and not on a personal, individual basis. It included tribal groups, political parties, social clubs, et cetera. The Council soon changed its name to 'National Council of Nigeria and the Cameroons' to accommodate tribal groups from the Cameroons, which at that time was part of Nigeria. Notably, the N.Y.M. did not affiliate, but Herbert Macaulay's N.N.D.P. did. When Macaulay died, Azikiwe assumed leadership of the N.C.N.C. Since the leadership was Ibo, and the Ibo

Union, one of many affiliates, was especially active in the Party, the
N.C.N.C. came to be regarded in certain quarters as an Ibo affair.[60] In
1945 Chief Awolowo, then a law student in London, formed the *Egbe
Omo Oduduwa* (Descendants of Oduduwa, the mythical founder of the
Yorubas). The *Egbe* was a pan-Yoruba cultural organisation. Its objective,
like that of the Ibo Union, was educational. But it was also 'to accelerate
the emergence of a virile modernised and efficient Yoruba State with its
own individuality within the Federal State of Nigeria . . . to unite the
various clans and tribes in Yorubaland and generally create and actively
foster the idea of a single nationalism throughout Yorubaland.'[61]

The fall of the Yoruba-led N.Y.M. gave rise to a general sense of
frustration and disillusionment among that people, especially as the Ibo
State Union and the Ibibio State Union, constituents of the N.C.N.C.,
continued to make progress. The *Egbe* therefore arose to renew Yoruba
solidarity. As the founder, Chief Obafemi Awolowo says:

> The Yorubas were a highly progressive, but badly disunited group. . . . [As a result of
> Dr. Azikiwe's propaganda] the Yorubas indulged in mutual recrimination and
> condemnation. The younger elements thought the Yorubas were inferior to the go-
> ahead Ibos, and that whatever may have been the past glories of the Yorubas, they
> had become effete and decadent. To cap it all, it was freely bandied [about] that the
> Yorubas were no longer capable of leadership in any sphere of life. . . . I decided
> therefore to do all in my power to infuse solidarity to the disjointed tribes that
> constituted the Yoruba ethnic group.[62]

From the start the *Egbe* and the Ibo State Union antagonised each
other. Such statements as 'Ibo domination is a question of time', attributed
to a prominent Ibo, did not improve things, nor did statements such as:
'We never knew the Ibos, but since we came to know them we have tried
to be friendly and neighbourly. Then came the Arch-Devil himself
[Azikiwe] to sow the seeds of distrust and hatred.'[63]

The *Egbe* was to form the infra-structure on which Chief Awolowo
built his party, the Action Group, in 1951. 'When the idea of starting a
political party occurred to me in 1949,' wrote Awolowo,

> and I began to make contacts, I had frequent contacts with members of the *Egbe*. . . .
> If the new Party was to make any appreciable showing at all at the regional elections
> it must make use of the branches and organisation of the *Egbe Omo Oduduwa* through-
> out the West Region. Besides, party organisation does cost money; and the people to
> whom I looked for financial support were to be found at the head of the *Egbe*. . . . It
> was when they gave their blessing that I convened the first meeting at which the Action
> Group was formed.[64]

The Action Group contested and won the elections to the Western
House of Assembly in 1951 and remained in power in Western Nigeria
until 1963. At Independence, therefore, in 1960, the pattern of the distribution of political parties in Nigeria was: the Yoruba-dominated Action
Group formed the government in the West, the Ibo-dominated National

Council of Nigerian Citizens that in the Eastern Region, and the Hausa-Fulani Northern Peoples' Congress, that in Northern Nigeria.

So far attention has centred on Southern Nigeria, where Yoruba–Ibo antagonisms of the late 1940s crystallised into the political parties of the 1950s and 1960s. This antagonism arose partly because political leadership was originally in the hands of Yorubas, but had become at least shared, if not usurped, by the Ibos.

The position of Northern Nigeria will become a little clearer later on; suffice it to say that at this stage and until 1951 little political contact was made between the North and the South, the result of separate developments early in the country's history. It will be remembered that the 1929 Hussey educational Memorandum (see Chapter 5) also allowed for a separation of Southern and Northern Nigeria. Second, and more important, the Northern Region had about half the total population in the country and was therefore entitled to about half of the seats in the Federal Parliament, where representation was on the basis of population. Since all but a few of the Northern seats were won by the Northern People's Congress, that party needed to form a coalition with a Southern Nigerian Party in order to form the Federal government. In such coalitions the N.P.C. was nearly always the senior partner.

The next stage of development was the Action Group crisis of 1962. In 1959 Chief Awolowo resigned as Premier of Western Nigeria to become Leader of the Opposition in a Federal Parliament controlled by a N.P.C.–N.C.N.C. coalition. Thus he relinquished the Premiership of the Western Region to Chief S. L. Akintola who had also held office in the Nigerian Youth Movement.

With their position firmly secure in the Western Region but contested at the centre, two courses of action were open to them if they were to gain control of the Federal Parliament. The Action Group must either team up with the other Southern party, the N.C.N.C., and thus overcome the numerical supremacy of the North, or agree to join the N.P.C. and the N.C.N.C. in forming a national government. Chief Awolowo, leader of the Party, favoured the first course, whilst Chief Akintola, the Premier of the West and deputy leader of the A.G., favoured the second. Thus the Party split into two: the more radical elements turned towards Awolowo and the more conservative to Akintola. Awolowo's new left-wing sympathies crystallised themselves in the Manifesto on Democratic Socialism which the Party published in 1960. In preparing this he had solicited the aid of certain non-party intellectuals, notably Dr. Oyenuga, Professor of Agriculture, and Dr. S. A. Aluko, Lecturer in Economics at the University of Ife, and others, many of whom belonged to the Committee for Civil Liberties—a non-political group of intellectuals. In October 1961 Awolowo also formed the National Reconstruction Committee, which included university lecturers and professors, some of whom may have had A.G. sympathies but did not belong to the Party. The Committee prepared papers on various aspects of the economy, including extravagance in public expenditure. This immediately prompted some of Awolowo's opponents in the Party to allege that Chief Awolowo had fallen into the hands of 'communists'.

After a long series of events which are described elsewhere,[65] Akintola was dismissed from the Party. But he soon formed a new group, the United People's Party, which remained in power by teaming up with the N.C.N.C. The Federal Government showed sympathy towards Akintola and following disturbances in the Western House of Parliament dissolved that body. Meanwhile the Federal Government attempted to destroy Awolowo politically by examining the activities of certain statutory corporations during Awolowo's Premiership. This enquiry under Justice Coker found Chief Awolowo guilty of misappropriating public funds. Dr. Aluko, who has already been mentioned in this chapter, wrote an article on 'what disgusts me in the Coker Enquiry',[66] implying in it an unnecessary partiality to Chief Akintola. For this he was prosecuted. This apparent sympathy for the Action Group would have marked him for eventual 'disciplinary action', had he not resigned with Professor Oyenuga, also well known for his sympathy for that Party.

The split within the Action Group and the subsequent polarisation of the Party into the 'radical' pro-Awolowo group and a 'conservative' pro-Akintola group (which later formed the core of Akintola's United Peoples Party) was the cause of the Oyenuga crisis. As the Professor himself recorded soon after his dismissal in 1964, plans to get rid of him had been afoot since 1962.[67]

Awolowo was later tried for treasonable felony, convicted and sentenced to ten years imprisonment. With the Chief out of the way and his Action Group reduced in strength, Akintola was now free to conduct affairs his own way. The subsequent turn of events explains the political basis of the Lagos University Crisis in 1965.

In July 1963, the Mid-West agreed in a plebiscite to form their own Region. The creation of the new Region resulted in excision of the non-Yoruba element of the Western Region. Moves were made by prominent Yorubas to effect unity in the tribe and early in 1964 they formed a new Yoruba society, the *Egbe Omo Olofin*, which was now claimed to be the correct name of the Yorubas' ancestor.[68] The keynote of Yoruba unity must be seen as a move by Akintola to retain power in the Region. With the non-Yorubas gone, it naturally followed that anyone who wished to unite the Region would attack other Nigerians at such meeting points as the federal institutions. Meanwhile Chief Akintola had rechristened his former United People's Party as the Nigerian National Democratic Party. To this new party flocked the Yorubas in the N.C.N.C. almost to a man, as did some from the Action Group. The new N.N.D.P. introduced itself in a government White Paper on the political alignment in Western Nigeria thus:

A careful study . . . would reveal a reorientation of ideas and a new basis of inter-Regional relations in the country. . . . The new Government Party, that is the N.N.D.P., or in other words the Government of Western Nigeria, based its irrevocable decision [to form a new Party] on the fact that unless the people of Western Nigeria [now consisting entirely of Yorubas] made conscious efforts to unite and work out their salvation, then they would never be able to enjoy a fair share of the riches and good heritage of their own country and fatherland, in comparison with the people of the other Regions of the Federation, where greater degrees of internal cohesion have been made.

This white paper unveils another gloomy picture of the activities of the N.C.N.C. which prove beyond doubt that its leaders from another Region have been taking their erstwhile Yoruba colleagues for a ride. . . . Numerous cases of nepotism and other irregularities against the interest of Westerners in the appointments to Federal Boards and Corporations have been unearthed.

The *White Paper* then went on to list Federal Government institutions where the Yorubas had not been given their due share. Every conceivable Federal institution was mentioned: the railways, port authority, the airways, the electricity corporation and even admission of children to primary schools in Lagos. Naturally the University of Ibadan and its teaching hospital, the University College Hospital, came in for mention.

In a publication subsequently issued on the University of Ibadan, the N.N.D.P. said:

The Yorubas have always been in the majority on the staff of the University of Ibadan up to the beginning of the 1960/61 session, when Dr. Dike (Ibo) was appointed the Principal of the University College, Ibadan; facts abundantly indicate that tribe did not influence appointments. Merit was then the only consideration.

Counter-publications were prepared by the Ibos but these need not be dealt with here. The above declaration by the N.N.D.P. was an important indication of what was coming in Lagos University which, with Ibadan, makes up the two federally-supported universities in the country.

To fight the Federal elections of 1964, Akintola's N.N.D.P. teamed up with the N.P.C. and a number of minor parties to form the Nigerian National Alliance, while the A.G. and the N.C.N.C. formed the United Progressive Grand Alliance (U.P.G.A.).

The N.N.D.P. was determined to carry out its objective of re-instating Yoruba supremacy, and it was widely believed during the election campaigns that the Party would remove the Vice-Chancellors of the two Federal Government universities, Lagos and Ibadan (Professor Njoku and Dr. K. O. Dike), both of whom were Ibos.

Dr. Aluko, a Yoruba who resigned from Ife University and subsequently declared for the Action Group and who was at the time lecturing in economics at the University of Nigeria, Nsukka, warned of the impending Njoku crisis:

If the N.N.A. wins the Federal Election it is going to interfere more and more with the academic rights of the universities. The N.N.D.P. has not hidden it determination to appoint Vice-Chancellors of Universities on the basis of tribe, in its public statement

L

NIGERIAN POLITICAL ORGANISATIONS AND PARTIES 1908-1966

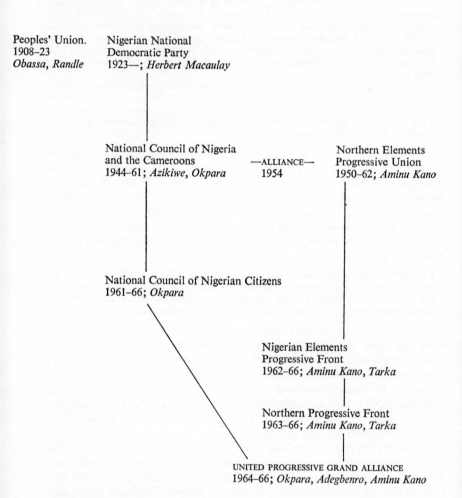

Peoples' Union. Nigerian National
1908–23   Democratic Party
Obassa, Randle   1923—; *Herbert Macaulay*

National Council of Nigeria
and the Cameroons   —ALLIANCE—   Northern Elements
1944–61; *Azikiwe, Okpara*   1954   Progressive Union
                                                  1950–62; *Aminu Kano*

National Council of Nigerian Citizens
1961–66; *Okpara*

Nigerian Elements
Progressive Front
1962–66; *Aminu Kano, Tarka*

Northern Progressive Front
1963–66; *Aminu Kano, Tarka*

UNITED PROGRESSIVE GRAND ALLIANCE
1964–66; *Okpara, Adegbenro, Aminu Kano*

Source: Modified from R. L. SKLAR in
Politics in Africa (ed. G. Carter), 1966, p. 159

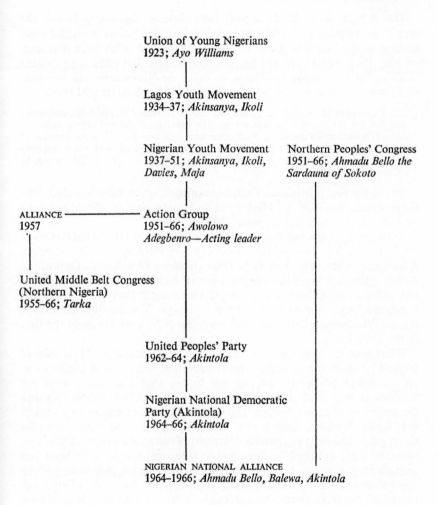

Union of Young Nigerians
1923; *Ayo Williams*

Lagos Youth Movement
1934–37; *Akinsanya, Ikoli*

Nigerian Youth Movement   Northern Peoples' Congress
1937–51; *Akinsanya, Ikoli,*   1951–66; *Ahmadu Bello the*
Davies, Maja   *Sardauna of Sokoto*

ALLIANCE ——————————— Action Group
1957   1951–66; *Awolowo*
                         Adegbenro—Acting leader

United Middle Belt Congress
(Northern Nigeria)
1955–66; *Tarka*

United Peoples' Party
1962–64; *Akintola*

Nigerian National Democratic
Party (Akintola)
1964–66; *Akintola*

NIGERIAN NATIONAL ALLIANCE
1964–1966; *Ahmadu Bello, Balewa, Akintola*

challenging the rights of the Ibos to the Vice-Chancellorships of Ibadan and Lagos
Universities. It has lined up puppets to replace one or both of these illustrious Nigerians, should the N.N.D.P. win.

The N.N.A. won the December 1964 Federal election, although the
results were disputed. Clearly thereafter Njoku did not have much longer
to serve as the Vice-Chancellor of Lagos. At the end of his three year term
on May 1965, he relinquished his post. No wonder that when appeals were
made to the government to intervene during the Njoku crisis the Minister
of Education, who was N.N.D.P. member for Ibadan, refused thus:

This Parliament in its wisdom, passed the Lagos University Act of 1962, and under
that Act the Provisional Act was set up. The Provisional Council acting within its
powers, takes certain decisions. No matter what one may feel about the decision of
this Council on the Lagos University, the Provisional Council, which is a statutory
body acting within its powers and having every right to do what it did, cannot be
validly challenged.

But of the ten Provisional Council members, seven were Yorubas. The
Government was N.N.A.; Njoku was an Ibo. In view of all that has been
said above, the implications were obvious.

Thus the Oyenuga and Njoku crises were precipitated by tribal factors in
Nigerian politics. That of Ife University was intra-tribal with Oyenuga,
Aluko and others who had *Egbe Omo Oduduwa* (Awolowo's Opposition
Action group) sympathies ranged against Akintola's *Egbe Omo Olofin*
(Akintola's ruling, Nigerian National Democratic Party). On the other
hand, the Lagos University crisis was a straight Yoruba–Ibo affair, with
many of the leading Yorubas in the coalition N.N.A. and most of the Ibos
in the U.P.G.A.

What were the issues involved in the Lindsay affair at the University of
Nigeria? It does appear that the most important factor is that Lindsay was
an expatriate European. This is not to say that Europeans were not
welcome in Nigeria. But the peculiar history of Nsukka is closely tied with
the history of Nigerian politics. The Chancellorship, an executive post, was
held by Dr. Nnamdi Azikiwe (see chapters 3 and 8), whose aspiration for
thirty years had been to found a university. Professor Lindsay's criticisms,
some of them couched in intemperate language, would have been bad
enough from a Nigerian, but coming from a European, they were nothing
more than a sort of 'neo-colonialism' reflecting the older form of colonialism which Nigerian politicans had fought from 1908 onwards. It would not
be tolerated in a university whose Chancellor had laboured to 'Restore the
dignity of (Negro) Man' by its founding.

It will be recalled that during the Lagos University crisis violent attacks
had been launched against the European expatriate staff. This was not
merely a question of xenophobia, but of a continued deep-seated distrust
of apparent reminders of colonial days. This political distrust is naturally
more pronounced in Nigerians who had played active roles in pre-

independence politics, with its sustained and continuous attack on the British 'imperialists'. It is perhaps a little more than coincidental that Chief H. O. Davies should have been the first to attack expatriates publicly during the Lagos University crisis:

> The unwarranted 'butting-in' of the Deans [all six were expatriates, British, American] amounts to a naked form of neo-imperialism. Divide and rule was the method of the imperialists and we thought we had seen the last of that.

It will be remembered that Chief H. O. Davies was the 'sole genius', according to Chief Awolowo, who thirty years earlier, in 1936, had helped to reorganise Nigeria's first modern nationalist party. He was, with Dr. Azikiwe, one of the famous 'volcanic nationalist quartet' of the Nigerian Youth Movement in the 1930s who drew crowds when they were billed to speak.[69]

At the University of Nigeria, issues were not complicated by tribal factors. It was a straight forward affair. But Lindsay did not appreciate the aspirations behind the foundation of Nsukka, which, like Nigeria's independence, was only four years old in 1964.

The extent of the violation of academic freedom

Academic freedom has been earlier defined as pertaining to the freedom of an institution of higher learning to decide who, what, and how to teach or what research to undertake. When this freedom exists autonomy automatically follows, but autonomy cannot exist without academic freedom in the modern sense.

With this in mind we will now examine the three cases under study and see to what extent, if at all, academic freedom was violated. Inevitably the discussion must involve an examination of the Constitutions of Nigerian universities, a topic which will be dealt with more fully in Chapter 13.

A feature common to, and which is indeed necessary for, the functioning of universities, is that the teachers themselves (the Senate) should control the academic affairs of the university. When this is so a basis is established for the existence of academic freedom.

Of the three cases under study, seemingly the most glaring case of an infringement of academic freedom was that of Professor Lindsay. This case was complicated by his claim to be Head of the History Department. But the issue which triggered events leading to termination of his employment was that he criticised the University of Nigeria for being 'naïve and grandiose' in the introduction of certain courses. According to him, the University was either not at that time in a position to teach these subjects because of staff shortage, or that they would be better taught in a university better positioned geographically. Clearly Professor Lindsay, as he quite correctly pointed out, was exercising his right as a Senate member under Clause 14(1) of the University Law, 1961. This clause places responsibility for the 'development and supervision of all academic matters' on the Senate. Professor Lindsay's memorandum to his colleagues in the Senate was an exercise of a right legally conferred on him. In this instance he could not agree with the Council that Archeology and the subjects mentioned in his letter could be efficiently taught in the University at that time.

Yet as has been shown earlier, the possession of academic freedom also demands of university teachers a certain decorum of conduct and an awareness of the peculiarities of the environment. Professor Lindsay did not show this. The cantankerous criticisms, for example of the upkeep of the University campus, and the tone of his letters reflected less than a sense of respect for the authorities of the University. Ohe is immediately aware of the contrast between Professor Lindsay's letters and the constructiveness of that of Professor Oyenuga.

The cases of Professor Njoku and Professor Oyenuga are not easily shown to have been evidences of breaches of academic freedom. In the case of Professor Njoku, notwithstanding any political or other motives behind the decision of the Council to appoint Dr. Biobaku rather than Njoku, the Council was acting completely within its legal rights. It is true that the Council did not accept the recommendation of the Senate, thereby breaking a convention firmly established in British universities, but not, so far, in Nigeria. There was, however, no interference with that autonomy which arises from 'the freedom to decide what and how to teach or study and whom to teach'. The Vice-Chancellor is the Head of the university, including the teachers and the administrators. The possibility of a breach of academic freedom and therefore of autonomy could be remotely inferred in the Lagos University controversy in that Professor Njoku was also regarded as being a teacher, by virtue of his Vice-Chancellorship. In that case the teachers themselves (the Senate) had decided in accordance with their freedom who should teach amongst them.

It may be observed in this connection that the University of Nigeria Law, 1961, contravenes the basic principle of academic freedom. For although Section 14(1) states that 'Subject to the Provisions of this Law and the Statutes, the Senate is responsible to the University Council for the development and supervision of all academic matters.' the power to decide who shall teach is vested legally in the Council, thus (Statute 7d):

> Where a vacancy occurs in any position on the academic or administrative staff, other than the Vice-Chancellor, the Council shall after advertisement appoint a suitable person to fill such a vacancy and may, for adequate cause, suspend the person so appointed from his duties or terminate his appointment.

The convention, however, is that the academics themselves choose the new teacher, having considered his academic and other credentials. A member of the Council is usually present on the board of interview, but the panel consists predominantly of teachers; often the Council is represented in that a member representing the Senate is on the Council.

Academic freedom is an institutional freedom and if the Council is regarded as the legal embodiment of the university any interpretation of its legal right to appoint staff as being a breach of academic freedom becomes invalid.

In the case of Professor Oyenuga, an Ibadan High Court awarded him damages against the Provisional Council for salaries and emoluments due in lieu of notice of the termination of his appointment. But suppose he had been given the appropriate notice, and then dismissed: would there still have been a breach of academic freedom? Unless it had been shown by his colleagues that he was not fit to teach either because his work was inadequate or for some other reason, then there would indeed have been such a breach: the charge against Professor Oyenuga was 'insubordination', not 'academic incompetence'.

The award of damages to Professor Oyenuga's colleagues who resigned in protest is a landmark in the history of Nigerian academic freedom. Dr. Aluko and the other lecturers concerned resigned voluntarily and their employment was not terminated by the Provisional Council. The Ibadan Court was thus creating a precedent which may have far-reaching consequences in the future entrenchment of academic freedom in Nigerian Universities.

Notes

[1] RALPH F. FUCHS in *Academic Freedom*, ed. HANS W. BAADE and ROBINSON O. EVERETT, New York 1964, p. 1.
[2] ROBERT M. MACIVER, *Academic Freedom in our Time*, Columbia University, 1955, p. 6.
[3] FUCHS, *loc. cit.*
[4] *Ibid.*, p. 5.
[5] JOHN S. BRUBACHER and WILLIS RUDY, *Higher Education in Transition*, New York, 1958, pp. 171–2.
[6] *Ibid.*, Chapters 6 and 11, *passim;* see also Fuchs, *op. cit.*, p. 2, note 5.
[7] MACIVER, *op. cit.*
[8] LORD CHORLEY, 'Academic Freedom in the United Kingdom', in BAADE and EVERETT, *op. cit.*, p. 232.
[9] ERIC ASHBY and MARY ANDERSON, 'Autonomy and academic freedom in Britain and in English-speaking countries of Tropical Africa', *Minerva*, 4, 1966, pp. 320–1.
[10] *Ibid.*, p. 317.
[11] *Ibid.*, p. 321.
[11a] P. MACKINTOSH, *Nigerian Government and Politics*, 1966 p. 459.
[12] *Daily Express*, Lagos. 23 November 1963, p. 2.
[13] Except where expressly stated, the events leading to the dismissal of Professor Oyenuga are taken from *Minerva*, 2(3), 1964, pp. 395–9.

[14] *Daily Express*, Lagos, 25 November 1963.
[15] *Ibid.*, 21 December 1963.
[16] *Ibid.*, 21 and 23 December 1963. *Minerva*, 2(2), 1964, p. 269.
[17] *Minerva, loc. cit. The Daily Service*, Lagos, 27 December 1963; *The Daily Times* Lagos, 6 February 1964.
[18] *Minerva, loc. cit.*
[19] *Minerva*, 3(2), 1965, p. 272.
[20] *University of Nigeria—Lindsay Correspondence*, complete correspondence, 12 May 1964 to 2 March 1965, privately printed, Jamaica, 1965.
[21] *Ibid.*, pp. 1–2.
[22] *Ibid.*, p. 2.
[23] *Ibid.*, p. 3.
[24] *Ibid.*, p. 5.
[25] *Ibid.*, pp. 5–6.
[26] *Ibid.*, p. 7.
[27] *Ibid.*
[28] *Ibid.*, p. 8.
[29] *The Daily Times*, Lagos, 1 March 1965.
[30] *Ibid.*, 5 March 1965.
[31] *Daily Express*, Lagos, 3 March 1965.
[32] *Ibid.*, 2 March 1965.
[33] *Ibid.*, 11 March 1965; *Daily Times*, Lagos. 11 March 1965.
[34] *The Daily Express*, Lagos, 12 March 1965.
[35] *Ibid.*, 17 March 1965.
[36] Nsukka release.
[37] *The Daily Express*, 3 March 1965.
[38] *Ibid.*, 18 March 1965.
[39] *Ibid.*, 3 March 1965.
[40] *Ibid.*, 5 March 1965.
[41] For the details of the various manœuvres by the Senate, Council, Senior Staff Association, the Association of University Teachers, and an 'internal' attempt at reconciliation by the Prime Minister, see the various publications produced at the time by the different sides. *Change in Vice-Chancellorship: An Official Publication, University of Lagos*, Lagos, n.d.; *The Truth about the Change in Vice-Chancellorship, University of Lagos* by Berrie, Fielstra, Nicholson, Nsugbe, Nwabueze and Nwaefuna, published by the authors, Lagos, n.d.; *The Crisis over the appointment of Vice-Chancellor of University of Lagos*, by the Senior Members of the staff of the University, Lagos, 19 March 1965; *The Crisis at the University of Lagos: Implications and Way Out*, by the Senior Members of the Staff, the University of Lagos, Lagos, 5 May 1965; *The Inspired Crisis over the Appointment of Vice-Chancellor of the University of Lagos*, by the other Senior Members of Staff, The University of Lagos, Lagos, 24 March 1965.
[42] JAMES COLEMAN, *Nigeria: Background to Nationalism*, California, 1960, pp. 178–9.
[43] R. L. BUELL, *The Native Problem in Africa*, London, 1928, Vol. 1, p. 662.
[44] DAVID KIMBLE, *Political History of Ghana*, Oxford, 1962, pp. 381–3.
[45] COLEMAN, *op. cit.*, pp. 196–200.
[46] NNAMDI AZIKIWE; *The Development of Political Parties in Nigeria*, London, 1957, p. 6.
[47] OBAFEMI AWOLOWO, *Awo*, Cambridge, 1960, p. 131.
[48] *Ibid.*, p. 133.
[49] *Ibid.*, p. 134.
[50] *Ibid., passim*, esp. Chapter 11.
[51] COLEMAN, *op. cit.*, pp. 227–9.
[52] RICHARD L. SKLAR, *Nigerian Political Parties*, Princeton University, 1963, pp. 52–55.
[53] AWOLOWO, *op. cit.*, p. 132.

[54] P. E. H. HAIR: 'An analysis of the Register of Fourah Bay College, 1827–1950'. *Sierra Leone Studies*, New Series 7, 1956, pp. 157–8.

[55] The impression is confirmed by looking at the newspapers published in Nigeria up to the 1920s and early 1930s.

[56] K. A. B. JONES–QUARTEY, *A life of Azikiwe*, London, 1965, p. 115.

[57] COLEMAN, *op. cit.*, p. 333.

[58] *Ibid.*, p. 341.

[59] *Ibid.*, p. 340.

[60] *Ibid.*, pp. 264–5, 341.

[61] *Ibid.*, p. 344.

[62] AWOLOWO, *op. cit.*, p. 166.

[63] OLUWOLE ALAKIJA, *Egbe Omo Oduduwa*, 1, December 1948, p. 4; quoted in COLEMAN, *op. cit.* p. 30.

[64] AWOLOWO, *op. cit.*, p. 220.

[65] The events from the split of the Action Group in 1962 to the crisis following the Federal elections in 1964 have been well-covered in great detail by RICHARD L. SKLAR, 'Nigerian Politics: The Ordeal of Chief Awolowo, 1960–65', *Politics in Africa—7 Cases*, Gwendolin M. Carter, ed., New York, 1966, pp. 119–65.

[66] *The Sunday Express*, Lagos, 27 January 1963.

[67] *The Daily Times*, Lagos, 6 February 1964.

[68] SKLAR, 'The Ordeal of Chief Awolowo', in CARTER, *op. cit.*

[69] AWOLOWO, *op. cit.*, p. 133.

12 Courses, Degrees, Certificates offered by Nigerian Universities

It is important that the curricula of the universities be examined, for these form the most direct areas of relations between the teachers and students. The choice and organisation of degree courses develops that contact between 'senior' and 'junior' scholars which is one of the main tasks of universities anywhere.

The curricula also afford the university the opportunity to show awareness of the needs of its environment. In other words, the curricula of a university provide an important area for adaptation in any country, but especially so in countries which like Nigeria are not only new to university tradition but have had to introduce the systems of other countries without much initial opportunity for adaptation.

The entrance qualification

The minimum qualifications for the Universities of Ahmadu Bello, Ibadan, Ife, and Lagos are five subjects at the General Certificate of Education, two of which must be at the Advanced Level; *or* four subjects, three of which are at Advanced Level. One of the subjects must be the English language. But at Ibadan, Lagos, and Ahmadu Bello, this English language requirement may be given special consideration where candidates show special ability in the science subjects if such candidates intend to study for a degree in agriculture, engineering, medicine or science.

In addition, these four universities have concessional entry for students fresh from school who hold the G.C.E. Ordinary Level in five subjects including English and mathematics. Such candidates sit an entrance examination and if successful, undergo a year's preliminary course (at Ahmadu Bello, two years) before being admitted to the Degree Courses. The concession extends especially to students in the science subjects, including agriculture, forestry and medicine. At Ibadan it extends to Arts and at Ahmadu Bello there is also a preliminary course in Arabic and Islamic Studies.

The University of Nigeria, Nsukka, differs from the others in having a minimum entrance qualification of passes in six subjects at the G.C.E. Ordinary Level (or five credits in the West African School Certificate), provided that these subjects are passed at one and the same sitting and include a language and either mathematics or an approved science subject. The minimum qualifications are thus the same as those necessary for admission to a preliminary course at the other universities.

At the University of Nigeria students admitted by entrance examination spend four years to obtain a degree in most subjects, excluding engineering, which takes five. Those who come in by direct entry, i.e. who have a minimum of two Advanced Level and three Ordinary Level subjects in the G.C.E., spend three years. Thus the system is similar in essence to that adopted in the other universities.

The institution of 'Concessional Entry' at the four Nigerian universities, and the provision of an entrance examination for 'O' Level students at the University of Nigeria, have been necessitated by the lack of a sufficient number of sixth-form schools, expecially in science. It reflects also a commendable awareness of the great shortage of scientists in the country in that some universities are prepared to waive the English language as a requirement for those would-be science students who exhibit special ability in the appropriate subjects. The preliminary course in Islamic Studies at Ahmadu Bello also fulfils an important need in introducing Islam as a university subject in a country where a large proportion of the inhabitants are Muslims.

These concessions do not in any way indicate a lowering of standards, for Concessional Entrance operated at Ibadan even when that University was under 'special relationship' with the University of London. They are temporary measures and are bound to disappear as more and more schools with 'Sixth Forms' come into operation. That there is a genuine shortage of such schools in the *sciences* is indicated by the preponderance in three successive years (Table 7) of those who applied to enter Nsukka by entrance examination, over those who wished to do so by direct entry.

In general then the minimum entrance qualification into four Nigerian universities is similar to that required for entrance into United Kingdom universities, whereas that of Nsukka resembles rather that for admission to universities in the United States of America.

The Vice-Chancellors' Committee is stated to have agreed in principle to a proposal for a Common Entrance Board for all the universities.[1] It is doubtful if such a move would achieve any useful purpose. Different universities in any country, and even different departments within the same university, may demand different qualities—dexterity in dissections for instance—provided the candidate possesses a certain minimum intellectual ability.

Degree structure and courses offered

The length of the degree course in most subjects (excluding the professional subjects, e.g. medicine) in Nigerian universities where the entrance

Table 7

Applications received from students qualified to enter the various Faculties of the University of Nigeria by direct entry and by entrance examination

	1962/63				1963/64				1964/65			
	Direct Entry		Entrance Exam.		Direct Entry		Entrance Exam.		Direct Entry		Entrance Exam.	
	M*	F*	M	F	M	F	M	F	M	F	M	F
Agriculture	–	–	–	–	34	1	10	2	44	1	131	13
Arts	247	6	71	10	139	11	178	7	218	15	74	21
Business Administration	–	–	–	–	–	–	–	–	496	1	149	26
Education	–	–	–	–	126	–	125	2	129	3	130	22
Engineering	–	–	–	–	45	–	10	–	80	–	134	1
Law	–	–	–	–	31	–	44	–	49	11	17	4
Science	150	3	253	10	51	4	21	1	76	6	205	29
Social Studies	731	3	163	10	538	4	476	4	–	7	53	4
Technology†	65	–	85	7	–	–	–	–	–	–	–	–
Grand totals	1193	12	572	37	964	20	864	16	1092	34	893	120

* Male/Female
† The Faculty of Technology was abolished after 1963. It consisted of the following departments: Architecture, Engineering, Fine Arts, Home Economics, Music, Physical Education, Secretarial Studies, and Surveying.

Source: *Annual Report, University of Nigeria, 1962–63; 1963–64; 1964–65*

qualification is three 'A' Level subjects, is three years; the period spent in undergoing a preliminary course does not count towards a degree. At the University of Nigeria, Nsukka, when the student is admitted with 'O' Level qualifications (i.e. by entrance examination), he spends a total of four years. Those admitted with 'A' Level qualifications (i.e. by direct entry), complete the degree in three years.

In all Nigerian universities, single subject Honours degrees in Science and Arts are the exception rather than the rule. Until recently Ibadan followed closely the pattern of its senior associate, London University, and gave single-subject Honours degrees, a situation which earned it strong criticism[2] in some quarters. The trend, even in Britain, has been for a broadening of the degree course. Undoubtedly influenced by practice in the United States of America, this trend is apparent in the United Kingdom in the new English universities—Keele, Sussex, et cetera. A similar tendency is recently noticeable in Nigerian universities—including Ibadan. In Ahmadu Bello, Ibadan, Ife and Lagos, the typical 'A' Level entrant who spends three years, studies three subjects in his first year and continues with two of these in his second and third years. At one end of the scale is Ahmadu Bello, where the student also does a subsidiary subject in his second and third years; at the other end is Ife, where after the first year the student may choose *one* or two subjects for study in the remaining two years.

At the University of Nigeria, there is a broadening of the curricula, which is ensured not only by the general studies programme but also by the system of electives. The programme of that University will be discussed in greater detail below. The courses offered by the universities are given in Tables 8 and 9.

General education at Nigerian universities

To discuss the topic of general education one must ask what indeed are the aims of higher education? These aims must vary in detail from one society to another, and even in the same society from one phase of its history to another. Broadly, however, they may be put down under four heads. First there is the acquisition of skills, which will reward successful participation in higher education with employment and a means of sustenance. Second, there is the advancement of learning, which though quite practicable outside, is most rewarding, due to the student-teacher contact, inside the universities. Third, a training of the mind takes place which makes it possible for even narrow specialists to develop cultivated minds, able to see problems in their wider contexts. Finally, higher education, like the other forms of education, should provide the students with a common citizenship, with an opportunity to transmit the best in the accumulated culture of the society.[3]

All universities, to exist at all, carry out the first and second functions. Where universities have not efficiently fostered the growth of the third and fourth, they have been rightly accused of being mere factories for turning out degree holders or technicians. Under such conditions the universities, to use the words of an eminent Nigerian academican, 'fail to bring about that development and enrichment of the individual which should foster in him a sense of social and civic responsibility as well as appreciation of beauty in art, music and ethics'.[4] In Nigeria, as in the rest of Africa with a history of colonialism and with a large illiterate population, the need arises

Table 8

Degree courses offered in Nigerian Universities as in 1965/66

Degree course	Ahmadu Bello	Ibadan	Ife	Lagos	Nigeria
Accountancy				√	√
Agriculture		√	√		
Agricultural Economics					√
Agricultural Engineering					√
Agricultural Mechanisation					√
Anatomy		√			
Animal Science					√
Anthropology					√
Architecture	√				√
Arabic and Islamic Studies	√	√			
Biochemistry		√			
Botany	√	√	√	√	√
Business Administration	√ *			√	√
Chemistry	√	√	√	√	√
Classics		√			
Drama		√			
Economics	√	√	√	√	√
Education	√	√		√	√
Engineering (Civil)	√			√	√
Engineering (Electrical)	√			√	√
Engineering (Mechanical)	√			√	√
English	√	√	√	√	√
Fine Arts	√				√
Forestry		√			
French (Language)	√	√		√	√
Geography	√	√	√	√	√
Greek		√			
History	√	√	√	√	√

Degree course	Ahmadu Bello	Ibadan	Ife	Lagos	Nigeria
Home Economics					√
Journalism					√
Laboratory Technology		√			
Land Economics					√
Languages†	√	√			√
Latin		√			
Law	√		√	√	√
Mathematics	√	√	√	√	√
Medicine		√		√	
Music					√
Nursing		√			
Pharmacy		√			
Pharmacology		√			
Philosophy			√		√
Physical Education					√
Physics	√	√	√	√	√
Physiology		√			
Physiotherapy		√			√
Plant-Soil Science					√
Political Science (Government)		√	√	√	√
Psychology		√		√	√
Radiography		√			
Religion		√	√		√
Sociology		√			√
Statistics		√			
Vocational Teacher Education					√
Veterinary Science		√			√
Zoology	√	√	√	√	√

* B.A. (Administration) with option to specialise in Business Administration, International Affairs or Public Administration.
† Including Nigerian Languages.

Cource: 1964/65 Calendars of the five Universities.

for graduates who are not only so broadly educated that they appreciate their local cultures in the larger context of the world, but also are able to provide the leadership necessary in a largely illiterate society. Indeed the need for education outside that essential for the acquisition of skills is becoming recognised the world over.

Table 9

Certificates/Diplomas awarded by the various Nigerian Universities in 1965/66

	Ahmadu Bello	Ibadan	Ife	Lagos	Nigeria
Diploma/Certificate in Arabic	√	√			
Diploma in Librarianship		√			
Diploma/Certificate in Education	√	√		√	
Advanced Post-graduate Diploma in the teaching of English as a second language		√			
Certificate of Proficiency in Modern Languages (French, Hausa, Ibo, Yoruba)				√	
Diploma in Public Administration	√		√		
Diploma in Physical Education	√				
Diploma in Co-operative Management	√				
Diploma in Law	√				
Diploma in Music Education					√
Diploma in Animal Health and Husbandry					√
Diploma in Religious Studies		√			√
Diploma in Secretarial Studies					√
Post-graduate Diploma in Drama		√			
Post-graduate Diploma in Phonetics and Linguistics		√			
Post-graduate Diploma in Analytical Chemistry		√			

	Ahmadu Bello	Ibadan	Ife	Lagos	Nigeria
Diploma in Tropical Health	✓				
Diploma in Public Health	✓				
Post-graduate Diploma in Agricultural Extension	✓				
Post-graduate Diploma in Statistics		✓			
Associateship Certificate in Education		✓			
Certificate in Education and Adult Education		✓			

In England higher education was originally mainly the preserve of the aristocracy and the wealthy, and was imparted at Oxford and Cambridge. The young student entering these institutions already had some education from the very company he had at home. He went to the university as it were, to become rounded off as a 'gentleman' through contact with other students, through imbibing the traditions of the ancient institutions and through the guidance of a senior member of the university, his tutor. For about six centuries, Oxford and Cambridge remained the only universities in England, until Durham was founded after the pattern of the other two. When London University was founded in the nineteenth century it began first as a correspondence college. Obviously the informal general education at Oxford and Cambridge could not be imparted. The pattern then developed in England and British Commonwealth countries that no special provision be made by the university for the general education of students, apart from their own discussion with fellow-students, from attending lectures outside their degree requirement, and so on—in short, through their own efforts.

In the United States, due again to historical reasons and especially the need to weld together the various nationalities which their population comprises, it became necessary to arrange consciously a system of general education for the student.

What is the need for general education in Nigerian universities? If there is one, how are the universities meeting it? Nigeria is a new state and one made of many differing ethnic groups. Therefore a general education which *inter alia* teaches the student something of the culture, traditions and the attributes of the various groups would be an undeniable asset in fostering mutual respect and harmonious co-existence among them.

Furthermore, Negro Africa has been at the receiving end of the

M

devastating and ruthless exploitation of human beings through slavery. The 'civilising' imposition of the culture of the colonising foreign (European) powers over its own has led to the attrition and stunted growth in some areas of Africa's indigenous culture. Negro Africa therefore needs to restore some of its lost self-confidence by a proper appreciation of its own culture and that of other peoples. A well-planned general education can achieve this end, and nowhere more so than in the training of its would-be leaders. Besides all this is the fact that, in a largely illiterate society, the general populace looks upon its educated countrymen for leadership in fields outside those in which the university graduate may have received his major university training.

A final reason for conscious general education is that specialisation in narrow fields of study is becoming the trend, with increased knowledge. The non-specialist is therefore often helped to communicate or to begin to understand the specialist if he has some knowledge, no matter how small, of how the specialist thinks. Thus general education at a university must be seen partly as equipping the student for an education which he will develop and acquire himself in later life.

Of the Nigerian universities, the University of Lagos and the University of Nigeria, Nsukka, stand out as those where general education is consciously introduced into the programme. At the University of Lagos, according to the University's Calendar for the 1965/66 session, all students, irrespective of their courses of study, undertake in the first year a course on General African Studies. In the second year the Law and Arts students and some in the Faculty of Business and Social Studies take, besides their major subjects, an Introduction to Science and Technology. French (occasionally, German or Russian) is studied at some point in the training of these students. The science and engineering students, after taking the General African Studies course in the first year follow a course in Introduction to Modern Thought in their second and may be required to study French, German, or Russian in the third.

At the University of Nigeria, Nsukka (in 1965/66), students who complete the four-year Degree programme must attain a minimum aggregate of 192 credit hours (see below for explanation) and, except in architecture, engineering and surveying, not more than 220 credit hours. Usually of these, 48 credit hours must be spent in the Division of General Studies. The Calendar for 1965/66 states the function of the Division of General Studies, as being 'to establish the broad basis of knowledge required for effective modern citizenship and to indicate the unity of existence by stressing the interrelationship of all knowledge. Thereby, in conjunction with the student's major studies, the Division of General Studies prepares the graduate for useful service to Nigeria and mankind, in any place or in any capacity in which he finds himself.'[5] The General Studies programme is divided into four sections: Use of English (9 credits),

Natural Science (12 credits), Humanities (12 credits) and Social Studies (15 credits). Students who enter the University by direct entry do not take two of these courses; if they are direct entry Science students they usually do not take Natural Science. Studies relevant to Africa are introduced in these courses.

At the other end of the scale are Ahmadu Bello, Ibadan and Ife, which do not offer any general education courses at all.

Defending the Ibadan situation, the then Vice-Chancellor of Ibadan, told the Congregation on 17 November 1965:

> It is true that we have not, as in some West African universities, introduced a General Studies Course in African History and Culture. We have considered the idea and rejected it on the grounds that a compulsory course in African Culture will defeat its purpose: it will stimulate just those students who would have chosen the course in African Studies anyway, and create positive distaste for African Studies in the minority it is seeking to convert. We chose instead to spread African Studies throughout our courses and emphasized the necessity of teaching all courses in a way relevant to African conditions. The chances are now very narrow indeed of a student passing through the Faculty of Arts without studying some material bearing on indigenous African culture and institutions. Even if he does not take African History or Geography, he would do African Traditional Religion, Literature, Politics, Economics, Sociology, or Linguistics. Even if he does Classics, he could still [be] offer[ed] one of these subjects in his first year. His Classics would also include some ancient history of North Africa and some comparison between classical institutions such as Oracles and the politics of the City States and those of traditional African Societies.[6]

A number of points emerge from this. First, it appears that African Studies are a course of study meant only for Arts students. But the arguments put forward earlier indicate that a broadening of outlook beyond that necessary to fit one into a particular type of employment is particularly essential in an African environment. Non-Arts students, e.g. medical students, whose subjects may be highly specialised, equally need African studies. Perhaps they need them more, as such a course may be the only form of non-science general education they are ever likely to encounter.

Second, the idea that a compulsory course in African Studies will defeat its purpose by instilling a dislike of the subject into unwilling students, stems from an incomplete acceptance on the part of that University of the central importance of introducing the students to the history and heritage of their continent. It is similar to saying that the compulsory study of French for some Arts degrees necessarily induces a dislike in the language for those who go on to specialise in, say, geography.

Third, while it is true that all subjects taught in African universities should, where relevant, make the local situation the centre of their studies, there is a major difficulty. Most university textbooks are written in and for other countries, especially Europe and America. Examples and illustrations are usually drawn in these textbooks from these non-African countries. At present there is not enough material to re-write and/or adapt these textbooks to African conditions. In the interim period, what material there is on Africa should therefore be presented as far as possible in a single course or courses. Where such material is available then a compulsory course should be instituted. At the University of Ife, for instance, the optional subjects for Part I Law students were African history, Nigerian history, economics, or philosophy. Perhaps a compulsory course in African or Nigerian history would be of immense benefit to the Nigerian lawyer who practices in Nigeria, rather than either economics or (European) philosophy.

As one European observer put it in 1962:

> It is clearly one of the most important functions of West African universities to put African Studies at the core of the curriculum—I would say of all university curricula including those in science and technology. Othersise universities [having been imported from Europe] will not take root in West Africa . . . An African can graduate with a B.A. knowing practically nothing about the intricate political and social structure of his own race: the fascinating and complex network of organization among the Kede on the Niger . . . the reverence for the earth among the Tallensi and the ingenious checks and balances which protect them from autocracy and which contribute to good government; the economics of Yoruba trading; the laws of ownership and inheritance of land among the Ibo. . . . And this is not just interesting antiquarian knowledge: it is essential knowledge for the African intellectual who will become a civil servant or a teacher and who has the challenging responsibility of leading the common people from the old Africa to the new.[7]

At Ife University, the Faculty of Arts attempts to educate non-Science students by providing a series of lectures for them on science topics. The course is optional and does not count towards the degree. No reciprocal course is organised for science students.

Equivalence and standard of degree courses at Nigerian universities

Not only must the curricula of the various Nigerian universities reflect local conditions, but these universities must simultaneously strive to attain internationally recognised standards. It is for the purpose of attaining such standards that the 'Asquith University Colleges', of which Ibadan was one, originally granted, not their own degrees, but those of the University of London, with which they had a 'Special Relationship'. This pattern was in vogue in England during the 1940s when the Asquith Commission met. After the Second World War the pattern in that country changed. For instance, the University College of North Staffordshire (it became the University of Keele in 1962) received its charter in 1949 and was allowed to grant its own degrees from the beginning. Instead of attachment to another university by special relationship, an Academic Council, the majority of whose members were representatives of some of the older universities, oversaw the academic programme of the new university. The pattern in England now appears to be one in which Academic Councils of the above type supervise for a limited period the academic activities of new universities.[8]

But a period of sponsorship of whatever type does not necessarily guarantee a continuous maintenance of high standards at the expiration of that sponsorship. In Britain something of an equivalence of standards among universities is maintained by the system of 'external examiners' in which teachers from other universities are present for, and participate in, all or part of the degree examinations of a university.

Nigeria has copied that pattern and external examiners are drawn not only from Nigerian universities but also from other countries, notably the United Kingdom and the United States. Indeed, the Laws establishing the Universities of Ahmadu Bello and Ibadan enjoin that their respective Senates arrange for external examiners.

The Ashby Commission, which recommended the founding of new Nigerian universities, thought that 'it would not be in the national interest if one single pattern were to be imposed on all Nigerian higher education. The hope for Nigerian higher education lies in its diversity.'[9] Nigerian universities founded after Ibadan (i.e. Nsukka, Lagos, Ahmadu Bello and Ife) all granted their own degrees from the start. Thus the danger of evolving a single pattern was arrested, since each of the universities went its own way with no period of tutelage.

Other methods of maintaining an equivalence of degrees exist in other parts of the world. For instance in the United States, where there is no extensive official inter-university organisation, an equivalence of degrees is maintained by a free and voluntary system of 'accreditation' in which some universities set high standards for themselves and admit other universities only if they measure up to this standard.[10]

The equivalence of degrees earned in four years with G.C.E. 'O' Level and those earned after three with G.C.E. 'A' Level has been a source of argument. The first type pertains at Nsukka and also exists in many non-European countries, e.g. South Africa and the United States. The second type, adopted at the other Nigerian universities, is the practice in England. There have been claims and counterclaims for the superiority and draw-backs of each system. According to an English academic, Sir Charles Morris, since the English degree is taken five years after 'O' Level or School Certificate (SC) and that of the non-European countries just mentioned in four years, the first degrees in these countries is broadly speaking one year behind the English degree.[11]

On the other hand, an American writing on the topic said 'Most Americans, and some British, maintain that an American Bachelor's Degree, certainly one from a leading institution, ranks as high as a Bachelor's Degree from a British oriented institution; that it is obtained in sixteen years of schooling in lieu of the British seventeen years, thereby indicating one year "wasted" under the British-type system.'[12]

In Nigeria, the National Universities Commission, in discussing the issue, doubted whether four years from 'O' Level at Nsukka would be equivalent in academic achievement to three years from 'A' Level at other universities, notwithstanding the General Studies given at Nsukka.[13] But this comparison stems from a lack of appreciation of the organisation of courses at Nsukka. At Nsukka, duplication of teaching is eliminated through careful and lengthy discussions between departments. Thus, although part of the student's career is spent reading General Studies, the portion of the course which is spent studying his major subject in depth is not substantially different from that in other universities. Moreover, a comparison of the actual periods spent on their studies shows that students work slightly harder than at the other universities. Nevertheless it would seem that there is a case for reducing the length of time spent on General Studies courses if only to allow more time for students to pursue their own extra reading interests.

In a country whose educational system is strongly British-influenced and where 'foreign (i.e. non-British) ways used, until recently, to be suspect, Nsukka with its association (1960–70) with an American university (Michigan State University) met at the initial stages a lukewarm, almost hostile, reception from the Nigerian public. Two events have helped the acceptance of that University. The first was the system discussed above of external examiners, which permitted some form of assessment of Nsukka *vis à vis* the other Nigerian universities. The second was the positive involvement of a leading British institution, London University, in an advisory role. Every year in January or February, two representatives each from London University, Michigan State University and the University of Nigeria itself meet for a week at Nsukka. This body, the Joint University Advisory Committee, which first convened in 1962, discusses and makes recommendations on the broad principles of the University's academic programme.

African Studies

The need for African Studies was stressed by the Ashby Commission:

> The future of Nigeria is bound with the future of Africa; and Nigeria's past lies in African history, folklore and language. It should be the first duty of Nigerian universities, therefore, to foster the study of African history and antiquities, its languages, its societies, its rocks and soils and vegetation and animal life. We know this will not be easy; before African Studies can be taught they must be codified. The textbooks still have to be written. But a start must be made and we recommend that every university should have a department or institute of African Studies, doing at first mainly research, but building up a body of knowledge which will be the material for undergraduate courses in the future. We suggest such an institute should as far as possible be inter-disciplinary, and should co-ordinate research by various departments in this vital field.[14]

African Studies have recently become a growing field in many universities all over the world. In Nigeria two universities, Ibadan and Ife, have thriving African Studies Institutes. The University of Nigeria does not seem to be making the impact it should. Ahmadu Bello and Lagos Universities in 1965/66 had no Institutes of African Studies.

The Ibadan Institute is inter-disciplinary and is financed by the Rockefeller and Ford Foundations. Its main role is to provide a common meeting ground for all those disciplines of the University which have concern with African Studies in the widest sense. In 1965/66 the Institute employed research fellows, and had three chairs in Archaeology, Linguistics and Sociology. Truly inter-disciplinary, it has appointed research fellows to work in Nigerian history, geography, oral literature and industrial relations. It also offers grants to members of the University. It holds learned meetings, symposia, lectures either alone or in conjunction with the other departments of the University, especially the Faculty of Education and Extra-mural Studies. It publishes books and a number of regular journals including *African Notes*, *Archaeological Newsletter*, and *Journal of West African Languages*.[15]

The other vigorous, active Institute is that at the University of Ife. Although this was in 1965/66 a purely research institute and hoped to attract interested research scholars from all over the world, it also has as its aim undergraduate teaching. The latter aim cannot yet be accomplished because of paucity of material.

The Institute is organised into the following six divisions:

1. Anthropology and Sociology
2. Archaeology
3. Ethno-history, Art and Folk Culture
4. Languages and Linguistics
5. The Maghreb and Arabic Influences
6. Africa-in-Transition.

Each division, although not forming a water-tight compartment, is an academic entity and offers scope for future development of academic units.

The Institute has also organised seminars, symposia, lectures, conferences and exhibitions, and publishes the journal, *Odu*.[16]

The University of Nigeria, Nsukka, has an African Studies Institute, concerned mainly with post-graduate research. In 1965/66 its activities included the production of annotated bibliographies, anthologies and readings in Africana, and the acquisition of oral and written pictorial and cartographic source material for the study of the history of government, law, religion, et cetera of Nigeria.[17]

Notes

[1] *University Development in Nigeria*, Report of the National Universities Commission, Federal Ministry of Information, Lagos, 1963, p. 11.
[2] See SIR ERIC ASHBY, *African Universities and Western Tradition.* Oxford, 1964, *passim.*
[3] *Higher Education:* Committee under the Chairmanship of Lord Robbins, Cmd. 2154, H.M.S.O. London, 1963; pp. 6–7.
[4] ENI NJOKU, *General Education in the University,* Speech delivered by the Vice-Chancellor at the formal opening of the University of Lagos Medical School, 1962, p. 2.
[5] Speaking to the Congregation of 18 September 1965, the Head of the General Studies division of the University of Nigeria explained this programme thus:

Today's world is a world filled with men who are increasingly dependent upon each other. Citizens depend upon other citizens, regions depend on other regions, nations depend on other nations. At the same time that this is true men have been increasingly separated from one another by the fragmentation of specialized training. Such a situation obviously produces a crisis in education. How can universities prepare students to live in *one world* and yet produce graduates who have no knowledge in common? This is a problem for all universities everywhere and many outstanding universities throughout the world have incorporated into their curricula general courses required of all students. The idea of such courses is an old idea, but the implementation of it in the modern world is new. Today's intellectual world is a world of esoteric specialists who speak a language only they and their fellow specialists understand, who possess a knowledge beyond the comprehension of ordinary men, and who pride themselves on the incomprehensibility of their discipline. In order to bridge the gap between such specialists it is necessary to have some common knowledge which all educated men, the world over, share with each other. Thus in our programme in General Studies at the University of Nigeria we are giving our students an opportunity to belong to a world-wide intellectual and moral community which includes men from all the nations and races of the world. When they have completed their degree programme at this University, they will recognize as fellow members of their community men from Europe, Asia, India, America, as well as men from other parts of Africa. Such a world community of like-minded citizens was desirable in the past but today it is a necessity for survival, for unless men can join with other men in a common human ideology they will separate into hostile groups and destroy one another by means of the unbelievably destructive instruments of modern warfare.

All men today want to understand the world of science. They live daily surrounded by the products of science and it is natural for them to desire to understand the intellectual institution which has made these remarkable products possible. The general studies course in natural science attempts to give students such an understanding. We want to gain a basic knowledge of the physical world in both its animate and its inanimate expressions. Whether we consider physics or chemistry, biology or astronomy, all science has a method and structure in common. It is this method and structure we are primarily concerned with. The twentieth century has no place in it for ancient superstititions, provincialisms or intolerances. One of the best ways of overcoming these is by an intensive study of modern science.

In addition to the physical world, today's student needs to understand the complex social world of which he is a part and which is a part of him. No man can separate himself from this social world. He could not exist without his fellow men; his very nature and character are formed by the social groups to which he belongs. To recognize this fact and to choose on the basis of knowledge rather than chance to which group one belongs, is a distinguishing feature of an educated man. The social science course studies the social life of man and relates the student articulately and explicitly to the many social groups which exist today.

But man is more than a physical and social being; he is also a *telic* being. Man is an animal who lives by purposes, values, and goals. The *telic* dimension of life is expressed in men's religions, arts, philosophies, and literatures. We concern ourselves with these institutions in the humanities course. Throughout our work we keep in mind that the students of this University are Nigerian students who belong to Africa, but we do not forget the relation of Nigeria to world religions and arts.

In the house of intellect there are many rooms for many kinds of people. But some of the rooms are shared by all men. The better we understand these common rooms the more humane and distinguished our lives will be and these qualities of humaneness and distinction are the mark of an educated man.

But none of the general studies is more important than the use of English. Men cannot think or communicate without symbols, and the symbol structure we all share in Nigeria is the English language. Thus our effectiveness as citizens and as human beings is measured to a large extent by our ability in using English. For this reason we all make every effort to master the skills of English usage.

[6] K. O. DIKE, *Addresses by the Vice Chancellor and Citations in support of Honorary Graduates in Trenchard Hall*, University of Ibadan, 1965, p. 5.

[7] SIR ERIC ASHBY, *The West African Intellectual Community*, Ibadan, 1962, p. 54.

[8] S. J. CURTIS, *History of Education in Great Britain*, University Tutorial Press, 1965, p. 644.

[9] *Investment in Education*, Lagos, 1960, p. 25.

[10] FRANCIS M. ROGERS, *Higher Education in the United States*, Harvard, 1963, pp. 60–62.

[11] SIR CHARLES MORRIS, 'The Functions of Universities Today' in *The Expanding University*, ed. W. R. Niblett, London, 1962, p. 20.

[12] C. WALTER HOWE, 'African Approaches to Higher Education', in *Post-primary Education and Political and Economic Development*, Duke University, 1964, pp. 165–6.

[13] *University Development in Nigeria, op. cit.*, p. 13.

[14] *Investment in Education*, Lagos, 1960, p. 23.

[15] *Calendar 1965/66*, University of Ibadan.

[16] *Calendar 1965/66*, University of Ife, Ibadan.

[17] *Calendar, 1965/66*, University of Nigeria, Nsukka.

13 Universities and Government in Nigeria: The National Universities Commission

The Ashby Commission recommended the establishment of a National Universities Commission to advise the government on the distribution of the limited funds available for higher education. It suggested that the Universities Commission should be set up by an Act of Parliament and should consist of a chairman and nine members, all part-time, giving their services free. The chairman should be a distinguished Nigerian citizen chosen for the confidence placed in him by all Nigerian citizens. Two members of the Commission, who should serve for a limited period, should be distinguished and experienced scholars from abroad. The other seven should be non-partisan Nigerians. Heads of Nigerian universities should not be eligible nor should there be any government representatives amongst the members, though the Permanent Secretary of the Federal Ministry of Education could attend as an observer. The body once established should, in consultation with the Heads of the universities, suggest a list of its own successors, while the final choice should be left to the Federal government. However, retirement from the Commission should be so arranged that continuity was ensured. A full time secretary would be required.[1]

In effect the idea of a National Universities Commission derived from Britain's University Grants Committee. The Ashby Commission recognised that while this pattern had been exported to Commonwealth countries, e.g. Australia and New Zealand, it had to be adapted to the peculiar situation of Nigeria.

The Federal government accepted the recommendation and appointed a Commission with the following terms of reference:

1. To assist in consultation with the universities and other bodies concerned in planning the balanced and co-ordinated development of the universities in order to ensure that they are fully adequate to the national needs.

2. To enquire into (and advise the government on) the financial needs, both recurrent and capital, of university education in Nigeria.

3. To receive annually a block grant from the Federal government and to allocate it to universities with such conditions attached as the Commission may think advisable.

4. To act as an agency for channelling all external aid to the universities throughout the Federation.

5. To take into account, in advising the Federal government, such grants as may be made to the institutions, both at home and abroad.

6. To collate, analyse, and publish information relating to university finance and university education both in Nigeria and abroad.

7. To make, either by itself or through committee, such other investigations relating to higher education as the Commission may consider necessary; and, for the purpose of such investigations, to have access to the records of universities seeking or receiving Federal grants.

8. To make such other recommendations to the Federal government or to universities relating to higher education as the Commission may consider to be in the national interest.[2]

The first Commission, appointed in October 1962, consisted of the following:[3]

Mallam Mohammadu Tukur, O.B.E., Emir of Yauri (Chairman);
Mr. Alvan Ikoku, President, Nigerian Union of Teachers;
Mr. E. E. Esua, Secretary, Nigerian Union of Teachers;
Mr. S. O. Wey, Secretary to the Prime Minister;
Mr. E. A. Osindero, Chairman, Federal Board of Inland Revenue;
Alhaji Addurrahman Okene, Provincial Secretary, Sokoto;
Alhaji Audu Gusau, Resident Engineer, Sokoto;
Dr. the Hon. S. E. Imoke, Minister of Education, Eastern Nigeria;
Mr. J. O. Udoji, Chief Secretary to the Premier, Eastern Nigeria;
Dr. F. Ogunro, Medical Practitioner, Benin City;
Mr. C. O. Komolafe, Executive Director, Western Nigeria Development Corporation, Ibadan;
Mr. Okoi Arikpo, Secretary to the National Universities Commission;
Sir Eric Ashby, Master of Clare College, Cambridge (Honorary Adviser).

The inaugural meeting of the Commission was held on 11 October 1962. Between mid-January 1963 and May 1963, it had visited all five universities, meeting the faculties, the administrative staffs, and students in order to obtain a comprehensive picture of all aspects of the life and problems of the universities. In the early stages of the work of processing and costing the capital programmes submitted to the Commission, the help of the recently retired Assistant Secretary of the London University Grants Commission was engaged for a brief period.[6]

The first report of the Commission was a comprehensive document which dealt with all aspects of university affairs in the country, ranging from student members and their distribution, entrance qualifications, academic staff and university finances, through buildings for teaching, halls of residence, and general financial policies.

Its main recommendations for the quinquennium 1963–68 were as follows:

1. That the universities should aim at a maximum target of enrolment of 10,000 by 1967–68, distributed as shown in Table 10.

2. That priority be given to the development of the scientific and technological departments of universities; and that of the total student population of 10,000 recommended, 7,580 should be taking courses in pure and applied sciences.

3. That for the present only three Engineering Faculties be developed, i.e. at Ahmadu Bello, Nsukka and Lagos.

Table 10

Distribution of students among Faculties by 1967/68

Faculty	Enrolment
Agriculture, Forestry & Fisheries	1,250
Pure Science	2,830
Veterinary Science	500
Medicine	1,000
Engineering	2,000
Arts	1,420
Others (Business, Social Studies, Management)	1,000
Total	10,000

4. That veterinary science be developed jointly by the Universities of Ibadan and Ahmadu Bello, the pre-clinical course at Ibadan and the clinical at Ahmadu Bello (Zaria).

5. That there should be only two Faculties of Medicine, at Lagos and Ibadan, in 1963–68.

6. That all Nigerian universities except Lagos should develop strong Faculties of Agriculture; the University of Ibadan should build up a vigorous post-graduate school in agriculture and the three Regional universities should each develop an Agricultural Extension Department in co-operation with the appropriate Regional Ministry of Agriculture.

7. That all the governments of the Federation should make most of their undergraduate scholarships available in Nigerian universities in order to increase the number of scholarships available to Nigerians and in order that the income of the universities may be increased.

8. That the University of Lagos Act be amended to enable the Senate of the University to have an overall responsibility for the academic affairs of the University of Lagos Medical School.

9. That the University of Ife should move to its permanent site at the earliest practicable date and that it should be compensated for the loss of its Ibadan campus buildings which should be taken over by the University of Ibadan.

10. That the universities should be assured of a capital grant of £17·63 million and a recurrent grant of £30·00 million during the quinquennium 1963–68.

11. That the Federal Government should provide for the entire financial needs of the Universities of Ibadan and Lagos together with fifty per cent of both the capital and recurrent needs of the three Regional universities.

12. That there should be a National Universities Fund into which all grants and subventions to the universities should be paid.

13. That the National Universities Commission be converted into a statutory body with the same terms of reference as those set out for the Commission and with responsibility for managing the National Universities Fund.

14. That each of the Laws establishing the Regional universities be amended so as to provide for nominees of the Federal government to be members of the Governing Councils of each of these universities.

Before taking any decisions on the recommendations, the Federal government called for the views of the Regional governments. The Federal government accepted most of the recommendations of the Commission. It rejected two of them, however: first, the government refused to convert the National Universities Commission into a statutory body, but agreed that it should remain an administrative body directly responsible to the Prime Minister. Second, the government decided not to ask to be represented on the Governing Council of the Regional universities.

It accepted the target of 10,000 full-time students provided that the number of part-time students should not exceed half of this number and the Federal government's grants to the Regional universities be based only on their respective quotas of the maximum enrolment target of 10,000 full-time students.[8] It also accepted the Commission's emphasis on science subjects, its suggestion that the Lagos Medical School be brought by law under the academic supervision of the Senate of the University, Ife's speedy movement to a permanent site, the award of scholarships for studies in Nigeria, the emphasis on agriculture in all universities (except Lagos) and on the development of medicine. It referred the Commission's recommendations on veterinary science and engineering for further study.

On the financing of universities, the Government decided that:

1. It would provide for the entire financial needs of Ibadan and Lagos;

2. It would provide the Regional universities with fifty per cent of their capital grant of £17.63 million;

3. It would provide the Universities of Nigeria and Ife with 30 per cent of their shares of the recurrent grant of £30 million;

4. In view of the fact that seventy-five per cent of the students of the branch of the Nigerian College of Arts, Science and Technology at Ahmadu Bello University came from outside Northern Nigeria, whilst the North had not at present as many students in the other universities, and that that was likely to be the position for some years to come, the Federal government should provide Ahmadu Bello with fifty per cent of its share of the total recurrent grant of £30 million in order to enable the government

of Northern Nigeria to make available more funds for the provision of sixth forms in Secondary Schools and thus increase the number of potential university entrants in Northern Nigeria;

5. The capital and recurrent grants to the universities be made available by all the governments within the Federation in accordance with Table 11:

Table 11

Proposal for contributions towards the capital and recurrent grants to the universities for the quinquennium 1963–68 in £ million

	1963/64	1964/65	1965/66	1966/67	1967/68	Total	Grant Total Recurrent and Capital
Federal Govt. share	3·555	3·875	4·220	4·470	4·735	20·855	34·289
Northern Govt. share	0·425	0·450	0·500	0·550	0·575	2·500	4·200
Eastern Govt. share	0·700	0·770	0·840	0·910	0·980	4·200	5·850
Western Govt. share	0·420	0·455	0·490	0·525	0·560	2·450	3·450
Total	5·100	5·550	6·050	6·455	6·850	30·005	47·789

6. All external grants and subventions to the universities should first be notified to the Commission and thereafter passed on to the universities concerned, and that all internal grants and subventions should be paid into a fund to be known as the National Universities Account, to be maintained by the Federal Ministry of Finance subject to the control of the Cabinet office; the grant payable to each of the universities from time to time should be reduced by the amount of any external aid or subvention, including the cost of all valuable equipment received by each university.[9]

Internal government and functioning of the universities

As may be seen from the various laws establishing them, Nigerian universities exhibit a welcome and remarkable diversity in their internal organisations, although they broadly follow the pattern usual with universities elsewhere. The laws operating in December, 1965 and on which this discussion is based are *The Ahmadu Bello University Law, 1962; The University of Ibadan Act, 1962; The University of Ife (Provisional Council) Law, 1961;* (as amended 1963 and 1964); *The University of Lagos Act, 1962;* and *The University of Nigeria Law, 1961*. (In March 1967 *The University of Lagos Degree 1967*; this is discussed in the post-script.)

AIMS

All the universities are legally open to anyone, irrespective of tribe, race or religion, and are all committed to the promotion of research, science and learning and the provision and extension of an education of university standard. They all have the power to confer their own degrees and diplomas.

THE GOVERNING COUNCILS

The Councils of the five universities are charged by law with the general control and superintendence of the properties and policies of the universities to which they belong. They may do anything in their power which in their opinions is calculated to facilitate the carrying on of the activities of their respective universities.

The Councils are thus very powerful bodies, but they may function, subject to unwritten traditions and conventions, only as laid down by the governments which established them. Although they may suggest alterations, they are not allowed to actually alter the statutes without permission.

The composition of the Councils is given in Table 12, and it will be seen that the members are predominantly nominees of the various Nigerian governments. The Law of Ahmadu Bello was unique in making provision for a Federal government appointee although the University itself is sponsored by the Northern government. It will be recalled that the Federal government rejected the suggestion of the National Universities Commission that the Federal Government should be represented on university councils.

The Councils are permitted to delegate their administrative powers to persons or committees. According to the Laws establishing the Universities of Nigeria and Ahmadu Bello, the Councils of these universities may delegate any of their powers, except the making, altering or annulling of statutes, to the Chancellor (University of Nigeria) or Chairman of the Council (at Ahmadu Bello) or to any committee appointed by the Council, provided that such a committee consists of at least one member of the Council. In this way, no doubt the Council and hence the government which appointed it is able to review the more important affairs of the University.

There is also at Ahmadu Bello, Ibadan, and Nsukka a Finance and General Purposes Committee of the Council which, subject to its direction, exercises control over the property and finances of the University. This Committee at Ahmadu Bello and Ibadan is made up of the Chairman of the Council, the Vice-Chancellor, and eight other Council members including two members of the academic staff. At Nsukka, besides the Chancellor and Vice-Chancellor, the Committee includes three of the five members of the Council appointed by the East Regional Government.

The Councils meet a minimum of two to four times a year and during

Table 12

Composition of the Governing Councils of Nigerian universities

		Ahmadu Bello	Ibadan	Ife	Lagos	Nsukka
1	Chairman[1]	1	1	1	1	1
2	Vice-Chancellor	1	1	1	1	1
3	Pro-Vice-Chancellor or Deputy Vice-Chancellor	1	1	1	–	–
4	Provost of Abdulahi Bayero College	1	–	–	–	–
5	Appointed by the Chancellor	4	–	–	–	–
6	Appointed by the Federal Government	1	4	–	5	–
7	Appointed by the Eastern Nigeria Government	–	2	–	–	5
8	Appointed by the Western Nigeria Government	–	2	15	–	–
9	Appointed by the Northern Nigeria Government	4	2	–	–	–
10	Appointed by the Mid-Western Nigeria Government	–	2	–	–	–
11	Appointed by Senate	4	4	2	1	2
12	Appointed by Congregation	2	2	–	–	–
13	Appointed by Convocation	–	1	–	–	–
14	Co-opted by the Council (maximum)	10	4	–	–	–
15	Appointed by the Lagos Medical School	–	–	–	2	–
	Total (maximum)[2]	29	26	20	10	9

Sources:
  University of Ahmadu Bello Law (1962);
  University of Ibadan Act (1962);
  University of Ife Law, (Provisional Council), (1962) (Amended 1963 and 1964);
  University of Lagos Act, (1962);
  University of Nigeria Law, (1961).

[1] At Ibadan the Chairman of Council is the Pro-Chancellor; at Nsukka, he is the Chancellor.

[2] The minimum members are 19 and 22 at Ahmadu Bello and Ibadan respectively.

the interval the Finance and General Purposes Committee manage any urgent affairs of the University. This Committee is really the core of the power in the University since it is smaller, easier to manage, and meets more often than the rest of the Council.

The Finance and General Purposes Committee of the University of

Nigeria is particularly interesting. Teachers, except the Vice-Chancellor, are completely excluded from it. It is easy to see therefore why decisions have been made in the past by the Council (through its Finance and General Purpose Committee) without the necessary concurrence of Senate, since the Council usually acts by resolution passed by a simple majority of the members present and voting, and the only academic, the Vice-Chancellor, could be easily outnumbered. Also at Nsukka, by the 1961 Law, unless requested by three members, the summoning of a meeting was left in the hands of the Chancellor (or in his absence the Visitor). At Ahmadu Bello, the Chairman or the Vice-Chancellor or ten members of the Council may convene a meeting of that body.

CONTROL OF ACADEMIC AFFAIRS

The Laws all relegate the development and supervision of academic matters to the Senate (Academic Board at Ife). The Senate is constituted by law mostly of the more senior members of the teaching staff (Vice-Chancellor, Deputy Vice-Chancellor, professors, readers, Heads of Departments), and a small number (usually two to four) of members elected from the rest of the staff, as well as the Librarian, and Directors of Institutes within the universities.

The Laws establishing the Universities of Ahmadu Bello, Ibadan and Lagos specify in some detail the functions of their Senates. These will be discussed more fully in later sections. Faculty Boards are also established at all the universities, except Ife. These Boards are headed by Deans, chosen by the Boards themselves from among the Professors of their departments for a period of two years. At the University of Nigeria, a Dean is appointed by the Council and 'The Deans of the several Faculties shall constitute the Council of Deans which shall be advisory to the Vice-Chancellor on all academic matters, and on particular matters referred to the University Council by the Senate.' (Section 13.)

RELATIONSHIP BETWEEN COUNCIL AND SENATE

1. *Appointment of staff*

It is one of the cardinal points in the existence of academic freedom that the institution should be able to choose who should teach. Only the teachers themselves within the institution may be expected to be able to determine competence or lack of it among its own members and the choice of a teacher in the institution in effect boils down to a choice made by the teachers. It is necessary to make this point as it may be argued that since, the Council is legally part of the university and especially since the said Council is charged with the function of superintendence of the university, it could, and would, be exercising academic freedom if it undertook to

N

appoint staff. Looking at the letter of the law, the Laws establishing Ife and Nsukka do not make any concessions to the consultation of Senate in the appointment of staff.

The Ife Law reads:

> The Council may employ such academic and administrative staff as may appear to it to be necessary for the purposes of the University and for the due exercise of the powers and functions of the Council under this Law.

The University of Nigeria Law states (Statute 7, Section 11, sub-section 1):

> (a) The number and status of persons to be employed by the University, whether members of the academic or administrative staff, . . . shall be such as the Council may from time to time determine.
>
> (b) Whenever a vacancy occurs in the academic staff or in the offices of Registrar, Librarian, Bursar, or Director of Extra-Mural Studies, the Council shall except for good reason, cause the vacancy to be advertised and a suitable person to fill any such vacancy shall be chosen by the Council.
>
> (c) Where a vacancy occurs in any position on the academic or administrative staff other than the office of Vice-Chancellor, the Council shall after advertisement appoint a suitable person to fill such vacancy and may for adequate cause, suspend the person so appointed from his duties or terminate his appointment.

At the University of Lagos, by the 1962 Act, the Senate has the duty of 'recommending in any appropriate case the appointment of members of the academic staff.' (Section 3, sub-section 1g).

The Laws of Ife and Nsukka do not reflect conditions in Nigeria where, owing to the newness of the university tradition of academic freedom, Councils may interpret the laws literally and with full legal right decide to appoint academic staff without the backing of the academics themselves. It is not enough merely that Senate should recommend, as is the case at the University of Lagos. Council should be made to accept, unless there are serious reasons otherwise, the recommendations of Senate in the appointment of academic staff.

The Act establishing Ibadan is more realistic in that it states that 'it shall in particular be the functions of Senate to make provision for the appointment and promotion of teachers at the University.' (Section 5, sub-section 2a).

The near-ideal is achieved, however, at Ahmadu Bello, where the compositions of the Boards of Selection are set out by a statute of the Law establishing that University, and there can be no question whatever therefore of the Council appointing academic staff without the concurrence of the teachers. As will be seen below the Council is represented on these boards but Council members are always in the minority. It may be mentioned in passing that most Nigerian universities benefit from the independent assessment of candidates, sometimes offered on request, by the Inter-University Council for Overseas Universities.

Table 13

The composition of Appointment Boards as established by the University of Ahmadu Bello Law, 1962

Appointment	Composition
1 Professorship and Directorship of Institute of Administration and of Agricultural Research and Special Service	a, b, c, d, e, f
2 Readership	a, b, c, d, e, f, g
3 Lecturership	a, c, d, e, f, g
4 Assistant Lecturership	a, d, e, g
5 Other junior appointments	a, d, e, g
6 Librarian	a, b, c, d, f
7 Registrar	a, b, c, d

Source: *Statute 8, Ahmadu Bello University Law, 1962.*

Notes:
a = Vice-Chancellor or Deputy appointed by him; b = The Chairman of Council; c = Two members of Council not being members of Senate; d = Two members of the Senate being also members of the Council, who shall have been nominated by the Senate to serve on a particular Board or on Boards of selection; e = The Dean of the Faculty/Director of Institute concerned; f = Two external experts nominated by Senate, who are not University personnel; g = Head of Department or Institute of appointment.

2. *The setting up of new Faculties or areas of study*

Like the appointment of teachers, the setting up of new Faculties or areas of study could be a source of trouble between the Senate and the Council as was clearly seen in the case of Lindsay at the University of Nigeria. One of the essentials of academic freedom is the freedom to decide what to teach. But clearly whoever finances a university cannot be an onlooker when decisions are being made about what the areas of study shall be.

The Council of the University of Nigeria, for instance, 'may at any time establish all or any of the Faculties or Colleges described in the Statutes' (Section 6). The Council is not required to consult the Senate, but since the Senate are the body competent to teach, lack of consultation could lead to trouble.

Except a vaguely defined function, 'the formulation and execution of academic policy' (Section 17a), the University of Ife Law gives the Senate no hand in determining the areas of study, which must therefore be under the jurisdiction of the Council. Similarly the Law establishing the University of Lagos is silent on the Senate's role in this issue.

The Senates of the Universities of Ahmadu Bello and Ibadan are given considerable power in the establishment of Faculties, etc.

At the Ahmadu Bello, the Senate is *inter alia* required to:

> formulate, modify, or revise schemes for the organization of Faculties and to assign to such Faculties their respective subjects; also to report to the Council on the expediency of the establishment at any time of other Faculties, or as to the expediency of the abolition, combination or sub-division of any Faculties. (Statute 5, sub-section 6, clause ix).

At Ibadan the Senate has full control and is not even required to report to the Council (Section 5, sub-section 2a):

> [It shall be the function of the Senate to make provision for] the establishment, organization and control of faculties and other departments of the University, and the allocation to different departments of responsibility for different branches of learning.

The above again indicates that some form of communication between Senate and Council, quite apart from members of Senate on the Council, is an obvious necessity. For the government, which provides funds for the running of a university, needs to transmit its wishes through the Council to the Senate. The argument here is that quite apart from any convention which may grow, the Law needs to specify in detail the process of such matters as establishing new Faculties, in order to avoid the considerable friction which might arise in an environment like that of Nigeria, new to university organisation and still evolving one peculiar to itself. Such provision should bear in mind the requirements of academic freedom.

STUDENT DISCIPLINE AND WELFARE

At Ibadan, student discipline and welfare is under the supervision of the Senate, under which also come the establishment, organisation and control of halls of residence. The power to suspend, rusticate, or dismiss students is, however, vested in the Vice-Chancellor. At the other universities the Vice-Chancellors are generally responsible for the students' welfare, but at Nsukka the Vice-Chancellor acts through a Dean of Student Affairs.

RELATIONSHIP BETWEEN THE GOVERNMENT AND THE UNIVERSITIES

The Constitutions of the Nigerian universities enable the governments which have established them to wield a large amount of influence in these universities. To begin with, although the Councils are corporate bodies, they may be dissolved (and this has occurred at least once) should the government feel its aim thwarted. In this respect it is quite meaningless to talk of autonomy in the context of Nigerian universities.

Besides appointing a majority of the members of the Councils of universities, (such appointed members usually have sympathy for the official point of view), the governments have other means of ensuring a constant watch over their universities. For example, the Laws stipulate that the Governors of the Northern and Eastern Regions shall be the Visitors of Ahmadu Bello and Nsukka Universities respectively, and that the President of the Republic should act in similar capacity for the University of Ibadan. At both Ibadan and Ahmadu Bello Universities the Laws state that their Visitors may conduct a visitation from time to time for the purpose of ensuring that the Universities are fulfilling the functions for which they were set up.

At Ibadan also the Council

> Shall prepare and submit to the (Federal) Prime Minister, not later than the thirty-first day of January in each year, a report in such form as the Prime Minister may direct on the activities of the university during the period of twelve months ending with the preceding thirty-first day of August, and shall include in the report a copy of the last accounts audited . . . and a copy of the auditor's report on the accounts; and the Prime Minister shall cause a copy of each report made to him in pursuance of this sub-section to be laid before each House of Parliament (Section 4, sub-section 9).

Similarly at Ife, the Chairman of the Council and the Vice-Chancellor will furnish the Chancellor such information as he may desire to receive.

The Chancellors, appointed as they are by governments as Heads of the Universities, are naturally pro-government in their sympathies. The Chancellor at Nsukka is also Chairman of the Council and holds office for life.

In all the ways illustrated above the governments which have established Nigerian universities have ensured that they are able to 'keep an eye' on them. Due to ignorance of university affairs, or to score political points, governments or their agents have been known to stick to the letter of the law with disastrous consequences. It does appear then that framing of laws which recognise the political temperament of the country could do more to avert the crises which occasionally threaten to arise. In other words, the laws should state clearly and unequivocally the functions of the Council, Senate, etc.

Notes

[1] *Investment in Education*, Lagos, 1960, pp. 32–33.
[2] *University Development in Nigeria*, Report of the National Universities Commission, Lagos, 1963, pp. 1–2.
[3] *Ibid.*
[4] *Ibid.*, p. 6.
[5] *Ibid.*, pp. 42–43.
[6] *Ibid.*, p. 21.
[7] *Decisions of the Government of the Federal Republic of Nigeria on the Report of the National Universities Commission*, Sessional paper No. 4, of 1964, Lagos, p. 8.
[8] *Ibid.*, p. 5.
[9] *Ibid.*, pp. 7–8.

14 Conclusion

Modern universities, as has been shown, have their origins in the Europe of the Middle Ages. Yet they have not remained stereotypes from one country to another, nor indeed, from one university to another within the same country.

At any period in history it is possible to give a general indication of the distinguishing characteristics of the universities of any particular country. University development then may be seen as an evolutionary process in which a gradual change occurs in the university's nature so as to suit the environment in which it exists. When a university has attained equilibrium with the historical, social, economic and other factors around it, it bears the distinguishing characteristics of those surroundings. What, if any, are the characteristics which make the universities in Nigeria today peculiarly Nigerian? To what extent may these universities be said to have become so attuned to the history of the country that they differ from universities elsewhere? The answer to these questions must await the verdict of time. But there are phenomena noted in the succeeding Postscript which are a reflection of the Nigeria of today. The country itself is just over half a century old, and the oldest university has existed for less than half this period. The purpose of this final chapter is to examine some of the factors which have so far been operational in the 'character' development of these institutions in Nigeria.

It will be shown that besides the internal factors of the country itself, compelling influences have emanated from two English-speaking countries, namely Britain and the United States. The extent to which these countries have influenced the emergence of a 'Nigerian' university will be examined.

First the United States will be dealt with, as the long-standing influence of that country on Nigerian educational matters is not always appreciated, whilst the political influence on Nigerian *leaders* is better known. The earliest means of transporting this transatlantic influence was via Negro slaves returned to West Africa. Up to the late nineteenth and early twentieth centuries many of the leading figures in West African affairs were descendants of returned Negroes, by whom the earliest two demands for a university in West Africa were made. It was natural that they should have kept in touch with their kin in the United States. The activities of these American Negroes were keenly followed by nineteenth-century West

Africans, as may be seen from the newspapers of those times. For instance, when in 1895 Booker T. Washington, the Negro educational leader from the South, made his famous Atlanta Speech, it re-echoed in the Lagos newspapers. Washington, a great advocate of vocational (industrial) education, went to Tuskegee in 1881, and made that institution the famous Negro vocational institution that it became.

Washington, realistic and pragmatic, knew that in the spirit of the late nineteenth-century southern United States, co-operation and a certain amount of conformity with white Southerners was the most likely avenue for bringing his fellow Negroes the greatest utilitarian benefits, safety as well as security. This policy he enunciated publicly in the speech he made at the Atlanta Exposition in 1895, urging Negroes to co-operate with people of all races by whom they were surrounded. It was extreme folly, he considered, for the Negro to claim social equality with these other people; the Negroes' place was in agriculture, in mechanics, in commerce, in domestic service and in the professions—in other words, in what came to be regarded in Lagos as 'industrial' pursuits. The exposition and Washington's speech were advanced by *The Lagos Weekly Record*, in argument for the Lagos Literary and Industrial Institute, as the greatest thing that had happened to the Negro since his advent to the Western world.

The Negroes, claimed *The Record*,

> erected their own buildings designed by their own architects and contributed to and controlled solely by their own race. . . . Mr. Booker T. Washington, a Negro, was the man chosen by the managers—and we should say by God—to voice the feeling which it was becoming to express on that occasion. . . . We in Africa hail him as our messenger [who] was inspired to speak for Africa.

The main impression produced by the Exhibition, according to *The Record*, was that the most genuine progress of the Negro in America had been in the industrial field and not in spiritual, literary, and commercial affairs: his labours were chiefly manual. It was along these lines of 'industrial training and skilled labour' that the African needed to be educated.[3]

Nevertheless, argued *The Record*, 'material development is not humanity's last word. There are loftier utterances yet to be made; and there is no reason why Africa should not share in these utterances.' A form of education other than vocational was clearly in the mind of this advocate of the Lagos Institute, but the vocational type so recently 'successful' and welcomed in the States was the type most wanted.

Thus the idea of a vocational emphasis in education which the Southern American once needed for his existence was absorbed by the Lagos educated class and incorporated into the proposals for the Institute.

We find later, in the 1920s, that even when education was completely in the hands of missionaries who were in the main based in England, British government interest in African education was inspired by the Phelps-Stokes Foundation of the United States, which had sent out commissions to study education in the continent. At the meeting called on 6 June 1923 to advise the Colonial Office, Dr. Jesse Jones, a Welsh-born American who had chaired the Phelps-Stokes Commission to West Africa, was present, as were also the Governors of African territories, representatives of missionaries, and Colonial Office officials. Dr. Jesse Jones, an authority on Negro education in the States, was President of Hampton Institute, an organisation famous for industrial education for Negroes, and the *alma mater* of Booker T. Washington. Not unnaturally, therefore, the Phelps-Stokes Commission reflected a preference for this type of education for the African. Thus the Commission reported:

> For an example of the working of essentials of education in moulding the life of individuals and communities, we can turn to a demonstration successfully made by a man of African origin. The services of Booker T. Washington, as the founder of Tuskegee Institute, the promoter of education related to the life of the people, and an exponent of co-operation are recognized throughout the world. Those who are concerned with the welfare of Africa will do well to study the life and work of this great man.[5]

Additionally, for some time the Advisory Committee on Education in Africa, subsequently set up by the Colonial Office in London in 1925, ran on funds provided by the Carnegie Foundation, an American body.

It has been made evident that the emphasis on vocation had its origin in the educational ideas of Negroes in America and became accepted not only by the nineteenth century Nigerians, but by British planners of African education in the early twentieth century. But there was a counter-current of opinion opposed to vocational training. In the United States Dr. W. E. B. Du Bois, after an initial period of discipleship, was already arguing in his *Souls of Black Folk* in 1903 that 'Mr. Washington's programme practically accepts the alleged inferiority of the Negro races'[6]. In a bitter attack on 'Mr. Booker T. Washington and others' he came out strongly against industrial education and eventually 'conquered' Washington.[7]

Soon the industrial education earlier advocated by Blyden and his Lagos associates was also to be discredited in West Africa. Dr. Du Bois' triumph over Washington assured that. His presence and ideas were represented at Pan-African Congresses held in London (1900), Paris (1919), London and Brussels (1921), London and Lisbon (1923), and New York (1927).[8] Although Nigerians were not represented at these conferences, the proceedings were followed in the local press and added to the build-up of nationalism in Nigeria in the early decades of the present century.[9]

This nationalism, stimulated as it was by the ideas of Dr. Du Bois (and Garvey[10]), could no longer accept a form of education which Nigerians judged inferior. Hence the rejection of industrial training in secondary schools,[11] but more especially that of the Yaba Higher College. Thus the United States, whence had come the idea of the importance of industrial education, 'geared', in the words of the 1925 *Memorandum* of the Advisory Committee, 'to the mentality and aptitude of the African', was also the country to supply a reason for its rejection.

The most important influence in recent years, however, has been in the sphere of higher education. This has come about *via* two channels, namely the Ashby Commission and the University of Nigeria.

We find in the Ashby Commission that for the first time in Nigeria's history a commission studying higher education included members from outside the United Kingdom; specifically it included opinion from the United States of America. As has been noted in Chapter 12, one important idea introduced by Ashby into Nigerian higher education was the award of university degrees for subjects which at the time, following the tradition inherited from Britain, would have qualified for non-university diplomas.

Moreover, the Ashby Commission's favourable disposition towards the American land-grant college facilitated public acceptance of the University of Nigeria, which, as has been indicated, was modelled on similar lines.

But what is the land grant system? Why did it flourish in the United States when it did? In order to understand the place of this system in Nigeria's educational set-up, it is necessary to answer these questions briefly, although there is a huge literature[12] on the growth of the American state university and the land grant system in general.

The first important thing to note about the control of American education is that no strong national or central organisation has ever been created to regulate, standardise, or even to advise educators. For among the powers and functions allotted by the United States Constitution to the Federal government, education is not mentioned. Education in all its phases and levels has therefore always been the responsibility of each state.[13] The young states of the early nineteenth century were, however, unable to support adequately the institution of higher learning, as their financial resources were too slender. At the same time there was a good deal of dissatisfaction in the second quarter of that century regarding the traditional 'colonial' colleges which America had inherited from Oxford and Cambridge, not one of which was 'designed to furnish the agriculturist, the manufacturer, the mechanic or the merchant with the education that will prepare him for the profession to which his life is to be devoted.'[14] Furthermore, following the British and European tradition, higher education was reserved for a minority of the intellectual élite or for those born into wealthy families. The colleges themselves were private and sectarian and taught classics oriented towards the past. The result was Justin Morrill's introduction in Congress in 1856 of a Bill calling for federal aid to agricultural and mechanical colleges. Parochial disagreements led to the Bill being vetoed by the President (though passed by Congress) in 1859. At last in 1862, the Land Grant Act was passed. It provided for the donation by the Federal government of public land 'to the several states and territories which may provide colleges for the benefit of agriculture and the mechanic arts.' Each state which benefited under this Act was required to establish at least one college where the leading object shall be, without excluding other scientific and classical studies, and including military tactics, to teach such branches of learning as are related to agriculture and the mechanic arts . . . in order to promote the liberal and practical education of the industrial classes in the several pursuits and professions in life.'[15] A second Morrill Act passed in 1890 provided annual Federal grants for the colleges and operated to encourage the states to provide similar finances. The Morrill Acts gave higher education in the states a new sense of direction and responsibility. Knowledge was for use, not snobbery. The Acts stimulated work along vocational lines. Some of the land-grant colleges were established *de novo*, whereas in other cases, Federal government grants augmented the coffers of an already existing state university. The land-grant funds, important at the initiation of the scheme, at present form only a small proportion of college revenue, the rest coming from taxes, state and Federal.

The important features of the system were:[16]

1. An emphasis on study of items which were immediately beneficial to the people, on practical utility and vocational emphasis—the idea of service to the state—and a simultaneous embracement of the universality of learning.

2. A concomitant democratisation of higher education which made it available to a much wider public than hitherto.

3. The widening of the curriculum to dignify many studies with university attention, i.e. the satisfaction of the need for respect of all occupational groups.

According to American authors, the land-grant idea is that country's contribution to higher education. It was a factor introduced into an infrastructure derived from two European sources. The first was the sixteenth- and seventeenth-century English university (specifically, Oxford and Cambridge) which in turn transmitted the inheritance that reached it *via* the Paris, Salerno and Bologna universities of the European Middle Ages. The second was the German tradition of learning which flourished in the nineteenth century Germany university with its impersonal search for knowledge for its own sake, its introduction of the laboratory and the seminar, its unrelenting pursuit of research and scientific experimentation in the climate of academic freedom. To these two European importations then, the American university has added the novel land-grant idea.

Nevertheless, two modifications have become more or less permanent features of American higher education. The first is the principle of electives, whereby a student is free to choose, within limits, his courses from a range of subjects. In a way, of course, this is an aspect of *Lernfreiheit* (student academic freedom) for which the German university was known, and in this sense 'electives' are not therefore essentially American in origin.

The other innovation was the growth of general education, to provide consciously, through education, the common basis of living and working together.[17]

This system then, with its emphasis on vocational, utilitarian, rather than classical subjects, its democratisation of higher education, its wide range of subjects including General Studies, its electives and credit-system, was imported into Nigeria, where for just over a century educational ideas had been supplied mainly by Britain.

Educational contact between England and Nigeria began even before the country itself was created. As far back as 1841, the first schools were founded by missionaries from England, twenty years before Lagos was ceded to the British and at least fifty years before the unification of the country. Educational practice and organisation in Nigeria therefore largely bear the marks of this contact with the British. In the field of higher education Britain transmitted her ideas to Nigeria, through the Asquith and Elliot Commissions and the Fyfe Delegation, already discussed earlier in this book. Naturally Britain was encouraging in Nigeria a system she knew and understood.

At the time of these Commissions—during and immediately after the Second World War—the system included the following attributes, some of which persist. First, the system of higher education was geared at the time to an intellectual and social *élite* capable of leading an inert mass. The rigid class structure of English society is breaking, but the remnants are visible in the élitist higher educational system transmitted to Nigeria. It was a system which was criticised by Nigerians because it limited the number of entrants to the then single Nigerian university— University College, Ibadan—to the number of available beds in the halls of residence.

Second, it was a system which relegated certain areas of study to technical colleges. The Elliot Commission recommended Faculties of Arts, Science, Medicine, Agriculture—subjects which were to be found in British universities. The traditional English system assigned many other areas of study, such as accountancy and journalism, to technical colleges. One consequence of this is the existence in England of higher education qualifications awarded by societies, associations, or institutes other than universities. Because the earlier universities (Oxford and Cambridge) adhered too closely to the classical curricula to the neglect of the more vocational subjects, many professional organisations were forced to found their own qualifications.

Third, British universities, not having been founded by the government, enjoyed a considerable independence.

Britain and the United States have been the major sources of ideas in

Nigerian higher education. Other countries have contributed also, but to a much smaller extent than the two just mentioned; as has been remarked, for example, the UNESCO Commission which made recommendations on Lagos University included representatives from France and the USSR. These members no doubt contributed ideas based on the experiences of their own countries. As has been argued in the first chapter of this book every university must, however, adapt itself to environmental requirements. It is yet too early to speak of characteristics peculiar to Nigerian universities. Nevertheless even in its comparative youth the Nigerian university has demonstrated some awareness of its environment. Ibadan, founded as a result of the Asquith and Elliot Commissions, at a time when Nigeria was still a British colony, naturally bore from the start strong marks of its British origins. Similarly Nsukka, founded through the enthusiasm of Dr. Azikiwe, began as a copy of its American sponsor, Michigan State University.

There are already signs of deviation from the original patterns, many of which are in response to the needs of the local environment. At Ibadan, subjects which under the British system were not university courses are now offered for degrees. Examples are nursing, laboratory technology, physiotherapy and radiotherapy. This broadening of curricula stems from two causes. First is the dilemma which faces independent Nigeria when it continues to rely on examinations conducted by the City and Guilds, Institute of Secretaries, Nursing Council of England and Wales, etc. for vocational pursuits. Does it not constitute a negation of independence and a reflection of 'colonial mentality' when professional examinations designed for England are taken in Nigeria? On the other hand, how can the country ensure international recognition for a purely local qualification? One way out of the dilemma has been to raise the prestige of these qualifications by associating them with the name of the university. A second reason for the broadening of curricula is the influence of ideas from elsewhere, notably the United States.

At Nsukka, despite the presence of credits, electives, etc., the final degree is graded as in Britain. The other three universities are also slowly adapting, although all broadly follow the British pattern.

It will still be some time before one can speak or write of a university which is peculiarly Nigerian; the two influences which may continue to be important are those of Great Britain and the United States.

Notes

[1] J. COLEMAN, *Nigeria: Background to Nationalism*, California, 1960, *passim*.
[2] BOOKER T. WASHINGTON, *Up from Slavery*, New York, 1901, pp. 218–25; also *Negro Education in America* ed. by V. A. CLIFT, A. W. ANDERSON, and H. G. HULL-FISH, New York, pp. 47–49. The Southern whites were pleased that the Negroes did not

claim equality and the northerners were pleased that industrial education would fit the Negro better for work in their industrial establishments.

³ *The Lagos Weekly Record,* 23 May 1896.

⁴ W. ORMSBY GORE, 'Education in the British Dependencies in Tropical Africa', *Year-book of Education 1932,* London, p. 748.

⁵ *Education in Africa,* Report by THOMAS JESSE JONES, Chairman of Commission, Phelps-Stokes Foundation, New York, p. 13.

⁶ W. E. B. DU BOIS, *The Souls of Black Folk,* London, 1965, p. 33.

⁷ *Ibid.,* pp. 27–38; p. XI.

⁸ COLIN LEGUM, *Pan-Africanism,* London, 1962, pp. 24–30.

⁹ COLEMAN, *op. cit.,* p. 189.

¹⁰ Marcus Aurelius Garvey, a Jamaican who founded the Universal Negro Improvement Association, was a great antagonist of Du Bois. See COLEMAN, *op. cit.,* pp. 189–90.

¹¹ See however, J. F. ADE AJAYI, 'The Development of Secondary Grammar Schools in Nigeria', *Journal of the Historical Society of Nigeria,* 4, 1963.

¹² For example, JAMES L. MORRILL, *The Ongoing State University,* Minnesota, 1960; JOHN S. BRUBACHER and WILLIS RUDY, *Higher Education in Transition,* New York, 1958; RICHARD HOFSTADTER and WILSON SMITH, *American Higher Education,* 2 Vols., Chicago, 1960; FRANCIS M. ROGERS, *Higher Education in the United States,* Harvard, 1963; WILLIAM CLYDE DE VANE, *Higher Education in Twentieth Century America,* 1965.

¹³ DE VANE, *ibid.,* p. 1; ROGERS, *op. cit.,* p. 121.

¹⁴ BRUBACHER and RUDY, *op. cit.,* pp. 62–63.

¹⁵ MORRILL, *op. cit.,* pp. 3–4.
The best use of the funds made available under the Act was where they were given to a pre-existing state college. In states where funds were shared among more than one college the effect could not obviously be felt as much. HOFSTADTER and WILSON, *op. cit.,* pp. 568–9.

¹⁶ BRUBACHER and RUDY, *op. cit.,* pp. 373–86.

¹⁷ MORRILL, *op. cit.,* pp. 16–19.

Postscript: the Military Governments and the Universities

It has become clear in this book that Nigerian universities have not been insulated from the rough and tumble of politics.

On 15 January 1966 news was received that a 'dissident' section of the Nigerian Army had mutinied. Eventually it was learnt that this section had killed the Premier of the Northern Region, Sir Ahmadu Bello (Sardauna of Sokoto); the Premier of Western Nigeria, Chief S. L. Akintola; Chief Festus Okotie-Eboh, the Federal Minister of Finance; and the Prime Minister of the Federation of Nigeria, Sir Abubakar Tafawa Balewa.

Later on it was announced that the Council of (Federal) Ministers, or what was left of it, had voluntarily handed over power to the Head of the Army, Major-General J. T. U. Aguiyi-Ironsi, who became known as the 'Head of the Federal Military Government and Supreme Commander of the Armed Forces.' This hand-over created at the time a general sense of relief. For previous to the January *coup* there had been a wave of disturbances and menacing of life and property especially in Western Nigeria, following the alleged rigging of the elections held in that Region in October 1965. There had also been widespread corruption among the politicians and high government officials.

In the new atmosphere of idealism, political parties and tribal unions were banned. Politicians were discredited, and many of them were detained by the police while arrangements were made to try them. Plans were also made to clear the country of corruption and to expose it in public life. Sectionalism, as reflected in excessive tribal and regional loyalities, was deplored. This new mood could not but be reflected in the universities. It was soon announced that the universities would be re-organised to serve the larger interests of Nigeria. The Head of the Federal Military Government announced that his government would 're-appraise educational policies to ensure high and uniform standards throughout the country. Our universities will be re-oriented to serve the genuine needs of the people.'[1] The Governor of the Eastern Group of Provinces (the Regions became 'Groups of Provinces') promised that the Law establishing the University of Nigeria would be reviewed to leave academic matters entirely in the hands of academicians, subject to the overall requirements of the country's man-power needs, as directed by the National Universities Commission.[2]

Subsequently the Laws establishing the Universities of Nigeria and

Lagos were amended and the Provisional Councils of the University of Lagos,[3] Ife,[4] and the Council of the University of Nigeria were dissolved or re-organised and new appointments made.[5] The Law of the University of Nigeria had formerly invested the Chairmanship of the Council in the Chancellor. This Law was now amended to separate the offices of Chairmanship of Council from Chancellorship. Dr. Azikiwe, who had been Chancellor of the University of Nigeria, was replaced by a Northern Nigerian, Alhaji Bayero, the Emir of Kano, while the Oba of Benin, Oba Akenzua II, a Southern Nigerian, was appointed Chancellor of Ahmadu Bello University in place of the Sardauna of Sokoto, who had been killed during the Army *coup*.

These appointments reflected the new mood of inter-Regional friendliness and co-operation. Chancellors as well as members of the various University Councils were chosen from Regions other than those in which the universities were situated.

But this was not to last. On 29 May 1966, many hundreds of Southern Nigerians (especially Ibos) residing in Northern Nigeria were killed. It was generally held that this outrage reflected resentment at the military government's attempt to unify the country and rule it 'from Lagos', a reference to a Decree (No. 34) by General Ironsi abolishing the Regions and instituting a unitary government. Two months later, on 29 July 1966, there was a *coup* in the Army itself and not only did the Head of the National Military Government, Major-General Aguiyi-Ironsi and his Western Governor, Lt. Col. Fajuyi, disappear, but many Ibos in the Army were killed. Those who could escape did so. Soon the killing of civilians of Eastern Nigeria origin in the North, and occasionally in Lagos, became common, and thousands lost their lives. The climax of the killings was on 29 September when thousands more were killed in the North.

Following this most of the Ibo lecturers and students left Ahmadu Bello and many of those at Ibadan University and the handful in Lagos, feeling life insecure, returned to their Region of origin and were absorbed at the University of Nigeria. In all 1,036 students had been re-registered at Nsukka by mid-October 1966. It will be recalled that almost all the Nigerians who resigned in protest during the Njoku episode at the University of Lagos were Easterners, specifically Ibos. Many of them were also re-absorbed into the University of Nigeria, Nsukka.

Meanwhile the Military Governor of Eastern Nigeria (the old name reverted after the counter-coup) ordered in October 1966 that for their safety, non-Eastern Nigerians should leave the East. Students other than Easterners, Mid-West Ibos and Ijaws who had to leave as a result were found places at Ibadan, Ife and Lagos or abroad.

The net effect of these movements was a polarisation of university staff and students in institutions located in, or owned by, the Regions from where they originated. One result of this polarisation was that new departments and/or faculties had to be founded much earlier than would have been the case had not some universities suddenly found themselves with refugee staff in areas of study which were not being offered. This was certainly the case with the Faculty of Medicine which was established at the University of Nigeria early in 1967, a few years ahead of the planned time. The same is probably true also of the Faculty of Education at Ife and the Department of Journalism in Lagos.

As the Regions became more inward-looking, each of them set about making itself as self-sufficient as possible with respect to university places and courses. Two universities being proposed at the time of writing fall into this category.

The proposed University in the Mid-West

In April, 1967 the Mid-West Government announced that it had set up a nineteen-man committee to look into the possibility of establishing a university and a teaching hospital in that Region. This committee included two prominent academic indigenes of the Mid-West: Professor H. O. Thomas, Dean of the Medical School, University of Lagos, and Professor J. O. Edozien, former Dean of the Medical School at the University of Ibadan.

The proposed University of Science and Technology, Port Harcourt

Of all the Regions, Eastern Nigeria had the greatest number of refugees. The number was estimated at about 1·8 million and may well be larger when checking is complete. The government of that Region therefore decided to start its own interim three year economic planning, abandoning the six-year (1962–1968) plan devised for the whole country by the ousted civilian regime.

Increased scientific manpower was, in the government's view, a necessity in the economic 'take-off' the Region expected following its greatly augmented ('refugee') personnel. It decided to found a University of Science and Technology near the growing industrial port of Port Harcourt. The University is expected to concentrate on the applied sciences and is due to open in October, 1967.

The University of Lagos Decree, 1967

It will be recalled from Chapter 11 that the University of Lagos Act was not passed in December, 1964 due to political unrest following the Federal elections. In March 1967, the Federal Military Government passed the

University of Lagos Decree, 1967 and it came into operation on April 1st of that year.

The Decree seems to have combined all that is best in the laws establishing Ahmadu Bello and Ibadan. For instance, like the Ahmadu Bello Law it states clearly who shall sit on appointment boards for academic staff. It also delineates the functions and powers of the Senate. It has been stated in Chapter 13 that in an environment such as Nigeria where universities are comparatively new, functions need to be apportioned in the Laws establishing these universities, in order to avoid crises.

An important feature of the Decree is that the Medical School which was an autonomous unit of the university now became an integral part, redesignated the College of Medicine. Similarly, the former Federal Advanced Teachers College became the College of Education. The Law makes provision for the establishment of more colleges in future. Each is a body corporate and has a perpetual succession and a common seal. It would appear therefore that the University might become eventually a federation of colleges. Each college has a court of governors, but is subject to the control of the Council in non-academic matters and to the Senate in academic matters. In practice, therefore, the colleges may be no more than the faculties of other universities.

Notes

[1] *The Daily Times*, Lagos, 29 January 1966.
[2] *Ibid.*, 27 January 1966.
[3] *University of Lagos Act (Amendment) Decree, 1966*, Federal Military Government Decree No. 29, Supplement to Official Gazette Extra-Ordinary No. 43, 25 April 1966:
The new Council consisted of Mr. Justice C. D. Onyeama (Chairman), Mr. Justice Arthur Prest, Mallam Nuhu Bayero, Mrs. Aduke Moore, Mr. Chinua Achebe, Mr. R. I. Uzoma, Colonel Olutoye, the Vice-Chancellor, 2 members of Senate, the Permanent Secretaries of the Ministries of Finance and Education.
[4] *New Era at Ife University*, March 1960, Ibadan. The Vice-Chancellor, Dr. A. O. Ajose and the Chairman of the Council during whose terms of office Dr. Oyenuga had been dismissed, resigned and were replaced by Dr. H. A. Oluwasanmi and Dr. T. T. Solaru.
[5] *University of Nigeria Edict No. 12, 1966*. The edict also abolished the office of Secretary of the Council, the post being now occupied by the Registrar.

Table 14

Total Enrolment in Nigerian Universities 1964-5

University	Arts and Education	Pure Science	Social Science and Law	Technology	Med. and Pharmacy	Agric. and Forestry	Vet. Science	Post grad.	Total
Ahmadu Bello	225	77	139	253	–	25	–	–	719
Ibadan	859	464	251	–	390	155	10	155	2,284
Ife	253	107	180	–	61	39	—	19	659
Lagos	41	54	346	39	83	–	–	–	563
Nigeria	802	327	776	222	–	241	114	–	2,482
Total	2,180	1,029	1,692	514	534	460	124	174	6,707

Table 15

Staff Situation on 1 October 1965

University	Professors and Associate Professors		Senior Lecturers and Readers		Lecturers		Assistant Lecturers		Other		Total		Grand Total	Nig. Exp. Ratio
	NIG.	EXP.	NIG.	EXP.	NIG.	EXP.	NIG.	EXP.	NIG.	EXP.	NIG.	EXP.		
Ahmadu Bello	–	24	5	33	14	76	4	5	21	30	44	168	212	1:4
Ibadan	17	63	28	49	89	108	9	13	14	16	157	249	406	1:2
Ife	1	6	3	13	18	26	14	13	24	4	60	62	122	1:1
Lagos	6	24	11	12	42	3	7	6	6	2	72	47	119	1:1
Nigeria	3	31	11	26	74	35	14	17	7	2	109	111	220	1:1
Total	27	148	58	133	237	248	48	54	72	54	442	637	1,079	
Percentage of Total	2·5	13·7	5·4	12·3	22·0	23·0	4·4	5·0	6·7	5·0	41·0	59·0	100·0	

Table 16

Student/Staff Ratio 1964-5

University	Total Students enrolled	Total Teachers employed	Number of Students per Teacher
Ahamadu Bello	719	212	3·4
Ibadan	2,284	406	5·6
Ife	659	122	5·4
Lagos	563	119	4·7
Nigeria	2,482	220	11·3
Total	6,707	1,079	6·2

Table 17

Geographical Distribution of Students in Nigerian Universities by Institution and Sex: Academic Year 1964/5

Institution	North		East		West		Federal Territory		Mid-West		Non-Nigerian		Total		Grand Total
	M	W	M	W	M	W	M	W	M	W	M	W	M	W	
Ahmadu Bello	390	10	157	13	90	3	3	–	44	2	7	–	691	28	719
Ibadan	109	5	731	96	872	102	12	4	225	18	72	38	2,021	263	2,284
Ife	10	–	140	10	361	47	2	2	72	5	9	1	594	65	659
Lagos	30	–	227	9	164	18	9	1	88	2	9	6	527	36	563
Nigeria	4	2	1,713	136	249	28	5	1	279	10	23	32	2,273	209	2,482
Total	543	17	2,968	264	1,736	198	31	8	708	37	120	77	6,106	601	6,707
Percentage of total	8·4		48·2		28·8		0·6		11·1		2·9		100·0		

Source: *Annual Review of Nigerian Universities, Academic Year 1964–65.* Federal Ministry of Information Lagos.

Bibliography

Note: The more important sources are indicated by an asterisk.

BOOKS

AJAYI, J. F. ADE, *Christian Missions in Nigeria, 1841–1891*, London, 1965.
ASHBY, SIR ERIC, *Technology and the Academics*, London, 1958.
   African Universities and Western Tradition, Oxford, 1964.
*AWOLOWO, OBAFEMI, *Awo*, (Autobiography) Cambridge, 1960.
*AZIKIWE, NNAMDI, *Renascent Africa*, published by the author, Lagos, 1937.
   The Development of Political Parties in Nigeria, London, 1957.
   Respect for Human Dignity (Inaugural Address as Governor-General), Lagos, 1960.
   Zik, (Collected Speeches), Cambridge, 1961.
*BAADE, H. W. and EVERETT, R. O., (ed.) *Academic Freedom—its Basic Philosophy, Function and History*, New York, 1964.
*BLYDEN, E. W., *Liberia's Offering*, New York, 1862.
   The People of Africa, New York, 1871.
   Christianity, Islam and the Negro Race, London, 1887.
   West Africa Before Europe, London, 1905.
BUELL, R. L., *The Native Problem in Africa*, 2 vols., London, 1928.
BURNS, ALAN, *History of Nigeria*, London, 1948.
BRUBACHER, J. S. and RUDY, WILLIS, *Higher Education in Transition*, New York, 1958.
CARR, HENRY, *The Rebecca Hussey's Charity School at Lagos for Industrial and General Education*, Lagos, 1899.
*CARR-SAUNDERS, A. M., *New Universities Overseas*, London, 1961.
*COLEMAN, JAMES, *Nigeria: Background to Nationalism*, Berkeley, California, 1960.
COOK, A. N., *British Enterprise in Nigeria*, London, 1964.
CROWDER, MICHAEL, *The Story of Nigeria*, London, 1962.
DAVIDSON, BASIL, *Old Africa Rediscovered*, London, 1961.
DENT, H. C., *Universities in Transition*, London, 1960.
DIKE, K. O., *Trade and Politics in the Niger Delta, 1830–1885*, Oxford, 1959.
   Address by the Vice-Chancellor and Citations in Support of Honorary Graduands in Trenchard Hall, University of Ibadan, 1965.
DUBOIS, W. E. B., *Souls of Black Folk*, London, 1965.
EVANS, I. L., *The British in Tropical Africa*, Cambridge, 1929.
FAGE, J. D., *An Introduction to the History of West Africa*, Cambridge, 1962.
FLEXNER, ABRAHAM, *Universities: American, English, German*, Oxford, 1930.
*FYFE, CHRISTOPHER, *A History of Sierra Leone*, Oxford, 1962.
   Sierra Leone Inheritance, Oxford, 1964.
GROVES, C. P., *The Planting of Christianity in Africa*, London, 1948–58.
HAILEY (LORD), *An African Survey*, Oxford, 1957.
HASKINS, H. C., *The Rise of the University*, Cornell, 1963.
*HAYFORD, J. EPHRAIM CASELY, *Ethiopia Unbound*, London, 1911.
*HODGKIN, THOMAS, *Nationalism in Colonial Africa*, London, 1956.
*HORTON, JAMES AFRICANUS BEALE, *West African Countries and Peoples, British and Native: With the Requirements Necessary for Establishing that Self-Government Recommended by the Committee of the House of Commons, 1865; and a Vindication of the African Race*, London, 1868.
IKEJIANI, OKECHUKWU, *Nigerian Education*, London, 1964.
IKETUONYE, V. C. *Zik of New Africa*, London, 1961.
JONES-QUARTEY, K. A. B., *A Life of Azikiwe*, London, 1965.

KERR, A., *Universities of Europe*, Cambridge, 1962.
*KIMBLE, D., *Political History of Ghana*, Oxford, 1962.
LAWRENCE, A. W., *Trade Castles and Forts of West Africa*, London, 1963.
LEGUM, COLIN, *Pan-Africanism*, London, 1962.
LUGARD, F., *The Dual Mandate in Tropical Africa*, London, 1929.
MACIVER, R. M., *Academic Freedom in Our Time*, Columbia, 1955.
MBADIWE, K. O., *British and Axis Aims in Nigeria*, New York, 1942.
MELLANBY, KENNETH, *The Birth of Nigeria's University*, London, 1958.
MORRILL, J. L., *The Ongoing State University*, Minnesota, 1960.
NDUKA, OTONTI, *Western Education and the Nigerian Cultural Background*, Oxford, 1964.
*NJOKU, ENI, *General Education in the University*, speech delivered by the Vice-Chancellor at the formal opening of the University of Lagos Medical School, 1962.
PHELPS-STOKES COMMISSION, *Education in Africa*, New York, 1922.
*RASHDALL, H., *The Universities of Europe in the Middle Ages*, (1895) ed. by F. M. Powicke and A. B. Emden, Oxford, 1936.
ROGERS, FRANCIS M., *Higher Education in the United States*, Harvard, 1963.
*SAUNDERS, J. T., *University College, Ibadan*, Cambridge, 1960.
SAUNDERS, J. T. and DOWUONA, M., *The West African Intellectual Community*, Ibadan, 1962.
SHAW, FLORA, *A Tropical Dependency*, London, 1906.
*SKLAR, R. L., *Nigerian Political Parties*, Princeton, 1963.
TRIMINGHAM, J. G., *A History of Islam in West Africa*, Oxford, 1962.
TRUSCOT, BRUCE, *First Year at the University*, London, 1964.
WASHINGTON, BOOKER T., *Up from Slavery*, New York, 1901.
WILKINSON, A., *The African and Christian Religion*, London, 1892.
*WISE, C. G., *A History of Education in British West Africa*, London, 1956.
WILLIAMS, C. K., *Achimota: The Early Years, 1924–1948*, London, 1963.

ARTICLES

AJAYI, J. F. ADE, 'The Development of Secondary Grammar Schools in Nigeria,' *Journal of the Historical Society of Nigeria*, **4**, 1963.
'Henry Venn and the Policy of Development', *Journal of the Historical Society of Nigeria*, **1**, 1959.
'Nineteenth Century Origins of Nigerian Nationalism,' *Journal of the Historical Society of Nigeria*, **2**, 1960.
AKINWOWO, AKINSOLA, 'The place of Mojola Agbebi in the African Nationalist Movements: 1890–1917', *Phylon Atlanta*, 1966.
AZIKIWE, BENJAMIN NNAMDI, 'Ethics of Colonialism', *Journal of Negro History*, **16**, 1931.
'In Defence of Liberia', *Journal of Negro History*, **17**, 1932
'Origins of the University of Nigeria' in *The University of Nigeria Appraises Itself*, (a collection of four speeches delivered at the University on Alma Mater Night., 9 June 1963), published by the University.
*ASHBY, SIR ERIC and ANDERSON, MARY, 'Autonomy and Academic Freedom in Britain and in English-Speaking Countries of Tropical Africa', *Minerva*, **4**, 1966.
*AYANDELE, E. A., 'An Assessment of James Johnson and his Place in Nigerian History', *Journal of the Historical Society of Nigeria*, **2**, 1963.
ELIAS, T. O., 'Makers of Nigerian Law', *West Africa*, 19 November 1955 to 7 July 1956.
FISHER, H. J., 'The Ahmaduja Movement in Nigeria' in *St. Anthony's Papers No. 10: African Affairs*, London, 1961.

GRAVES, I. B., 'The Education Front in British Tropical Africa', *Yearbook of Education*, 1950.

HAIR, P. E. H., 'E. W. Blyden and the C.M.S., Freetown, 1871–1877', *Sierra Leone Bulletin of Religion*, 4, 1962.

HARBISON, FREDERICK, 'The African University and Human Resource Development' *Journal of Modern African Studies*, 1, 1965.

JOHNSON, H. C., 'Are our Universities Schools?', *Harvard Educational Review*, 35, Harvard, 1965.

JONES-QUARTEY, K. A. B., 'A note on J. M. Sarbah and J. E. Casely Hayford: Ghanaian Leaders, Politicians and Journalists, 1864–1930, *Sierra Leone Studies*, New Series, 14, 1960.

JULY, ROBERT, 'Nineteenth Century Negritude: Edward W. Blyden', *Journal of African History*, 5, 1964.

KILSON, M. L., 'The Rise of Nationalist Organisations and Parties in British West Africa', in *Africa As Seen by American Negroes*, Paris, 1958.

*LYNCH, HOLLIS, R., 'The Native Pastorate Controversy and Cultural Ethnocentricism in Sierra Leone, 1871–1874', *Journal of African History*, 3, 1964.

'Edward Blyden: Pioneer African Nationalist', *Journal of African History*, 6, 1965.

MUMFORD, W. B., 'Some growing points in African Higher Education', *Yearbook of Education*, 1936.

NICOL, ABIOSEH, 'West Indians in West Africa', *Sierra Leone Studies*, New Series, 4, pp. 14–23.

ONWUTEAKA, VICTORIA C., 'The Aba Riot of 1929 and its relation to the system of Indirect Rule', *Nigerian Journal of Economic Social Studies*, 7, 3, 1965.

ORMSBY GORE, W., 'Education in the British Dependencies in Tropical Africa', *The Year book of Education*, 1932.

RYDER, A. F. C., 'An early Portuguese trading voyage to Forcados River', *Journal of the Historical Society of Nigeria*, 1, 1959.

'Missionary Activity in the Kingdom of Warri to the early 19th Century', *Journal of the Historical Society of Nigeria*, 2, 1960.

Book Review in *Journal of African History*, 3, 1962.

SCOTT, H. S., 'Educational Policy in the British Colonial "Empire"', *Yearbook of Education*, 1937.

'The Development of the Education of the African in Relation to Western Contact. 2. Education by Europeans', *Yearbook of Education*, 1938.

'Educational Policy and Problems in the African Colonies', *Yearbook of Education*, 1940.

*SKLAR, R. L., 'Nigerian Politics: The Ordeal of Chief Awolowo, 1960–1965', in *Politics in Africa—7 Cases*, ed. by Gwendolen M. Carter, New York, 1966.

*WEBSTER, J. A. B., 'The Bible and the Plough', *Journal of the Historical Society of Nigeria*, 2, 1960.

WILKS, IVOR, 'A medieval trade-route from the Niger to the Gulf of Guinea', *Journal of African History*, 3, 1962.

SHEPPERSON, G., 'Notes on Negro American Influences on the Emergence of African Nationalism', *Journal of African History*, 1, 1960.

GOVERNMENT PUBLICATIONS AND REPORTS

*NIGERIA *Legislative Council Debates*, 1929–1944.

Memorandum on Educational Policy in Nigeria, Lagos, 1930.

Report of a Technical College Organisation for Nigeria, Lagos, 1950.

FEDERATION OF NIGERIA *House of Representative Debates*, Lagos 1954–65.

The Economic Development of Nigeria, Report of a Mission organised by the International Bank for Reconstruction and Development, Lagos, 1954.

Investment in Education, Report of the Commission on Post-School Certificate and Higher Education in Nigeria (Chairman: Sir Eric Ashby), Lagos, 1960.

Decisions of the Government of the Federal Republic of Nigeria on the Report of the National Universities Commission, Sessional Paper No. 4 of 1964, Lagos, 1964.

Annual Report of National Manpower Board, Lagos, 1964–1965.

Educational Development 1961–70, Sessional Paper No. 3, Lagos, 1961.

Gazette, 1965–66.

*University Development in Nigeria, Report of the National Universities Commission, Lagos, 1963.

*EASTERN NIGERIA Economic Rehabilitation of Eastern Nigeria, Report of the Economic Mission to Europe and North America (by Nnamdi Azikiwe and L. P. Ojukwu), Enugu, 1954.

University of Nigeria Law, 1961, Enugu, 1961.

Gazette, 1966.

*WESTERN NIGERIA White Paper on the Establishment of a University in Western Nigeria, Western Nigeria Legislature, Sessional Paper No. 12 of 1960, Ibadan, 1960.

White Paper on the political alignment in Western Nigeria, Ibadan, 1964.

Report of the Committee on the Proposed University of Western Nigeria, Mimeographed, Ibadan, n.d.

PROTECTORATE OF UGANDA *Annual Report of the Department of Education*, Entebbe, 1925.

UNITED KINGDOM *Education Policy in British Tropical Africa*, H.M.S.O., 1925.

*Parliamentary Debates: House of Commons, 1938–1945.

West India Royal Commission, 1938–1939, Cmd. 6174, H.M.S.O., 1940.

Statement of Policy on Colonial Development and Welfare, Cmd. 6175, H.M.S.O., 1940.

*Report of the Commission on Higher Education in West Africa, Cmd., H.M.S.O. 1945.

*Report of the Commission on Higher Education in the Colonies, Cmd. 6647, H.M.S.O. 1945.

Higher Education, Report of the Committee appointed by the Prime Minister under the Chairmanship of Lord Robbins, 1961–63, Cmd. 2154., H.M.S.O., 1963.

UNIVERSITY AND NIGERIAN COLLEGE PUBLICATIONS

*Calendars, 1965/66 of Ahmadu Bello University, Ibadan University, Ife University, Lagos University and University of Nigeria, Nsukka.

UNIVERSITY OF LAGOS *Change in Vice-Chancellorship: An official Publication*, n.d.

UNIVERSITY OF NIGERIA *Annual Reports*, 1958–1965.

*Nigerian College of Arts, Science and Technology, Calendar 1960/61.

UNPUBLISHED THESES

*BLYDEN III, E. W., Sierra Leone: The Pattern of Constitutional Development, 1924–1951, Ph.D. thesis, Harvard.

*FAFUNWA, A. BABS., An Historical Analysis of the Development of Higher Education in Nigeria, Ph.D. thesis, New York.

CORRESPONDENCE

*The West African University, Correspondence between Blyden and Hennessy, *Negro* Printing Office, Freetown, 1872.

The Lagos Training College and Industrial Institute, Correspondence between Edward
W. Blyden, LL.D. and His Excellency Sir Gilbert Carter, K.C.M.G., Governor and
Commander-in-Chief of Lagos and its Protectorates, Lagos, The Lagos, Standard
Office, 1896.

CARTER TO CHAMBERLIN Covering letter by Governor Carter of Lagos to the
Secretary of State to the Colonies on the Lagos Training College, C.O. 147/110,
Public Records Office, London.

University of Nigeria—Lindsay Correspondence, Correspondence between Professor
J. K. Lindsay and the University of Nigeria, 12 May 1964 to 2 March 1965, published
by the author, Jamaica, 1965.

NEWSPAPERS

Daily Express, Lagos 1964–1965
(Nigerian) Daily Times, Lagos, 1934–1965
Lagos Standard 1895–1897
Lagos Weekly Record 1895–1897
Lagos Daily News 1929–1934
Nigerian Tribune 1960–1965
West African Pilot, Lagos 1950–1965

MISCELLANEOUS

The Truth about the Change in Vice-Chancellorship, University of Lagos, by G. K. Berrie,
Fielstra, Nicholson, Nsugbe, Nwabueze, and Nwaefuna, published by the authors, n.d.

The Crisis over the Appointment of Vice-Chancellor of the University of Lagos, by the
Senior Members of the Staff of the University of Lagos, Lagos, 19 March 1965.

The Crisis at the University of Lagos: Implications and Way Out, by the Senior Members
of Staff of the University of Lagos, Lagos, 5 May 1965.

The Inspired Crisis over the Appointment of Vice-Chancellor of the University of Lagos,
by the Other Senior Members of the Staff of the University of Lagos, Lagos, 24 March
1965.

Minerva (A Review of Science, Learning and Policy), sections on 'Chronicle', 1964–
1966.

Index

Aba Riots, 16
Abayomi, Dr. K., 74
Abdullahi Bayero College, 122–3; *see also* Ahmadu Bello College; Ahmadu Bello University
Abeokuta, 11, 12, 60, 146
Aboh, 13
Aborigines Rights Protection Society, 38
Accountancy, 102, 105, 106, 164, 193
Accra, 38, 41, 73, 83, 144
Achimota, 89, 106
Achimota College, 41, 44, 83, 90, 114
Action Group, 93, 129, 136, 138, 142, 145, 148–50; *see also* United Progressive Grand Alliance
Administration, 106, 123, 132
Administrators, 80, 88, 118, 119
Advisory Committee on Education in Africa, 66–7, 78, 79, 190
Advisory Committee on Education in the Colonies, 70, 73–4, 83, 88
African Aid Society, 21
Africa-in-Transition Division (African Institute, Ife), 173
African National University, 37–8
African nationality, 35–6, 37, 40, 114
African Notes, 173
The African Review, 52
The African Slave Trade and its Remedy (Buxton), 12
African studies, 115, 122, 124–5, 131, 132, 168–70, 172–3
Africanus, Leo, 2
Agbebi, E. M. E., 74
Agbebi, The Rev. Dr. Mojala, 51–2
Agricultural economics, 164
Agricultural engineering, 164
Agricultural mechanisation, 164
Agricultural officers, 80
Agricultural science, 56, 94, 104
Agriculture, Advisory Committee recommendations, 68, 79; at Ahmadu Bello University, 123, 160, 178, 179, 185; Ashby Commission recommendations, 121; Economic Commission recommendations, 111, 116; Elliot Commission recommendations, 89, 193; at Ibadan University, 160, 164, 178, 179; at Ife University, 132, 138, 164, 178, 179; need for, 118, 119; National Universities Commission recommendations, 178, 179; at Nigerian College, 102–4, 107, 121; number of students (1967–8), 178; post-graduate courses, 167, 178; Thorp-Harlow recommendations, 101–2; at University College, Ibadan, 91,

94–5, 121; at University of Nigeria, 162, 178, 179; at Yaba Higher College, 69, 71, 78, 80; mentioned, 56, 58, 62, 69, 79, 80, 112–13
Agronomy, 123
Aguiyi-Ironsi, Major-General J. T. U., 196, 197
Ahmadu Bello College, 121, 122, 130; *see also* Abdullahi Bayero College
Ahmadu Bello University, courses at, 160, 161, 163, 164–7, 169, 173, 177–8, 200; effect of military government, 197; entrance qualifications, 160–1; financing of, 179–80, 181; foundation of, 4, 97; organisation of, 181–3, 184–5, 186, 187; staffing at, 200; students at, 200, 201; *see also* Institute of Administration (Zaria)
Ahmadu Bello University Law 1962, 122, 123, 171, 180, 181, 183, 184–7, 199
Ajayi, Professor J. F. Ade, 22–3, 24
Akenzua II, Oba, 197
Akintola, Chief S. L., 149–50, 196
Akinsanya, S. A., 75, 145–6
Akinyemi, Chief R. A., 136, 137
Alakija, O., 74
Alexander High School, Monrovia, 26
'Alfred Jones' Institute, New Calabar, 52
Aluko, Dr. S. A., 138, 139, 149, 150, 151–4, 157
America *see* United States of America
American Presbyterian Mission, 27
Analytical chemistry, 166
Anatomy, 25, 164
Anderson, Mr., 60
Anderson, Dr. Mary, 134–5
Anglican Native Pastorate, 60
Angola, 9
Animal health, 89, 166
Animal husbandry, 123, 166
Animal science, 164
Anthropology, 94, 164, 173
Arabic and Islamic studies, 94, 123, 160, 164, 166
Archaeological Newsletter, 173
Archaeology, 94, 139–40, 156, 173
Architecture, 104, 105, 111, 162, 164, 168
Arikpo, Okoi, 177
Aristotle, 2
Arochuka Riots, 16
Art, 173; *see also* Fine Arts
Arts Faculties, at Ahmadu University, 160, 161; Economic Mission recommendations, 111; Ellio Commission recommendations, 89, 193; at Ibadan University, 160, 161–2, 169; at Ife University, 132, 161, 170; at